MW01258172

A Poetics of Courtly Male Friendship in Heian Japan

Bo Ya Plays the Qin as Zhong Ziqi Listens. Attributed to Kano Motonobu (ca. 1476–1559). The Mary Griggs Burke Collection of Japanese Art. The Metropolitan Museum of Art. Photograph © 2000.

A Poetics of Courtly Male Friendship in Heian Japan

Paul Gordon Schalow

University of Hawai'i Press • Honolulu

Printed in the United States of America
12 11 10 09 08 07 6 5 4 3 2 1

Library of Congress Cataloging-in-Publication Data

Schalow, Paul Gordon.
A poetics of courtly male friendship in Heian Japan / Paul Gordon Schalow.
p. cm.
Includes bibliographical references and index.
ISBN 978-0-8248-3020-5 (hardcover : alk. paper)
1. Japanese literature—Heian period, 794–1185—History and criticism. 2. Male friendship in literature. I. Title.
PL726.2.S34 2007
895.6'114—dc22

2006020766

University of Hawai'i Press books are printed on acid-free paper and meet the guidelines for permanence and durability of the Council on Library Resources.

Designed by the University of Hawai'i Press production staff

Printed by The Maple-Vail Book Manufacturing Group

For Kiri, Eric, and Emlyn

Contents

Acknowledgments

The research and writing of this study was made possible over a period of years by a grant from the National Endowment for the Humanities, two semesters of sabbatical leave from Rutgers University, and a twelve-month fellowship in the School of Historical Studies at the Institute for Advanced Study in Princeton, New Jersey. I wish to express my deepest gratitude to each of these institutions for their generous support of the project.

I am also greatly indebted to mentors and colleagues in the field for their endorsement of the project at various stages along the way, especially Aileen Gatten, Howard Hibbett, the late Earl Miner, J. Thomas Rimer, and Haruo Shirane. Colleagues at Rutgers University who also deserve my deepest appreciation for their ongoing support of my work are Donald Roden, Ryoko Toyama, Ching-I Tu, and Janet Walker.

At the University of Hawai'i Press, I wish to thank the members of the Editorial Board and particularly acquiring editor Pamela Kelley for her strong interest in the manuscript and for helping me see it through to publication. I am grateful to two anonymous readers who took time to give the manuscript a careful reading. The insightful comments of one reader in particular spurred me to clarify certain key aspects of the study and are reflected in the finished book.

An earlier version of chapter 2 appeared in the *Harvard Journal of Asiatic Studies,* volume 60, number 2 (December 2000) under the title "Five Portraits of Male Friendship in the *Ise monogatari.*"

I wish to thank Eyal Ben-Ari at the Hebrew University of Jerusalem, Irmela Hijiya-Kirschnereit at the German Institute for Japanese Studies (DIJ) in Tokyo, Noriko Mizuta and Sumito Miki at Jōsai International University, Junko Saeki at Dōshisha University, and Rieko Wagoner at Trinity College for invitations to lecture on my work at their respective institutions. I am grateful for the thoughtful feedback of audiences there and at Georgetown University, the Institute for Advanced Study, and Rutgers University.

I am deeply grateful to Mrs. Mary Griggs Burke for allowing me to use two images from her collection of Japanese art: *Bo Ya Plays the Qin as Zhong Ziqi Listens* depicts the Chinese legend of the Broken Strings in a painting attributed to Kano Motonobu (ca. 1476–1559), and *Suetsumuhana: The Safflower* depicts a pivotal scene in chapter 6 of *The Tale of Genji* from an album attributed to Tosa Mitsuoki (1617–1691). I wish to thank Stephanie Wada at the Mary and Jackson Burke Foundation, Deanna Cross and Masako Watanabe at the Metropolitan Museum of Art, and Miyeko Murase of Columbia University for their assistance.

Introduction

This is a study of bonds of friendship depicted between noblemen in the literature of the Japanese imperial court during the Heian period (794–1185). It is not a description of real-life friendships between historical persons but rather an attempt to describe how what I will be calling "courtly male friendship" is depicted in a number of texts circulating in the late tenth and early eleventh centuries. The recurring patterns of this literary depiction constitute the "poetics" in the book's title. The texts under discussion are generically diverse and include a poetry collection (the *Wakan rōei shū,* or *Japanese and Chinese Poems to Sing*); two poem-tales (the *Ise monogatari,* or *Tale of Ise;* and the *Heichū monogatari,* or *Tale of Heichū*); a poetic memoir (the *Kagerō nikki,* or *Kagerō Diary*); and an extended work of imaginative fiction (the *Genji monogatari,* or *Tale of Genji*). Apart from *Poems to Sing,* all of the texts combine poetry and prose to varying degrees. My approach to the poetic element in the texts has been to focus on identifying motifs and rhetorical structures that recur in Chinese and Japanese poems about male friendship. In addressing the prose stories, I have focused on describing pairs of male characters created by the authors in their narratives of friendship. As we shall see, the nobleman's desires for erotic adventure with women and for friendship with men are not contradictory or mutually exclusive in these texts but are integrated and play off each other in interesting ways. In fact, to be both a lover of women and a friend of men comes to define the very notion of what constitutes a hero in the period. Such a hero seems to have provided Heian courtiers with hope for transcending the constrictions and disappointments of their admittedly privileged lives. In particular, this study is concerned with clarifying how Heian literature articulates the nobleman's wish to be known and appreciated fully by another man—or what may be termed the hope of transcendence through male friendship.

The ranked aristocracy of the mid-Heian court is estimated to have numbered no more than five thousand people whose ostensible purpose for existence was their service to the imperial household.[1] This small group completely dominated cultured life in the capital, called Heian kyō, the "City of Peace and Tranquility," from which derives the period name. Although courtly literature has come to symbolize Heian culture as a whole, the noblemen and noblewomen who produced it were but a tiny fraction of the population, a leisured elite. The court aristocracy rarely had to concern itself with earning a living, with child rearing, or with domestic chores. This is not to say that courtiers had easy lives, however. Political disgrace, rumor of personal misconduct, decline in family prestige, and even exile lay in wait for them; indeed, courtly literature was a forum where the collective fears inspired by the instability of their hierarchical world of finely tuned ranks could be explored, and it was also an island of elegance and well-being that they created to shelter themselves against those fears.

Any man born into one of the aristocratic families that served at court was among the most privileged on earth. He could expect to receive an elite continental-style education in Chinese poetry and the Chinese classics that would subsequently lead to his steady advancement in the elaborate court hierarchy. According to his abilities and the quality of his alliances, he might attain service to the imperial household or, even more desirable, become adviser to the emperor himself. But the competition for power and influence among the leading clans was fierce. By the time of the mid-Heian period one branch of the Fujiwara family—the *hokke,* or Northern House—had achieved overwhelming political dominance at court. This was accomplished through a system of marriage politics whereby the reigning Fujiwara chieftain of the Northern House was able to control the throne as regent *(sesshō)* by naming a daughter consort to the emperor and later installing his own grandson on the throne.

The almost complete domination of the court by the Northern House through the regency system *(sekkan sei)* meant that much of the court aristocracy was effectively disenfranchised. Members of the less successful branches of the Fujiwara and other clans were routinely sent out to the provinces for lengthy terms as provincial governors. Such a posting was prestigious enough, but it obligated the courtier to be absent from the capital for years at a time, and for that reason provincial governorships were generally not welcomed by high-ranking courtiers harboring political ambitions. Interestingly, it is from the class of provincial governors, on the periphery of court power, that many of the greatest Heian writers emerged, a result perhaps of the tendency for people on the margins to develop a critical perspective and analytical consciousness toward centers of power. Thus, while a nobleman's aristocratic birth provided little solace in the face of his lack of political clout, at least his literary attainments in the Chinese classics and Japanese poetry (or "Yamato song," *waka*) could provide the basis for his participation in a cultural and aesthetic regime of power that emerged in relation to the political power of the Fujiwara Regency. Verses and narratives depicting a disenfranchised hero who vied for the love of women and the friendship of men show that literature provided the Heian court with a cultural arena of the imagination, where power lost in the public realm might be recouped through the art of writing and reading.

Western scholars have heretofore tended to introduce questions of power and politics into their readings of Heian texts from the angle of feminism, placing special emphasis on the imbalance of power between men and women in the context of courtship.[2] The strategy has been to describe the ways in which Heian literature idealizes romantic love, or "longing," and then show it to be embedded within the marriage politics of the regency system. In general, feminist analysis has stressed the suffering of noblewomen and has looked for ways in which the literature nonetheless gives women hope of rising above or getting beyond the constraints of marriage politics through their experience of love or through some other means.[3] The present study inherits these concerns about the transcendence of love and the suffering of women from feminist scholarship and carries it into a new realm of inquiry—of the suffering of noblemen and the literary record of their hopes for transcendence through friendship. If feminist analysis of courtship and love has taken as its goal the politicization of feminine experience in canonical works of Heian literature, then this study of male friendship seeks to shift and deepen that analysis to include masculine experience as a subject of critical inquiry.[4]

Several of the narratives addressed in this study—namely, the *Tale of Heichū*, the *Kagerō Diary*, and the *Tale of Genji*—depict female characters playing a central role as mediators in friendships between noblemen. The central role of female characters can best be explained in terms of the ways that gendered perspectives inform Heian writing. In some scenes an author's depiction of male friendship is an expression of male interiority and highlights friendship as part of a man's inner life, whereas in other scenes such a depiction is an expression of female observation of men and frequently highlights the role of women in enabling the friendship. Heian depictions of male friendship inevitably embody the differing perspectives of male and female authors whose viewpoints on the subject were profoundly shaped by their gender roles in the court aristocracy.

The Chinese paradigm for male friendship is the story of Bo Ya and Zhong Ziqi, otherwise known as the legend of the Broken Strings (Chinese: *jue xian* Japanese: *zetsugen*). It appears for the first time in Han dynasty texts and was familiar to the Heian court as a theme of Tang dynasty painting and from the text of the *Lie-zi*.[5] According to the legend, Bo Ya was a skilled player of the zither, and Zhong Ziqi was his friend. Alone among all his listeners, Ziqi possessed a remarkable ability to appreciate the nuances of Bo Ya's playing. When Bo Ya played a passage that evoked mountains, Ziqi would grasp his intent immediately and say, "lofty like Mt. Tai"; when his playing evoked the sound of rushing water, Ziqi would say, "flowing like the Yangzi River and the Yellow River." When Ziqi died, Bo Ya cut the strings of his zither and never played again, "because there was no one else in the world that 'knew his sounds.'"[6] The legend of the Broken Strings came to exemplify the ideal of a nobleman's profound response to another man. Its echoes can be heard throughout Heian literature in stories that depict the nobleman's desire to be known and appreciated by a kindred spirit.

As the legend of the Broken Strings suggests, the Heian literature of courtly male friendship grew out of a bilingual and bicultural context involving aspects of both Chinese and Japanese literary languages. For members of the early Japanese (Yamato) elite, the ability to read and write was entirely a product of contact with continental culture, and originally Chinese literacy was the only type of literacy that existed for them. The reception of continental culture in the sixth century by the emerging Yamato state was controversial and followed an uncertain trajectory, characterized by military coups, political assassinations, and heated clashes among elite clans, but the forces favoring accommodation with Chinese cultural forces, and in particular with Buddhist teaching, ultimately prevailed. By the seventh century, powerful families within the Yamato court enjoyed the social and political advantages that Chinese literacy afforded them. At the same time, a desire to express themselves in the indigenous language led to creative experiments in literary production of Yamato texts, starting with renditions of Japanese poems called "Yamato songs" *(waka).* Initially, these experiments were conducted by literarily gifted members of the Yamato court and involved inventing ways to alternately use Chinese graphs for their sound (as phonetic graphs) and for their meaning (as logographs) so that an approximation of the indigenous language could be produced as text. Later, the phonetic use of Chinese graphs was systematized into a syllabic script (kana) that allowed relatively facile transcription of Yamato language as text. Phonetic graphs were at first used exclusively to transcribe names and *waka* within the context of Chinese prose, but with the later emergence of syllabic script it became possible to create extended narratives in the Yamato language.

The newfound ability of the educated elite at the Yamato court to write poems and prose in the indigenous language never displaced the court's interest in Chinese texts, however, and Chinese writing maintained tremendous prestige as an object of literary study and enjoyment. As Marian Ury once noted, "to the Heian Japanese, Chinese culture and its products existed apart from national boundaries as requisite tools of civilization and, to a very high degree, as the marks of civilization itself."[7] Furthermore, written Chinese continued to be used for all official communications within the Yamato court and between the Yamato court and the outside world, namely the Tang empire and the Korean kingdoms of Silla and Paekche. The Heian courtier's treatment of Chinese texts underwent a gradual change, however, whereby classical Chinese came to be read following Yamato-like diction and syntax. By the tenth century, Chinese texts were no longer something separate and foreign but were fully integrated into a system of literacy involving Japanese and Chinese frames of reference, what Thomas LaMarre has termed "the Yamato-Han or 'wa-kan' assemblage."[8] This assemblage allowed courtiers to integrate multiple forms of literary expression into a coherent, if slightly precarious, Yamato-Han literary culture. Although plagued by occasional glitches and inaccuracies, the hybrid literary apparatus nevertheless allowed most noblemen and a few elite noblewomen to read and compose texts at a sophisticated level within a dual literary environment.[9]

Because the literary depictions of male friendship addressed in this study are a product of a culture's history, they are inevitably bound to a specific time and place. We cannot assume that friendship's manifestation in Heian literature should automatically be intelligible to people living in the present day, one thousand years removed, for its epistemological underpinnings are not necessarily our own. Nevertheless, it would be a mistake to completely deny the comprehensibility of these narratives of friendship to people of today, for they manage to speak to us movingly about the Heian nobleman's desire to be known and appreciated by a kindred spirit. It is a desire that resonates convincingly across the temporal and cultural divide between the texts' creators and ourselves. The historical contexts that produce the wish for friendship and the depiction of that wish in literature will inevitably differ across cultures and time, yet it seems only human to wish for the intimacy of a friend, however elusive, who might understand us.

Chapter 1

Poems to Sing and the Hope for Transcendence

The *Wakan rōei shū* (Japanese and Chinese poems to sing) contains a sequence of seven poems on friendship that vividly illustrates the bilingual and bicultural *wa-kan* apparatus at work in the production and appreciation of Chinese and Japanese verse at the Heian court.[1] *Poems to Sing* was compiled by the courtier and literatus Fujiwara no Kintō (966–1041) in about the year 1013. Kintō's mother was the daughter of an Imperial Prince (the third son of Emperor Daigo) and his father was Fujiwara no Yoritada, who served the Emperors Kazan and En'yū as Chancellor *(kampaku)* from 977 to 986. On the basis of Kintō's illustrious lineage, he might have expected a stellar and unimpeded political career at court but for the fact that he was an exact contemporary of Fujiwara no Michinaga (966–1027), a man who eclipsed all of his kinsmen and became the defining political figure in the mid-Heian court. An examination of Kintō's career shows that his abilities in the composition of *waka* were recognized at an early age, and that as a young man he kept up a lively poetic correspondence with Fujiwara no Sanekata (?–998), Minamoto no Kanezumi (955?–?), and Fujiwara no Michinobu (?–994). In time, Kintō achieved in the poetic realm the same stature that Michinaga would achieve in the political realm and was widely regarded by his fellow courtiers as the preeminent arbiter of Japanese poetic taste in his day. He was principal compiler of the third imperial anthology, the *Shūi shū* (ca. 1005; Collection of gleanings), and between the years 1004 and 1012 he wrote several well-regarded poetic treatises, including the *Shinsen zuinō* (Essentials of poetry, new selection), the *Waka kuhon* (Nine styles of Japanese poetry), and the *Kingyoku shū* (Collection of gold and jewels), which served as study guides for courtiers in their poetic composition. None of these texts was to prove as important as *Poems to Sing,* which "served for many centuries not only as a source of beauty itself but also as a handbook of the arts, supplying poets and dramatists with lofty language, artists with subject matter, musicians with lyrics, and calligraphers with revered texts to copy."[2]

Poems to Sing was compiled probably as a celebratory gift on the occasion of the marriage in 1013 of Kintō's daughter to Fujiwara no Norimichi, Michinaga's third son, who himself reached the position of Chancellor in 1068.[3] The union was probably orchestrated in part to assuage Kintō's frustrated political ambitions. Michinaga, whose position at the time was Imperial Examiner *(nairan)*, was a master of using the literary and decorative arts as political capital, and the fine poetry Kintō collected and preserved in *Poems to Sing* undoubtedly enhanced the prestige of all parties to the marriage. The collection contains 803 entries consisting of Japanese and Chinese poems that were performed in a popular form of musical recitation, called *rōei* (thus the title *Poems to Sing*).[4] The majority of the entries are Chinese couplets on various themes composed by Heian and Tang court poets; these are matched with a smaller number of Japanese *waka* on related themes. Kintō organized the collection into two volumes of approximately equal length. The first volume contains 396 poems and poetic passages addressing the four seasons, beginning with spring. Each season is further subdivided into a total of sixty-five topics: twenty-one topics for spring, twelve for summer, twenty-three for autumn, and nine for winter. The second volume contains 407 poems and poetic passages divided among forty-eight miscellaneous topics. One of these miscellaneous topics is "Friends" (C: *jiaoyou* J: *kōyū*). The seven poems in the section allow us to glimpse in microcosm Kintō's literary formulation of male friendship within the complex linguistic environment of the Yamato-Han *(wa-kan)* nexus.

Poems to Sing consists of three general types of verses—*shi, kanshi,* and *waka*—that are grouped in a hierarchy according to type within each topical category. First in the hierarchy are couplets taken from *shi,* poems written in classical Chinese by Tang poets. Next come *kanshi,* couplets composed in classical Chinese as complete poems in two lines by Heian Japanese poets. Last in the typological hierarchy come *waka,* thirty-one-syllable Yamato songs, many of them gleaned from the first imperial anthology, the *Kokinshū* (or *Kokin waka shū,* 905; Collection of Japanese poems old and new).[5] The typological organization of poems suggests that Kintō made a conscious distinction between couplets composed in classical Chinese by Tang poets *(shi)* and those composed by Heian poets *(kanshi),* and that he treated those by Tang poets as primary, since they were the authentic source of poetic literacy. Kintō's juxtaposition of Heian *kanshi* following Tang *shi* couplets suggested a seamless connection between the Heian courtier and his Tang predecessors. Finally, the incorporation of *waka* into the hierarchy of poetic forms reveals Kintō's sense that Japanese poems resonated meaningfully with the themes of Chinese verse, despite the obvious formal differences of diction and imagery. This allowed him to treat *waka* as an integral element within a continuum of poetic expression alongside the *shi* couplets and *kanshi* that constituted the bulk of the collection.

Regarding Kintō's purposes in compiling *Poems to Sing,* J. Thomas Rimer has said, "It appears that Kintō was setting out to reinforce Japanese poetic values that had been established some or more [*sic*] hundred years previously. Rather than striking off in a new direction, he seemed to aim at establishing permanent standards on the basis of which the poets of his and successive generations should proceed."[6] In looking to the past for robust examples of *shi* couplets and *kanshi,* and matching them with *waka* on similar themes, Kintō acknowledged and made fine use of the integrative power of the Yamato-Han apparatus. His work of integration had one risk, however. It threatened to erase the very differences inherent in the separate languages that give the sequences their extraordinary poetic texture. As we shall see, this risk is especially well negotiated in the poetic entries included under the topic of "Friends."

There are approximately 240 *shi* couplets in the collection, attributed (some of them erroneously) to forty-three different Tang poets or Chinese literary sources. Most of these *shi* couplets are fragments of longer poems; in a few instances, they are derived from passages of classical Chinese prose. According to Rimer and Chaves, translators of *Poems to Sing,* the appreciation of Chinese *shi* couplets as a full-fledged poetic form represented a uniquely Heian approach to Chinese poetry and reached its apogee in the text of *Poems to Sing.* The collection favors one Tang poet, Bo Ju-yi (Po Chü-i, 772–846), who is credited with 140 entries (counting a few erroneous or doubtful attributions). Two of Bo Ju-yi's contemporaries and intimates are also well represented: Yuan Zhen (779–831), with 11 entries; and Xu Hun (791–854?), with 10 entries. Bo Ju-yi's overwhelming numerical superiority can be explained by Kintō's use of *Senzai kaku* (ca. 950, Splendid verses of a thousand years) as his source for many of the entries in *Poems to Sing. Senzai kaku* was compiled in about 950 by Ōe no Koretoki (888–963) and contains 1,083 *shi* couplets in classical Chinese. These are in the form of two-line couplets of seven graphs per line. The collection comprises works by 153 Tang poets, including four Korean poets from the kingdoms of Silla and Koryŏ.

Scholars believe that *Senzai kaku* was conceived of as a pair with *Nikkan shū* (ca. 945, Collection of Japanese views), a lost collection of *kanshi* by Heian poets. It is thought that Emperor Murakami (r. 946–967), when he was yet Crown Prince, commissioned the collection from his tutor, Koretoki, to serve in his study of Han composition. *Nikkan shū* contained the Chinese verses composed by ten major Heian courtier-poets who flourished in the ninety-year period between 834 and 923. The earliest Han verses in the collection are by Ono no Takamura (801–852) and his contemporary Korenaga no Harumichi (dates unknown). Their work reflects the immediate impact of the *Hakushi monjū* (Collected works of Bo Ju-yi), which reached Japan during Bo Ju-yi's lifetime in about the year 838, on the style of Chinese verse that came to be preferred by the Heian court.

According to the scholar Kimbara Tadashi, the very early admiration for Bo Ju-yi shown in the Chinese verses of Ono no Takamura and Koreyoshi no Harumichi went far beyond matters of literary style and into matters of lifestyle. They often composed in pairs and carried on an active exchange of verses that followed closely the literary example of Bo Ju-yi's own poetic friendships with Yuan Zhen and Liu Yu-xi (772–842).[7] The idea of "poetic friendships" between male poets thereby became entrenched among Heian courtiers in the ninth century, and the practice of such friendships continued well into mid-Heian. Other Heian courtiers whose works Koretoki included in *Nikkan shū* were likewise paired with each other: Sugawara no Koreyoshi (812–880) with Ōe no Otondo (811–877); Tachibana no Hiromi (837–890), who studied classical Chinese under Sugawara no Koreyoshi, with the legendary Miyako no Yoshika (834–879); Sugawara no Michizane (845–903), Koreyoshi's son, with Miyoshi no Kiyoyuki (847–918); and Ki no Haseo (845–912) with Ōe no Chifuru (d. 924), who was Koretoki's father. To the future Emperor Murakami, the text of *Nikkan shū* served as a fine introduction to much of the superior Chinese verse produced at the Heian court in the preceding four generations. When, a few years later, Koretoki turned to the task of compiling *Senzai kaku,* he similarly wanted to create a representative collection of superior Chinese verse produced in the Tang, Silla, and Koryŏ courts in the same generations. What distinguished the two anthologies was that the *Senzai kaku* focused on Tang, Silla, and Koryŏ poets, while *Nikkan shū* focused on Heian poets. Both volumes confirmed the Heian vogue for Bo Ju-yi's poems, and Kintō was greatly influenced by this vogue when he set out to compile *Poems to Sing* almost seventy years later.

In addition to the 240 *shi* couplets by Bo Ju-yi and other Tang poets, *Poems to Sing* contains approximately 350 *kanshi* by a total of fifty-two Heian male courtiers. The large number of poems—the largest of the three genres represented in the collection—is divided among a relatively small number of poets. Thirty-seven *kanshi* are by Sugawara no Michizane, 39 by his grandson Fumitoki (or Funtoki, 899–981), 30 by Minamoto no Shitagō (911–983), 30 by Ōe no Asatsuna (887–957), 22 by Ki no Haseo, 19 by Yoshishige no Yasutane (?–1002), 14 by Miyako no Yoshika, and 12 by Ono no Takamura. Of the Heian masters of Chinese verse, only Minamoto no Shitagō and Ōe no Asatsuna are represented with Japanese poems in the collection. They number among the few courtiers who had proved themselves capable of producing both *kanshi* and *waka* of excellent quality. As such, they represented the Heian ideal: men who were expert at manipulating both Yamato and Han frames of reference in the *wa-kan* apparatus. It was an elusive ideal, and in practice it seems that poetically competent men at court specialized in *kanshi* or *waka* but were rarely masters of both.

Kintō's most lasting contribution to Heian poetics occurred when he went against Koretoki's model found in *Senzai kaku* and *Nikkan shū* and integrated Chinese couplets by non-Heian and Heian poets as he did. The reason for Kintō's ability to reconceptualize the relationship between *shi* and *kanshi* owes much to changes in the Yamato-Han apparatus during the course of the tenth century, particularly regarding methods of reading Chinese verse. *Kanshi* are identical to *shi* graphically (both employ classical Chinese graphs) and formally (both are couplets consisting of two lines, and each line contains a specified number of graphs, usually seven). Kimbara Tadashi describes the fundamental difference between Tang *shi* and Heian *kanshi* in these terms: "Heian *kanshi* were produced in the realm of 'interpretive reading' *(kundoku),* and they therefore were fundamentally different from *shi* produced in China, because they lacked a natural sense of the rhythm of Chinese."[8] In the early years of the Japanese court, the educated elite probably read *shi* linearly as native Chinese would read them, following classical Chinese syntax, in an approximation of the original pronunciation (which varied depending on the dynasty when contact with the Japanese court occurred). This method of reading is termed *ondoku,* "phono-reading," but it appears to have fallen increasingly into disuse as the court became less and less familiar with the sounds of spoken Chinese in the course of the Heian period. In contrast to *ondoku,* the method of reading *shi* in Yamato language is termed *kundoku* (or *yomi kudashi*), "interpretive reading," and it was apparently the norm by mid-Heian. It is a nonlinear method of reading Chinese text, following Japanese syntax, wherein Chinese sounds are dispensed with and Yamato pronunciation is used instead. Reading *shi* and *kanshi* with the words and syntax of the Yamato language required a process of skipping graphs momentarily, then doubling back to retrieve skipped graphs until the sense of the poem was complete. Verb endings had to be added—in contrast to the Chinese language,

Japanese verbs are agglutinative—and a system of appropriate verb endings was developed that helped make Yamato-like syntactic sense of the classical Chinese lines. That Chinese verses were being read using Japanese words and syntax through a process of "interpretive reading" suggests that some of the incompatibility between *shi* composed by Tang poets and *kanshi* composed by Japanese poets that would have been apparent to Koretoki when he compiled *Senzai kaku* and *Nikkan shū* as two separate texts had, in Kintō's day, become blurred.

A vestige of the distinction between *shi* and *kanshi* remains in the form of Kintō's hierarchy that places *shi* first under each topical heading in *Poems to Sing,* but any essential difference is gone because of the homogenizing effect of "interpretive reading." After all, the aim of the Yamato-Han apparatus was to make Chinese intelligible to the Japanese court, not to preserve difference for its own sake, and thus the apparatus had built into it a bias toward the elimination or flattening out of difference. Kintō gives little evidence that the *shi* by Tang poets in any way represent a foreign poetic form in the Heian literary world or that *waka* represent native sentiment in contrast to them. Instead, the elements of *shi, kanshi,* and *waka* are integrated into a naturalized *wa-kan* text that de-emphasizes the logic of Han and Yamato as representing opposing cultural and ethnic entities. The only difference that remains in Kintō's compilation is in the historicity of the verses and songs. The Chinese nature of *shi* and *kanshi* in relation to Japanese poems is erased or domesticated, and their ancientness and their importance as a poetic origin remain; in fact, the value of ancientness—and all the virtues that it entails (precedent, authority)—is one of the important by-products of Kintō's effort in compiling *Poems to Sing.*

Joining the 240 *shi* and 350 *kanshi* in *Poems to Sing* are 210 Yamato songs by seventy-three different poets, drawn mainly from the *Kokinshū.* In comparison with the number of Chinese verses *(shi* and *kanshi),* a smaller number of *waka* are shared among a larger number of poets. The existence of such variety among *waka* poets indicates that there was a large group of competent poets of Japanese at court, including many elite women. By contrast, it was a smaller and almost exclusively male group of poets that could compose competently in Chinese verse. The individual poet with the most *waka* appearing in the collection is the *Kokinshū* compiler, Ki no Tsurayuki (872?–945), with 19 entries. Tsurayuki was known as a champion of Japanese poetry and prose at a time when the court was dominated by composition in Chinese verse. It should come as no surprise that Tsurayuki has no *kanshi* to his credit in the collection. There are 11 *waka* by Ōshikōchi no Mitsune (fl. 898–922), 8 by Taira no Kanemori (?–ca. 900), and 6 each by the female poets Ise (877?–940?) and Nakatsuka (920?–980). *Waka* is the only genre in the collection represented by female poets, reflecting the division along sex/gender lines that, with some important exceptions, discouraged women from composing in Chinese during the Heian period.

Scholars have sometimes argued that poetry in Japanese and Chinese followed a division between public and private spheres at court. According to this view, *waka* were composed primarily to express private or personal feelings, whereas *kanshi* were composed primarily in formal and ceremonial contexts and thereby acquired a public and political dimension that *waka* lacked. As evidence, scholars point to the widespread use of *waka* in the conduct of courtship and love affairs, which required ready exchange of Japanese poems between noblemen and women. In contrast, *kanshi* were aligned with the practice of recording all official and ceremonial activities at court in classical Chinese and were taught as part of a university curriculum in the Chinese classics that was sponsored by the court for the exclusive education of sons of the aristocracy. While this description contains much truth, it must be modified to include two important facts: first, that in the course of the Heian period *waka* came to play an increasingly prominent public role in the imperially commissioned anthologies and in court-sponsored poetry contests; and, more significant for the purposes of this study, that Chinese verse was clearly an important realm of private expression in the emotional lives of Heian noblemen, albeit outside courtship and love affairs, as is evident in the "Friends" sequence from *Poems to Sing*.

Friendship's Repertoire of Words and Rhetorical Devices

The seven poems on "Friends" (nos. 733–739, shown on page 13) in *Poems to Sing* tell us a great deal about how male friendship was conceptualized and articulated at the Heian court early in the eleventh century. The title of the section is written with two graphs (C: *jiaoyou* J: *kōyū*), meaning "friends." The overarching theme is friendship among men as defined through male poetic experience. For that reason, the friend who stands at the center of each verse is always a male figure, and each verse explores a specific dimension of male friendship, using a fairly limited set of poetic words and rhetorical devices. In several cases, friendship is signaled by the overt use of word-graphs for "friend" (C: *jiao* J: *kō* or C: *you* J: *tomo*). In other cases, friendship is indicated strictly through a two-pole rhetorical framework consisting of the pronouns "you" (C: *jun* J: *kimi*) and "I" (C: *wo* J: *ware*). Even in the absence of any word specifically denoting a friend, the graphs for "you" and "I" are capable of establishing a poetic context of male friendship.

The graph *jun/kimi* originally meant "prince" or "lord," and appears famously in early Taoist and Confucian texts to indicate a man of breeding, in the graphs often translated as "gentleman" (C: *junzi* J: *kunshi*). From these origins, it came to be used in the Tang as an honorific pronominal. The Yamato reading of the graph as *kimi* dates to the early stages of continental contact, when the preliterate Yamato world collided with the literate continental world. In preliterate Yamato, *kimi* was a respectful name for wealthy, powerful village chiefs. As proto-Yamato society became more highly structured under continental influence, *kimi* became the term for the ruler of a political entity, first of a village or a group of villages and then, with time, of larger regions or states. The ancient use of *kimi* in the poetry of the eighth-

Seven Poems on Friendship in *Poems to Sing*

- *Lute, poetry, wine—my friends all have deserted me;*
  snow, moon, flowers—these seasons, I most often think of you.
  Bo Ju-yi, poem 733
- *These songs of Yang-force in the spring: so noble, hard to echo!*
  Feelings of friendship like limpid waters only in old age I've come to know.
  Bo Ju-yi, poem 734
- *In former years you looked at me directly—pupils dark;*
  now, I meet you, and I find your hair has turned to white!
  Xu Hun, poem 735
- *K'uai-chi Magistrate Hsiao, on passing the ancient shrine, forged a friendship across eras;*
  Vice Director Chang, in valuing fresh talent, promoted it and formed a friendship transcending age.
  Ōe no Asatsuna, poem 736
- *Descendant of P'ei of the Bureau of Documents—I have heard of you for years!*
  Orphan of the attendant gentleman of the Ministry of Rites–you see me today for the first time.
  Sugawara no Atsushige, poem 737
- *You and I—What promises must we have made*
  In a former life?—How I would like to know!
  Unknown poet, poem 738
- *Who may I call my comrade now? For even the aged pines at Takasago*
  Cannot replace the friends of yore.
  Fujiwara no Okikaze, poem 739

Source: Rimer and Chaves, *Poems to Sing*, 219–221.

century *Man'yō shū* (Collection of ten thousand ages) to indicate or address the sovereign (later, the emperor) dates to this early time. By mid-Heian, however, *kimi* was being used as a second-person pronoun ("you") toward social equals and as a respectful third-person pronoun ("he," "she," "they") to indicate social superiors. It was also sometimes appended to the name of high-ranking male or female courtiers as an informal title. *Ware* (or *are*) had two uses, as the first-person pronoun "I," referring to oneself, or as the second-person pronoun "you," used toward social inferiors. In the poetry of male friendship, however, *kimi* and *ware* are used in a highly specialized manner, to establish a two-poled structure in which a male subject "I" addresses his male friend "you." Every poem in the section on "Friends" in *Poems to Sing* employs either a word for "friend," the two-poled rhetorical structure "you" and "I," or both, in order to construct a poetic context of male friendship.

The first three poems in the sequence are *shi* couplets by Tang poets Bo Ju-yi and Xu Hun. Kintō places the poems in a sequence based on three conventional Chinese contexts in which friendship may be experienced: longing for a friend in his absence, corresponding by letter with a friend, and meeting with a friend face-to-face. In doing so, Kintō follows the lead of Ōe no Koretoki in *Senzai kaku,* which similarly categorized friendship by type. Poem 733 appears in *Senzai kaku* under the heading "Longing for a Friend" *(tomo wo omou),* poem 734 under the heading "A Letter (or Pen) Friend" *(fumi no tomo),* and poem 735 under "Meeting a Friend" *(tomo ni au).* In each case, the heading of the poem identifies the context that inspired the composition.

• *Lute, poetry, wine—my friends all have deserted me;*
snow, moon, flowers—these seasons, I most often think of you.
Bo Ju-yi, poem 733

In this couplet, the poet Bo Ju-yi expresses his longing for an absent friend. The poem consists of two lines containing only seven graphs per line, but despite its brevity it is ranked as one of the most powerful and greatly admired expressions of male friendship in classical Chinese literature. A prose heading indicates that it was "Sent to Chief Musician Yin."[9] According to the standard interpretation of the poem, the poet's ("my") friends who formerly made music with him, composed poetry with him, and drank wine with him have now moved on to other places and other pursuits, but when the seasons come around and bring with them snowfall, autumn moonlight, and blossoming trees, they remind the poet of past times and particularly of Chief Musician Yin ("you"), the friend who once shared the three pleasures of playing the lute (C: *qin* J: *kin;* actually a zither), composing poetry, and drinking wine with the poet. "My" (the poet's) fond recollection of "you" (Chief Musician Yin) thus serves to comfort the poet even as it intensifies his longing and loneliness. Bo Ju-yi creates a parallel between the activities (lute, poetry, and wine) and the seasons when they are enjoyed (snow, moon, and blossoms) in order to establish and convey the poem's main point: that the seasons return unfailingly, and yet the times spent with this friend, and indeed the friend himself, are gone without hope of return. Simultaneously, Bo Ju-yi makes of the poem an affirmation of friendship, reassuring his friend, Chief Musician Yin, that he is remembered and missed. A poem on the theme of friendship becomes itself an enactment of friendship in the master poet's hands.

In another interpretation widely held at the Heian court, the lute, poetry, and wine are themselves the poet's "friends," and the poem's conceit is that these friends have now abandoned the poet, along with the human companions who once shared in these pleasures with him. There is good reason to believe that this alternate reading of the poem is a product of the mid-Heian courtier's method of reading Chinese verse. The opening line of poem 733 would have been read, using Japanese syntax in the style of "interpretive reading," as *kin shi shu no tomo wa mina ware wo nageutsu.* The phrase *kin shi shu* (lute, poetry, wine) is linked to the word *tomo* (friend) with the Japanese genitive particle *no,* which defines the relation of "friend" to the phrase "lute, poetry, wine" ambiguously. "Friend" may be interpreted in relation to the three items as a whole ("lute, poetry, and wine, *which are my friends*") or, as Bo Ju-yi intended, distributively in relation to each item individually (my lute-friends, poetry-friends, and wine-friends). By interpreting "friend" in relation to the three items as a whole, Heian readers of the poem took the items themselves to be the poet's friends and, for that reason, came to refer to "lute, poetry, and wine" as Bo Ju-yi's "three friends" (C: *san you* J: *san'yū*) in later literature. The process of "interpretive reading" using Yamato syntax in this case contributed to a novel interpretation of Bo Ju-yi's poetic text. Kawaguchi Hisao calls this a "slippage in meaning."[10] The mid-Heian *wa-kan* assemblage allowed the Heian courtier to read Chinese text as Yamato-language literature, but the process led to unintended apprehensions of meaning, as illustrated in this case. Such slippages proliferated within the *wa-kan* assemblage because the practice of "interpretive reading" created room for them. Individual courtiers educated in the Chinese classics may well have been capable of recognizing when such slippages occurred, but for the vast majority of mid-Heian readers of

Chinese texts the problem of semantic slippage was largely invisible. The example of Bo Ju-yi's "three friends" reveals one of the risks inherent in Kintō's conception of *Poems to Sing* as a text that could be read seamlessly in Japanese by relying on "interpretive reading": the Chinese text was glossed in Japanese and was thus no longer foreign at some level, but the familiarity and readability of the text was achieved at the cost of the poem's original meaning, which became a victim of the reading strategy employed at the mid-Heian court. If meaning was sacrificed, then Yamato and Chinese linguistic boundaries were not as permeable as the *wa-kan* assemblage pretended, and linguistic difference had a way of asserting itself against the homogenizing efforts of that assemblage, whether individual courtier readers were aware of it or not.

Kintō's decision to place Bo Ju-yi's poem 733 first in the sequence of seven poems accomplishes two tasks: it confirms the importance of the two-poled rhetorical structure of "you" and "me" in the Heian poetry of male friendship; and it acknowledges a particular aesthetic stance toward the friend, namely, that the deepest experience of friendship resides in the friend's absence, not in his presence. In a poem about friends who are absent, the reader is forced to imagine a moment when the pleasure of shared camaraderie is past—whether in the contexts of music, poetry, or wine or in the seasons of snow, moonlight, or flowering trees—and only then is he prepared to comprehend what Bo Ju-yi would have called the "truth" of friendship. We shall see in poem 735 by Xu Hun an opposite aesthetic choice that locates the experience of friendship in a friend's presence. By giving poem 733 pride of place in the sequence, Kintō suggests that the Tang poet and his Heian admirers shared a common aesthetic of longing for the absent friend. This fundamental aesthetic agreement allowed the Heian courtier to overcome trivial semantic slippages that may have occurred as a result of the interpretive mode of reading within the *wa-kan* assemblage and to achieve a profound comprehension of the poem's sense.

• *These songs of Yang-force in the spring: so noble, hard to echo!*
Feelings of friendship like limpid waters only in old age I've come to know.
Bo Ju-yi, poem 734

Bo Ju-yi's expression of fondness for his friend in this couplet is triggered by an exchange of poems. It thus describes a literary friendship, rather than a friendship based on longing for an absent friend as in the previous couplet. Poem 734 is formally identical to the preceding couplet, consisting again of two lines with seven graphs per line. The prose headnote to the couplet reads, "Supernumerary Chang [Zhang] the Eighteenth has sent me twenty-five of his new poems; in the Yamen tower beneath the moon, I chanted and enjoyed them all night long, and then inscribed this at the end."[11] The poet praises Zhang's poems, comparing them to "songs of Yang-force in the spring." This reference is to chapter 10 of the ancient Chinese text *Wen xuan* (Literary classics). But what most moves the poet is his realization of the special quality of Zhang's friendship; it is "bland" *(dan)* and, like water, pure and unadulterated. Only after a lifetime of friendship does the poet, now an old man, recognize this precious quality in his friend. The twenty-five poems function as an extension of Zhang himself and embody Zhang's friendship for the poet. By chanting them and enjoying them through the night, the poet comes to perceive the rare friendship that motivated Zhang's letter. Zhang is present through proxy in the form of his new poems, and they serve as a satisfying substitute for the poet. The resulting poem of gratitude and praise is Bo Ju-yi's response.

The phrase "feelings of friendship like limpid waters" refers to the "Mountain Tree" chapter of *Zhuang-zi:*

> The friendship of a gentleman, they say, is insipid [*dan*] as water; that of a petty man, sweet as rich wine. But the insipidity of the gentleman leads to affection, while the sweetness of the petty man leads to revulsion. Those with no particular reason for joining together will for no particular reason part.[12]

This discourse comes in the context of Confucius' questions to Master Sang-hu: Why was Confucius driven out of various states where he attempted to be of service? And why had his kinfolk, associates, friends, and followers abandoned him? Sang-hu answers the question with the example of Lin Hui, who threw away a disc of jade worth a thousand measures of gold but kept his little baby when fleeing the state of Jia. When asked why he did this, Lin Hui is said to have replied: "The jade disc and I were joined by profit, but the child and I were brought together by Heaven. Things joined by profit, when pressed by misfortune and danger, will cast each other aside; but things brought together by Heaven, when pressed by misfortune and danger, will cling to one another."[13]

The implication in Bo Ju-yi's poem is that friends are joined by something larger than themselves ("Heaven") and not by petty self-interest ("profit"). If misfortune and danger lead two friends to part, then they were in fact not friends but were merely joined to each other temporarily by the benefits derived from the relationship. The "insipidness" of the gentleman's friendship is a reflection of the selflessness of his association with his friend, and the "sweetness" of a petty man's friendship reflects his self-serving motives. The narrative suggests that selfless friendship that is insipid or "limpid" like fresh water can be trusted, whereas selfish friendship that has the alluring sweetness of wine quickly succumbs to self-interest, and the only way to distinguish the two is in the long term.

The diction and rhetorical structures employed in both of Bo Ju-yi's couplets are remarkably similar. Friendship is indicated overtly in poem 734 through the graphs translated as "feelings of friendship" (C: *jiaoqing* J: *kōjō*). This parallels the appearance of the graph for "friend" (C: *you* J: *tomo*) in the preceding couplet, number 733. Moreover, if we look beyond the couplet excerpted here in *Poems to Sing* to the complete verse as Bo Ju-yi wrote it, we find that the immediately preceding lines establish the context of the poet's friendship with Zhang through the pronouns "I" and "you."

> *Separated from me* [C: *wo* J: *ware*] *by 3,600 miles;*
> *[I] receive from you* [C: *jun* J: *kimi*] *twenty-five poems.*[14]

The two-poled formula of "me" and "you" establishes a rhetorical structure for male friendship in the complete poem, even though it is not evident in the excerpted couplet. Finally, Bo Ju-yi's stance as the poetic subject in poem 734 parallels his stance in the preceding poem, number 733. Both poems address absent friends and become enactments of the very friendship Bo Ju-yi is writing about. Whether recalling the seasons and Chief Musician Yin or admiring the poems of Supernumerary Zhang the Eighteenth, Bo Ju-yi's poems stand as proof of the power of poetry to unite distant friends, so that friendship becomes simultaneously the topic of the poems and what is enacted in them. The poems stand as powerful expressions of the hope that friendship can transcend the gulf of time and space that divides the men.

> • *In former years you looked at me directly—pupils dark;*
> *now, I meet you, and I find your hair has turned to white!*
> XU HUN, poem 735

The signs of aging we observe in a longtime friend can bring on stark emotions of pity and affection. This is the sentiment expressed beautifully in poem 735 by Xu Hun. As with Bo Ju-yi's preceding two verses, the couplet is taken from a longer *shi* and presents another perspective on friendship. The poem differs from them, however, in that it contains no explicit word designating the person of the "friend," neither C: *you* J: *tomo* found in poem 733 nor C: *jiao* J: *kō* found in poem 734. Instead, friendship is established solely with the pronoun pair "me" and "you." What makes Xu Hun's use of the two-poled rhetorical structure stand out is the way he links the pair of pronouns to two other sets of pairs contrasting time (past versus present) and color (dark versus white).

Time is divided in the poem between "former years" and "now." The poet remembers fondly that the two men have been friends since the friend's eyes were dark, an image signifying the passionate gaze of youth. The poet himself was the object of this long, dark gaze. Now the poet points out with surprise and perhaps amusement that his friend's hair has turned white with age. The use of contrasting colors in reference to the eyes and the hair is linked to the poem's chronological structure: dark eyes represent youth and the past, while white hair represents old age and the present. Another implied contrast is that time may have transformed the youthful friends into old men, but their friendship defies the ravages of time. Bo Ju-yi's preceding two couplets located the realization of friendship in the returning seasons (no. 733) and in the reading of a friend's poems (no. 734), but in Xu Hun's couplet the realization of friendship is triggered visually by the encounter with the face of the friend. The three couplets trace a trajectory of perception from the abstract to the concrete: from bodily absence (no. 733) to presence in surrogate form (through letters and poems, no. 734), to bodily presence (no. 735).

In each of the couplets by Bo Ju-yi and Xu Hun, the durability and ongoingness of friendship are its implicit subject: despite separation, friendship survives (no. 733); through a lifelong exchange of letters and poems, friendship thrives (no. 734); in the face of old age, the memory of youthful friendship revives and sustains itself (no. 735). This ability of friendship to offer hope of transcending the obstacles of time and distance is the focus of the next two poems in the sequence, both of which are *kanshi,* Chinese couplets composed by Heian noblemen.

- *K'uai-chi Magistrate Hsiao, on passing the ancient shrine, forged a friendship* [C: *jiao* J: *kō*] *across eras;*
  Vice Director Chang, in valuing fresh talent, promoted it and formed a friendship [C: *you* J: *tomo*] *transcending age.*
  Ōe no Asatsuna, poem 736

Can friendships be forged between men of vastly different ages and times? This seems to be the question implicit in this couplet, which argues that male friendships can indeed transcend time. Citing examples from Chinese histories, the poet presents an example of a friendship formed between an older man and a younger one, and between a man and a historical figure he admired. The couplet is by the Heian courtier Ōe no Asatsuna (887–957) and is atypical in form, in that it contains thirteen graphs per line instead of the usual seven. The poem is especially interesting in the context of the section on "Friends" because it is purely descriptive and not an avowal of fondness between two friends, as seen in the couplets by Bo Ju-yi and Xu Hun. For that reason, it is arguably the first poem to treat friendship as an abstraction. The poem describes two classical examples taken from the *Chen shu* (History of Chen) that illustrate the ability of friendship to transcend barriers that time imposes between men. A testament to Asatsuna's erudition, the poem befits his reputation as an expert in the Chinese classics.

The first verse of the couplet refers to an incident in the biography of Xiao Yun, who offered a sacrifice at the grave of Ji Zha, a famous sage-statesman from the Spring and Autumn Period, and whom he admired greatly. According to the poem's conceit, this act forged a connection between the men and thereby proved that friendship is indeed possible between men of similar convictions even if they lived in different historical eras. The second stanza refers to another incident from the *History of Chen* recorded in the biography of Jiang Zong. A Tang official named Zhang Zuan recognized Jiang Zong's talent and supported his advancement at court. Although Zhang was considerably his senior, the two men became friends. The poem presents their cross-generational friendship as further evidence of the remarkable ability of friendship to link two men across barriers of age and status. The poet, Ōe no Asatsuna, implies that the ability of men of different generations to experience friendship is a positive attribute, but when the incident in the *History of Chen* is looked at in context, it may well be that Jiang Zong's biographer meant the statement as a criticism. Certainly, cross-generational friendships could have violated a sense of decorum and represented a breakdown of the strict hierarchies of status that prevailed at court. Nevertheless, the Japanese poet has clearly chosen not to view the friendship between Jiang Zong and Zhang Zuan in a negative light, but instead regards it as a positive example of the ability of friendship to transcend the limitations on masculine intimacy imposed by hierarchical constraints and generational divisions.

The vocabulary of friendship in poem 736 is distinctive. First, the couplet lacks the formulaic rhetorical structure of male friendship built around the pronouns "you" and "I," as observed in the couplets by Bo Ju-yi and Xu Hun. Instead, this poem employs the two words for "friend" in a strict parallel structure: C: *jiao* J: *kō* at the end of the first line, and C: *you* J: *tomo* at the end of the second line. Through the device of parallel graphic cognates for "friend," the poet more than compensates for the lack of any pronominal two-poled structure in the poem. Asatsuna's poem is clearly an eloquent and erudite description of friendship. Is it meant simply as a poem in general praise of friendship? Or is it grounded in Asatsuna's personal experience and meant to justify or explain the poet's own experience of friendship? Lacking any contextual information regarding the poem's composition in the form of a headnote, none of these questions can be answered conclusively. What the poem suggests, however, is that male friendship was understood by the Heian courtier as possessing historical precedent and a historical context that could be deduced from Chinese histories, and that Japanese poets of *kanshi* such as Asatsuna looked to textual formulations of friendship in those histories as relevant to their experience of friendship in Heian court culture. By extension, whatever obstacles to friendship that existed between noblemen of different generations might be mediated—and potentially overcome—by their reading of friendship in Chinese histories. The poem suggests that Asatsuna and perhaps others manipulated the authority imputed in Chinese texts by the *wa-kan* assemblage for their own purposes, even to the extent of redrawing the boundaries of what sorts of friendships were considered acceptable at the Heian court. This manipulation of Chinese historical precedent to critique contemporary Heian court culture was a potent by-product of the *wa-kan* system of bilingual and bicultural literacy, and it probably served in this case to liberate the Heian nobleman in his pursuit and appreciation of friendship with like-minded men of his class.

• *Descendant of P'ei of the Bureau of Documents—I have heard of you for years!*
Orphan of the attendant gentleman of the Ministry of Rites—you see me for the first time.
SUGAWARA NO ATSUSHIGE, poem 737

Male friendship in poem 737 arises in an intercultural, interlingual setting. Two aristocrats from different courts, one Heian and the other in the kingdom of Bo-hai (between China and Korea), meet in their official capacities during an embassy to Heian, and the poet asserts that they are friends. The poem was written by Sugawara no Atsushige (d. 926) to welcome to the Heian capital the son of his father's friend, a diplomat named P'ei. The couplet consists of two lines of seven graphs each, identical in form to the couplets by Bo Ju-yi and Xu Hun seen earlier. Atsushige's father, Sugawara no Michizane,[15] had met the elder P'ei when he arrived on an earlier embassy to Heian in 883, and now the sons meet in similar circumstances during another Bo-hai embassy to Heian in 908.[16] When the poet addresses the envoy as "descendant of P'ei" and refers to himself as "orphan of the Minister of Rites," he is affirming that friendship is so transcendent and durable that it can be passed down from fathers to sons. That is why the poet can claim that even though they see each other for the first time, they have known each other for years. Friendship is again transcendent, in this case because it is capable of being passed down from one generation to the next.

The appearance of the pronouns "you" and "I" indicates that Atsushige has chosen to rely on the crucial two-poled structure for denoting friendship in the poem. The poem revolves around a contradiction: the two men have in a sense known each other all their lives ("I have heard of you for years"), even though they have never met ("you see me for the first time"). Their knowledge of each other is derivative or secondhand, a result of their fathers' friendship. The friendship of their fathers, officers of the Heian and Bo-hai courts, originally crossed the boundaries of their respective homelands, and now it crosses the generations to link the sons.

- kimi to ware ikanaru koto wo chigirikemu mukashi no yo koso shiramahoshikere

You and I—What promises must we have made
In a former life?—How I would like to know![17]
UNKNOWN POET, poem 738

This anonymous poem is the first *waka* in the "Friends" sequence, and the first time that the two-poled rhetorical structure appears in the Yamato language to denote male friendship, in the dramatic opening line, *kimi to ware* ("you and I"). The rhetorical structure mediates the linguistic shift from the preceding five poems in Chinese verse to Japanese song, thereby revealing rhetorical consistency in the face of linguistic difference. The poem draws on the Buddhist concepts of karma and past lives when it asks, "What promises must we have made in a former life?" Friendship in this life is conceptualized as a product of vows exchanged in former lives, and the karmic bond explains the intensity of the present friendship in this life. In the poetic vocabulary of *waka,* "exchanging vows" usually refers to vows of sexual love between a man and a woman. Frequently, the idea that bonds of love date from a previous life is drawn upon to help make sense of a relationship that is fraught with unusual peril or emotional suffering, for example, if it involves a man and a woman of very different social status. In fact, the poem appears in *Shin senzai shū* (1359, New collection of Japanese poems of a thousand years) as a poem on "Love" *(koi),* and it may have been composed originally as part of a poetry contest at court under the assigned topic of "Frustrated Love" *(awanu koi).*[18] Certainly, the poem would not be out of place in a collection of love poems, judging from its conventional focus on the exchange of vows *(chigirikemu)* and its reference to bonds from a former life *(mukashi no yo).*

The decisive factor in Kintō's appropriation of the poem into the sequence of poems on male friendship in *Poems to Sing* must have been the opening phrase, *kimi to ware* ("you and I"). For Kintō, who had been working thus far in the sequence exclusively within the masculine domain of Chinese verse, his encounter with the native words *kimi to ware* in this Japanese poem would have rhetorically signified friendship between men. Japanese poetry merges seamlessly with the preceding Chinese verses. That Chinese verses (both *shi* and *kanshi*) were being read in "interpretive reading" fashion at the Heian court probably explains why the Chinese graphs for "you" and "I" rang in Kintō's ear as an evocation of male friendship. The aura of masculinity inherent in the two-poled rhetorical structure in the poems on "Friends" served to disrupt Kintō's ability to read poem 738 as a love poem between a man and a woman. Transformed in its new context, the Japanese poem unmistakably and intriguingly becomes a poem about male friendship. Kintō's appropriation of the poem is nothing less than brilliant.

Some scholars argue that Kintō's use of poem 738 in the context of friendship was a mistake or was forced on him by a dearth of *waka* on the theme of male friendship. Certainly, the erotic intensity of the poetic diction and the reference to previous lives point powerfully to erotic love by traditional standards, and on that basis some commentators question its designation by Kintō as a poem on male friendship. Kaneko and Emi, for example, note that "although [this poem] is placed in the section on 'Friends,' it is clearly a statement about feelings of love between a man and a woman."[19] Donald Keene even suggests that Kintō had little choice but to appropriate the poem because there were few candidates on the topic of friendship in the *waka* repertoire: "Friendship, a frequent theme of Chinese poetry, is so rarely described in *waka* poetry that one of two *waka* on the theme (following five *kanshi*) is actually a love poem appropriated for the purpose, faute de mieux."[20] Ōsone and Horiuchi, cited by Keene, simply say that the poem's sentiments are recast in the context of poems on friendship—not inappropriately—as an expression of feelings of friendship *(kōyū no jō)*.[21] Likewise, Kawaguchi Hisao states, "It is originally a poem about erotic love between a man and woman *(danjo ren'ai)*, but here it is taken as being about feelings of friendship *(kōyū no jō)*."[22] Both opinions appear to accept one implication of Kintō's use of the poem in *Poems to Sing*, namely, that the poem's meaning could legitimately be reconceptualized through its new context in the poetic sequence of poems on friendship.

There are numerous examples suggesting that the poetic vocabulary in *waka* for expressing feelings of love and friendship was identical. Book 8 of the *Kokinshū* consists of "Songs of Parting" *(ribetsu no uta)*. Some are by male courtiers and addressed to their friends, and at the level of diction they are indistinguishable from love poems. *Kokinshū* poem 378, for example, uses the phrase *kayou kokoro* ("loving heart") to describe the intimate connection between the poet and his friend:

> kumoi ni mo kayou kokoro no okureneba wakaru to hito ni miyu bakari nari
> *no matter how great / a distance you may travel, / my loving heart will / never lag behind though it / may seem to have been parted*[23]

Even poetic place-names typically linked with erotic love, such as Ōsaka ("Meeting Hill"), are employed in expressions of friendship between men in the "Songs of Parting." *Kokinshū* poem 390, was composed by Ki no Tsurayuki, the headnote states, "while crossing Ōsaka when seeing off Fujiwara no Koreoka, who was taking up the post of Vice-Governor of Musashi."

> katsu koete wakare mo yuku ka ōsaka wa hitodanome naru na ni koso arikere
> *while still he crosses / over and journeys onward / leaving me behind, / your title Ōsaka— / Meeting Hill—is just a name*[24]

Another poem of friendship that is indistinguishable from a love poem is *Kokinshū* poem 399, by Ōshikōchi no Mitsune. It expresses feelings of longing for a Prince he has just met. The headnote reads, "Composed on parting from Prince Kanemi after first conversing with him."

wakaruredo ureshiku mo aru ka koyoi yori ai minu yori nani o koimashi
although we part / I am filled with happiness / for now I wonder / whom I might have thought I loved / before we two met tonight[25]

Similarly, poems expressing feelings of friendship appear in the sections on "Travel" (book 9) and "Grief" (book 16) in the *Kokinshū.*

The phrase *kimi to ware* ("you and I") was not exclusive to men in the diction of *waka,* either. There are several examples from both imperial anthologies and private collections that show it being used to denote a male/female pair. *Gosen shū* (ca. 951, Collection of later selections of Japanese poems) contains the first example of the phrase *kimi to ware* in a poem in an imperially commissioned anthology.

kimi to ware imose no yama mo aki kureba iro kawarinuru mono ni zo arikeru
You and I—when autumn comes to Mt. Imose [husband and wife], even there can we observe that the colors have changed.[26]

In the text of this poem, "you and I" refers to a husband and wife, although it is not obvious who is addressing whom. Typically, it is the role of the female figure in a *waka* to make accusations that a man's feelings have changed ("changing colors"), but whether the poem follows type is difficult to say. Moreover, it was not uncommon for male poets to compose accusatory poems, taking on the female perspective and voice, in *uta-awase* (poem matching) contests held at court, which meant that the sex of the poet did not necessarily coincide with the gendered viewpoint expressed in a poem.

A variant text of the imperial anthology *Gyokuyō shū* (1312–1313, Collection of jeweled leaves) contains a *kimi to ware* poem attributed to the famed poetess of love, Ono no Komachi (fl. ca. 833–857).

yo no naka wa asukagawa ni mo naraba nare kimi to ware to ga naka shi taezu wa
Should the world [of love] be the River Asuka, so be it; the bond between you and me shall never end.[27]

The River Asuka was a poetic place-name designating fickleness on the basis of the stream's unpredictable flow. The poem appears to be an assertion of the steadfastness of love between "you and me," presumably in the voice of a female poet addressed to her male lover. These two examples are the only to appear in the imperial anthologies with the phrases *kimi to ware* (five syllables) or *kimi to ware to ga* (seven syllables).

However, the words *kimi* and *ware* appear in separate lines in numerous *waka,* beginning with the first imperial anthology, the *Kokinshū,* thereby providing evidence that the two-poled structure of "you and I" was a common rhetorical device in *waka* about male and female lovers. A famous example in the *Kokinshū* is poem 645, which also appears in the *Ise monogatari* (Tale of Ise), episode 69. The poet is designated as "unknown" in the *Kokinshū,* but a headnote to the poem contradicts the anonymous designation and identifies the writer as Ise no Saigū, the unmarried Princess appointed to serve at the Ise Shrine and usually identified as Princess Tenshi (Yasuko, d. 913), who held that office from 859 to 876 during the reign of Emperor Seiwa. The identification is historically unreliable, and Helen McCullough is probably correct in calling it a "romantic myth."[28] The *Kokinshū* entry reads:

> Once, when Narihira was in Ise Province, he had a secret tryst with the Virgin of the Shrine. The next morning, as he was worrying about having no one to carry a message to her, this poem arrived from her.
>
> kimi ya koshi ware ya yukiken omōezu yume ka utsutsu ka nete ka samete ka
>
> *did you come to me / or did I go to you—I / cannot now recall / was it dream or reality / was I sleeping or awake*[29]

The structure of "you" and "I" as discrete entities that form a male-female pair is evoked powerfully here. The female poet's imagination ("did you come to me or did I go to you?") that makes the two lovers equally mobile partners probably reflects the poet's yearning for a mobility that she did not in fact possess. In the ninth century when the poem was composed, a high-born woman such as Ise no Saigū could rarely have traveled on her own to Narihira's bed for a night of lovemaking. Certainly by mid-Heian the idea of coming and going freely to her lover would have been in the realm of fantasy for a woman of exalted rank. The poem's power derives from the poet's expression of her wish that, rather than waiting passively for her lover's visits as dictated by the Heian social order, she could in fact have visited him freely at a time of her own choosing, in the manner of a male friend.

- tare wo kamo shiru hito ni semu Takasago no matsu mo mukashi no tomo naranaku ni

Who may I call my comrade now? For even the aged pines at Takasago
Cannot replace the friends of yore.
FUJIWARA NO OKIKAZE, poem 739

The final poem in the section on "Friends" tells us that death is the one obstacle friendship cannot overcome. It is a poem of grief by Fujiwara no Okikaze (early tenth century) from book 17 ("Miscellaneous Songs") of the *Kokinshū*. In some ways, it can be understood to contradict the preceding six poems in the section, all of which define friendship in terms of its ability to transcend the obstacles of time, distance, and history. The poem suggests that mortality is the one obstacle that cannot be surmounted and that even friendship is helpless against it. Put differently, the poem addresses the problem faced by the surviving friend, whose feelings of friendship may endure when the friend who was the object of those feelings has passed on. The poem acknowledges an ultimate human truth: that death takes our friends and leaves us bereft. The poem's imagery derives from a poetic legend of twin pine trees standing for a thousand years at Takasago along the coast of Japan's Inland Sea. The longevity of the pair of pines is contrasted to the mortality of the poet and his friend, parted in death. The Takasago pines survive together seemingly unscathed by the passage of years, but their image of constancy brings no comfort to the poet; instead, their existence only accentuates the poet's grief, for they force him to recognize that he is now alone and that nothing can replace the lost friend.

The poem defines what is a friend in terms of "knowing" *(shiru)*. A friend is, above all, someone I "know" and who in turn "knows" me. The line "Who may I call my comrade now?" in English translation captures nicely the ambiguity in the original, for the phrase *shiru hito* in Japanese implies both directions of knowing; it is "the person [I] know" and also "the person who knows [me]." This emphasis on "knowing"—or being known—is reminiscent of the legendary friends of the Broken Strings, Bo Ya and Zhong Ziqi. Recall that Bo Ya broke the strings of his zither when his friend died because there was no one else in the world who "knew his sounds." When a man loses his male soul mate, he calls out in grief, "Who may I call my comrade now?" This cry involves two dimensions of loss: the loss of the person whose soul the surviving friend comprehended most deeply, and the loss of the person who comprehended the surviving friend most deeply. The twin dimensions of knowing and being known are central to the poem's conception of male friendship and permeate the spirit of the poem.

Poem 739 can be thought of as transitional in nature. Coming at the end of the section on "Friends," it anticipates the next section, which addresses the topic of "Nostalgia for Men of the Past" *(kaikyū)*. In total, there are ten poems in the section on "Nostalgia for Men of the Past," and the connection to male friendship gets increasingly tenuous as the sequence progresses. What is important to realize is that Kintō compiled the poems on friendship in *Poems to Sing* with exquisite attention to subtleties of sentiment. In making two separate categories for poems of "Friendship" and poems of "Nostalgia for Men of the Past," Kintō makes an explicit distinction between the emotional experience of "friendship" and "nostalgia" that is highly instructive for understanding the parameters of male friendship in the work. The central figure in the sequence of poems on friendship is the "friend" (C: *jiao* J: *kō* or C: *you* J: *tomo*). In the poems on nostalgia for men of the past, the central figure changes to the "man of the past" (C: *guren* J: *kojin*), who may be living or dead. "Men of the past" are people who are transformed by separation, exile, death, or simply the passage of time into those whom the poetic subject remembers with nostalgia in his verses. Among them are numbered all manner of men with whom the poet may have consorted in former days, including friends, neighbors, colleagues at work, and cohorts in other endeavors. The "man of the past" is thus a figure created from the poet's recollection of the people he had contact with in former times. To the extent that the "friend" is also a figure of remembrance, there is a great deal of resonance between the idea of the "friend" and the "man of the past." If we look closely at the poems by Bo Ju-yi in other sections in *Poems to Sing,* we discover that he uses the word "men of the past" in his poetic vocabulary to refer to past acquaintances posthumously. This is particularly evident in Bo Ju-yi's poems of mourning for deceased acquaintances, which frequently retain the rhetorical structure of friendship in the pronoun pair "you" and "I."

> *Beneath the yellow earth, how could you know of me?*
> *With head of white hair, alone I think of you.*
> *All I can do is let my aged tears*
> *sprinkle these writings of yours, my friend.* [C: *guren* J: *kojin*]
> Bo Ju-yi, poem 740

Poem 740 resonates in interesting ways with poem 739 immediately preceding it, even though they appear under different topics. Poem 739 is the last poem in the section on "Friends," and it begins with the phrase *tare wo kamo shiru hito ni semu* ("Who may I call my comrade now?" or, more literally, "Who can I say I know [or knows me] now?"). As noted earlier, it is a cry of grief for a friend who has died. The first poem in "Nostalgia for Men of the Past," number 740, similarly begins with a cry of grief, using the same words "who" and "know" to express the poet's sense of loss: *shei zhi wo* ("Who knows me?"). The three graphs would be read in Japanese using the method of "interpretive reading" as *tare ka ware wo shiramu* ("Who might know me?"). The interpenetration of Chinese verse in number 740 and Japanese poem in number 739 is almost complete, both *shi* couplet and *waka* sharing identical diction and sentiment. As in poem 739, the object of the poet's grief in poem 740 is a specific individual who understood the surviving friend intimately. The poet recalls him here when he is looking at his writings—probably poems and letters addressed to the poet. Furthermore, poem 740 echoes the structure of poems in the section on "Friends" with its use of the pronoun pair "you" and "I." When considered in this light, the section on "Nostalgia for Men of the Past" clearly seems to be an extension of the section on "Friends," particularly in its depiction of grief that accompanies the death of a friend. The theme is continued in another couplet by Bo Ju-yi in the next verse, number 741.

> *Into the long night, you gentlemen have gone first;*
> *remaining years—how many left to me?*
> *Autumn wind, tears covering my shirt:*
> *beneath the Springs, so many of my friends!* [C: *guren* J: *kojin*]
> Bo Ju-yi, poem 741

While translated as "friends," the word Bo Ju-yi uses here is again "men of the past" (C: *guren* J: *kojin*), just as in poem 740. In spirit, however, the poem's sentiment is quite different from that in poems 739 and 740, which addressed specific individuals. Here, the grief is plural, amounting to many losses and compounded heartache because the poet has so many dead companions to mourn. Nevertheless, the poet's grief for "men of the past" is expressed once again within the idiom of friendship, employing the pronouns "you" and "I" for the second time in this section. The pronoun pair makes the poem an intimate, personal address from the poet to the memory of his deceased friends.

To understand the importance of this two-poled pronoun structure for our ability to interpret the word "men of the past" as designating deceased friends, it is interesting to consider an example of a poem that uses "men of the past" but without the two pronouns. In the section on "Living in Retirement" *(kankyo)* in *Poems to Sing,* the word appears in its general sense of "men of the past" in the second line of the following couplet by Bo Ju-yi:

When I open the crane's cage, I see the sovereign;
as I unfold my book scrolls, I encounter old friends. [C: *guren* J: *kojin*]
Bo Ju-yi, poem 616

Japanese commentators suggest that this poem expresses Bo Ju-yi's sentiments about his retirement, and in particular represents an attempt to describe what brings him comfort in the loneliness he experiences in his reclusion. The beauty and dignity of the crane make him feel he is in the presence of a gentleman (C: *junzi* J: *kunshi,* here translated "sovereign") who possesses great refinement and elegance. Through his reading of scrolls—books of poetry— he feels the vivid presence of their authors, serving in his retirement as companions from the past.[30] The English translation glosses C: *guren* J: *kojin* as "old friends," suggesting the possibility that the poet derives comfort in his retirement from reading the poetry of men who were once his actual intimates. More likely, however, "old friends" refers in general terms to authors from the past, whether known to the poet personally or not, whose well-loved writings bring comfort to the poet in his old age. This more general reading of C: *guren* J: *kojin* as "men of the [distant] past" rather than specific "old friends" may be preferable because the poem lacks the necessary intimacy of address that is conveyed in the poetry of friendship by the pronoun pair "you" and "I."

"Friends" in Context

It is worth turning to broader questions of how Kintō organized topics within *Poems to Sing* as a whole, in order to see the larger context in which the seven poems on "Friends" appeared. As noted earlier, *Poems to Sing* is divided into two volumes. Volume 1 consists of seasonal poems, while volume 2 consists of poems on forty-eight miscellaneous topics. The poems and prose segments in volume 2 are divided under topic headings in the following list. I have indicated the number of poems under each topic, and the distribution of Chinese *shi* couplets, *kanshi,* and *waka*—for example, 1-1-1 if a topic contains three poems, one of each type.

1. "Wind" (397–402; 6 poems: 1-3-2)
2. "Clouds" (403–409; 7 poems: 3-3-1)
3. "Clear Skies" (410–415; 6 poems: 1-4-1)
4. "Dawn" (416–420; 5 poems: 4-0-1)
5. "Pine Trees" (421–429; 9 poems: 2-4-3)
6. "Bamboo" (430–434; 5 poems: 2-2-1)

7. "Wild Grasses" (435–442; 8 poems: 2-3-3)
8. "Cranes" (443–453; 11 poems: 5-3-3)
9. "Gibbons" (454–461; 8 poems: 3-5-0)
10. "Pipes and Strings" (462–469; 8 poems: 4-3-1)
11. "Letters (with Bequeathed Letters appended)" (470–478; 9 poems: 4-4-1)
12. "Wine" (479–490; 12 poems: 6-5-1)
13. "Mountains" (491–498; 8 poems: 2-3-3)
14. "Mountains and Waters" (499–509; 11 poems: 5-5-1)
15. "Bodies of Water (with Fishermen appended)" (510–520; 11 poems: 5-4-2)
16. "The Forbidden City" (521–527; 7 poems: 3-2-2)
17. "The Old Capital" (528–529; 2 poems: 0-1-1)
18. "Old Palaces (with Deserted Mansions appended)" (530–539; 10 poems: 2-5-3)
19. "Immortals (with Taoists and Hermits appended)" (540–553; 14 poems: 3-10-1)
20. "Mountain Residences" (554–564; 11 poems: 3-6-2)
21. "Farmers" (565–571; 7 poems: 1-3-3)
22. "Neighbors" (572–577; 6 poems: 2-3-1)
23. "Mountain Temples" (578–586; 9 poems: 2-5-2)
24. "Buddhist Matters" (587–603; 17 poems: 3-10-4)
25. "Monks" (604–612; 9 poems: 2-4-3)
26. "Living in Retirement" (613–623; 11 poems: 6-4-1)
27. "Views and Vistas" (624–630; 7 poems: 1-5-1)
28. "Farewell Gatherings" (631–640; 10 poems: 1-6-3)
29. "Travel" (641–649; 9 poems: 1-5-3)
30. "Kōshin" (650–652; 3 poems: 1-1-1)
31. "Emperors and Princes" (653–665; 13 poems: 5-6-2)
32. "Princes (with Royal Grandchildren appended)" (666–673; 8 poems: 1-6-1)
33. "Prime Ministers (with Executive Officials appended)" (674–[677a]–680; 8 poems: 3-4-1)
34. "Generals" (681–688; 8 poems: 3-4-1)
35. "Provincial Governors" (689–692; 4 poems: 2-1-1)
36. "Singing of History" (693–696; 4 poems: 0-3-1)
37. "Wang Zhao-jun" (697–704; 8 poems: 1-6-1)
38. "Singing Girls (or Concubines)" (705–717; 13 poems: 4-8-1)
39. "Pleasure Girls" (718–721; 4 poems: 1-2-1)
40. "Old Men" (722–732; 11 poems: 3-6-2)

41. "Friends" (733–739; 7 poems: 3-2-2)
42. "Nostalgia for Men of the Past" (740–749; 10 poems: 4-3-3)
43. "Describing Sentiments" (750–764; 15 poems: 6-6-3)
44. "Congratulations" (765–772; 8 poems: 3-4-1)
45. "Felicitations" (773–776; 4 poems: 1-1-2)
46. "Love" (777–788; 12 poems: 5-4-3)
47. "Impermanence" (789–797; 9 poems: 3-3-3)
48. "Whiteness" (798–803; 6 poems: 1-4-1)

As shown by the numbers indicating the distribution among the three types of poems represented in the collection (*shi* couplets, *kanshi,* and *waka*), the linguistic and therefore poetic texture of each topic varies considerably. Only two topics have an equal representation of each type: topic 30, "Kōshin" (the practice of staying awake all night during a certain calendrical juncture), which is 1-1-1; and topic 47, "Impermanence," which is 3-3-3. Most other topics include representatives of all three types but are weighted more heavily toward one type than another. Topic 9, "Gibbons" (a monkey whose lonely cry in the mountains was thought to echo the traveler's longing for home), contains no *waka* at all, probably because monkeys were not considered to be an aesthetically appropriate subject for Japanese court poetry. Of the eight poems, all in Han verse, three are *shi* by Chinese poets and five are *kanshi* by Heian poets. The gibbon was a productive image for Heian court poets writing Chinese verse, even though the mournful cry of gibbons was outside the experience of the average Heian courtier. "Gibbons" represents a rare example of a topic that the Heian courtier took from Chinese poetry and reproduced in his own Chinese verse, but that he did not carry over into *waka.*

Conversely, sequences such as topic 17, "The Old Capital," and topic 36, "Singing of History," contain no poems by Tang poets, indicating that these topics were not perceived to be represented in Chinese verse. The categories presumably arose from the Heian courtier's own experience, which he expressed in Chinese verse or in Japanese poems. Several other categories seem to have been extraordinarily productive for the Heian courtier writing Chinese verse, such as topic 19, "Immortals (with Taoists and Hermits appended)," in which the distribution is 3-10-1; topic 24, "Buddhist Matters," with 3-10-4; topic 27, "Views and Vistas," with 1-5-1; topic 32, "Princes (with Royal Grandchildren appended)," with 1-6-1; and topic 37, "Wang Zhao-jun," also with 1-6-1. Heian poets were prolific in writing verses on these favorite topics, even though there were relatively few Tang examples, but they produced fewer *waka* on the same topics. Most of the other topics, including topic 41, "Friends," contain poems that are distributed across the three types relatively evenly. As we have seen, the seven poems in "Friends" are distributed as 3-2-2—that is, three *shi,* two *kanshi,* and two *waka.* The Heian courtier was inspired to compose poems of friendship in Chinese verses and in Japanese poems, suggesting that the theme of male friendship evident in Bo Ju-yi's and Xu Hun's poems was successfully integrated into poetic expression of the Heian male courtier's experience.

While it is impossible to make rigid generalizations about the thematic movement of these organizational categories, the earlier topics seem to focus on categories based on the poet's responses to nature (topics 1–9, 13–15) and subsequently move into areas of social experience that involve notable people and places. Topic 41, "Friends," appears in the context of nine other topics focusing in particular on aspects of male erotic or emotional experience, beginning with topic 38, "Singing Girls," and topic 39, "Pleasure Girls," and ending with topic 46, "Love." The three topics focusing on women bracket six categories (topics 40–45) that serve to focus more on men; in all cases, it is the male perspective on these topics that dominates. Topics 40–42 can be further subcategorized as sections covering a man's private experience: lamenting the aging process and the loss of youthful vigor (topic 40, "Old Men"), celebrating male friendship (topic 41, "Friends"), and longing for one's companions from the past (topic 42, "Nostalgia for Men of the Past"). Subsequently, topics 43–45 consist of poems expressing feelings related to a man's public experience: bemoaning the vicissitudes of the male courtier's career (topic 43, "Describing Sentiments"), offering congratulations to friends and colleagues for their advancement and promotions (topic 44, "Congratulations"), and celebrating the enthronement of a new emperor (topic 45, "Felicitations"). The six topics that focus on a man's private and public experience are framed by three topics focusing on his relations with women. This structure suggests that Kintō conceived of a man's experience as being divided into male-male and male-female realms, with friendship falling into the male-male realm of experience. Furthermore, Kintō's organization of topics suggests that a man's friendships were conceptualized as a component of his private life, while at the same time existing in relation to his public career at court.

The theme of male friendship is not entirely isolated under topic 41 on "Friends," and poems on the theme can be found under several other headings. Under topic 11, "Letters (with Bequeathed Letters appended)," for example, we find the following poem in Chinese verse by the Heian courtier Minamoto no Shitagō:

Yang Wang's eighth-generation descendant
Gathered the old writings of household supervisor Xu.
The lifelong friend of Chiang Yen
Collected the bequeathed works of administrative aide Fan.
MINAMOTO NO SHITAGŌ, poem 475

The translator notes, "The author here presents two examples of men of the past who collected and published the works of their predecessors. In the second case, it would also be grammatically possible to consider 'friend' and 'Fan' as being in apposition, which would yield '[He was] the lifelong friend of Chiang Yen: / [they] collected the bequeathed works of administrative aide Fan.'"[31] Of particular interest is the phrase translated as "lifelong friend" (C: *yi shi zhi you* J: *ichi ji no tomo*), indicating one of the defining characteristics of male friendship, namely, its durability over time.

In topic 20, "Mountain Residences," we find another *kanshi* verse about friendship discovered in nature. It is often the case in the poetry of friendship that the poet acknowledges his loneliness by referring to surrogate objects or phenomena as "friends." This seems to be the case in poem 560.

Among the flowers I seek for friends—Bush warblers exchange words with me;
Into a cave I move my home—Cranes become my neighbors.
KI NO HASEO, poem 560

The pairing of the words "friends" and "neighbors" in this poem reveals a fundamental search for intimacy; neighbors are intimate based on proximity, and friends are intimate based on mutual affection. An element of reciprocity is essential to friendship, and in fact the line "Bush warblers exchange words with me" employs as a verb the graph "exchange" (C: *jiao* J: *majifu*), which when used nominally means "friend" (C: *jiao* J: *kō*).

Two poems by Bo Ju-yi appear under topic 22, "Neighbors," and address a neighbor as if he were a friend.

On nights of bright moonlight, we will enjoy
Walking the three paths together;
Our green willows should share
A springtime of two households.
BO JU-YI, poem 572

Nor will it be only us two,
Visiting the rest of our lives:

Our sons and grandsons forever will be
Men who live next door.
Bo Ju-yi, poem 573

The translator notes, "This and the preceding couplet are from the same poem and allude to two famous retired scholars of the earlier periods: Chiang Hsü, who had three paths running through his place of hermitage, and Lu Hui-hsiao, whose residence shared two willows with that of his friend and neighbor, Chang Jung."[32] These poems are about neighbors with whom the poetic subject has developed a bond more normally associated with friendship. It suggests that the neighborly friendship shared by the two men will not end with them but will be passed down to the second and third generations. The transcendence expected of friendship here characterizes the ties between good neighbors.

Another important context for male friendship at the Heian court exists within the competition for power between clans and between individuals. The Heian court was in many ways a harsh place for noblemen, and friendship was useful in various ways to deal with the keen rivalries and animosities that sometimes divided the most powerful aristocratic families. The system of ranks within which the courtier lived and died meant that promotion defined one's status, and it was granted or withheld on the basis of harshly political realities. To be in favor at court was to be granted "human" status, and to suffer disfavor negated a courtier's fundamental worth. Self-exile from court life, in the form of taking the Buddhist tonsure (*shukke*—literally, leaving the household), was not uncommon in response to political setback, and the frustration and suffering of the politically marginalized courtier are a recurrent theme in the poetry. Topic 43, "Describing Sentiments," is one section in *Poems to Sing* that particularly highlights the marginalized courtier's feelings. One *kanshi* composed by Korenaga no Harumichi, who lived during the reign of Emperor Daigo (r. 897–930), gives voice to his suffering:

Hidden in people's words, secretly there burns
a fire to melt one's bones;
Cloaked in smiles, surreptitiously are sharpened
knives to cut one's flesh.[33]
Korenaga no Harumichi, poem 759

The poem is followed by another *kanshi* by Prince Kaneakira that expresses with bitter irony his severe disillusionment with life at the imperial court.

Riding in a carriage full of ghosts—What's so scary about that?
Rowing a boat down the gorges of the witch—That's not dangerous at all!
Prince Kaneakira, poem 760

As the translator's note explains, "Neither of these things can compare with the frightening dangers posed by the treachery or backbiting of one's enemies at court."[34] Kintō's organization of topics within *Poems to Sing* suggests that male friendship for the Heian courtier should be understood within a context of the brutal political realities of court life. A friend was a rare ally in what was otherwise a court full of rivals and potential enemies. Friendships might be a result of familial alliances or personal compatibility, but in every case a lasting friend was idealized as a treasure for life because in him a nobleman might find hope of transcending the oftentimes grim sociopolitical realities of his courtly world.

In *Poems to Sing,* we can see that the Heian courtier learned to hope for transcendence in friendship from the verse of Tang poets and incorporated that hope into his own poetic production of Chinese verse and Yamato song. The result was a hybrid *wa-kan* poetics of male friendship that was particularly suited to the Heian cultural milieu. The language of friendship existed within a dual cultural and linguistic environment, and *Poems to Sing* represented Fujiwara no Kintō's sublime attempt to capture the delicate bilingual texture of various topics for the education and enjoyment of the court aristocracy. In the section on "Friends," in particular, Kintō created a poetics of male friendship that remains a quintessential expression of the dual literary environment that existed in the mid-Heian period.

Chapter 2

Paradigms of Friendship in the *Tale of Ise*

The tenth-century *Ise monogatari* (Tale of Ise) is a poetic narrative in the Japanese language that features as its hero a Heian nobleman, commonly identified with the historical person Ariwara no Narihira (825–880). The tale depicts the hero's friendships with men in the context of his erotic adventures with women and posits a complementary relationship between love and friendship in the emotional life of the male courtier. The *Ise*'s depiction of courtly male friendship was widely admired by Japanese poets and writers of later centuries and helped establish the text as a canonical work in the late Heian and early medieval periods. The reason for the *Ise*'s success as a source of inspiration for later poets is twofold. First, it created a pair of influential models of male friendship: one the intimate friendship of equals centering upon the figure of the nobleman Ki no Aritsune (815–877), and the other the friendship of a Prince, centering upon Prince Koretaka (844–897), the eldest son of Emperor Montoku (r. 850–858). Second, inheriting the lesson of Chinese poetry about the hope for transcendence in male friendship and its ultimate betrayal in death, the *Ise* carried the Chinese model into a larger narrative in the Japanese language about a Heian nobleman's life.

Competing depictions of male friendship in texts written in the Japanese language circulated alongside the *Ise*, but they failed to elicit the same kind of admiration and never became canonical works. One such text is the now obscure *Heichū monogatari* (Tale of Heichū). If we compare the *Ise*'s and the *Heichū*'s depictions of male friendship, we find evidence that a heterogeneous discourse of male friendship existed at the Heian court. That the *Ise*'s representation of male friendship was remembered and the *Heichū*'s was largely forgotten suggests that aesthetic judgments by later generations favored the *Ise*'s. It also suggests that the process of canonization erased heterogeneity and produced orthodoxy with regard to representations of male friendship. This chapter explores the question of the *Ise*'s preeminence as a canonical text in relation to its depiction of male friendship.

The hero of the *Ise* is often said to embody the courtly ideal of the "erotic adventurer" *(irogonomi otoko),* a male courtier who seeks out the love of women as a form of self-cultivation and emotional expression.[1] The *Heichū* revolves around a similar hero, usually identified with the historical person Taira no Sadabumi (or Sadafun, 870?–923?). Both texts are thought to represent early efforts in composition in the Japanese language by male writers at court. The standard version of the *Ise,* the Tempuku-bon, was compiled by the nobleman Fujiwara no Teika (1162–1241) from a number of variant texts circulating at court and contains 125 episodes, many of which are only a few sentences in length. By contrast, the *Heichū* has 39 episodes, and most of them are several pages long. Judging from references to the texts in the early eleventh-century *Tale of Genji,* members of the mid-Heian court were equally familiar with the *Ise* and the *Heichū,* but the subsequent histories of each text diverged dramatically. The *Ise* survived in multiple copies representing multiple textual traditions, whereas the *Heichū* reemerged only in modern times with the discovery in 1931 of a single copy dating to the late thirteenth or early fourteenth century.

Even in mid-Heian, however, the hero of the *Ise* exerted far greater influence than the hero of the *Heichū* on the imaginations of writers at court. Scholars note that the *Ise*'s figure of Narihira was a major inspiration to the *Genji*'s author in the way she shaped her own hero, Prince Genji. Richard Bowring, for example, notes, "The *Ise* . . . has become a touchstone full of archetypal scenes, and its presence in the *Genji* is so all-pervasive that it may seem stretching a point to isolate specific instances. The dispossessed prince, the sexual transgression with an imperial concubine, the self-inflicted exile, and the link between poetry and sexuality: they all lie like shadows behind this peak of Heian literature."[2] In a similar vein, Haruo Shirane suggests that Genji's transgressive search for love in the *Tale of Genji* was motivated by the same feelings of disillusionment with aristocratic life that led the erotic hero of the *Ise* to seek love outside the institution of marriage: "Allusions [in the *Genji monogatari*] to the *Ise monogatari* draw a deliberate parallel between Genji and his literary precursor. Like the fictional Narihira, Genji is of royal blood, politically alienated, physically attractive, artistically talented, a superb poet, a man of deep emotions, and, above all, a passionate lover who discovers love where it is forbidden or most unlikely to be found or attained."[3] Norma Field interprets the *Ise*'s erotic hero in relation to another literary trope, the noble exile, when she argues, "*Ise* does not develop the hero's characterization beyond repeated display of prodigious amorousness and poetic gifts. What transcends mere repetition, giving him the suggestion of psychological continuity and retrospectively reinforcing the impression of a life, is his commission of a grave transgression."[4] For Field, the hero of the *Ise* would be little more than a frivolous gallant but for his association with the tragic fate of political exile.

One effect of the critical emphasis on the influence of the *Ise*'s depiction of erotic adventure on later literature has been to obscure the importance of its depiction of male friendship.[5] Several important episodes in the narrative emphasize the intensity of the hero's friendships, suggesting that the text of the *Ise* cannot be narrowly construed as being concerned with erotic adventure alone but must be understood as an exploration of the larger problem of male intimacy, inclusive of both erotic adventure directed at women and friendship directed at men. The hero of the *Ise* is not merely a passionate lover of women; he is also a devoted friend of men, and he possesses two complementary personae, *irogonomi otoko* (erotic adventurer) and *tomo,* or *tomodachi* (friend). It is the interplay between them that should be understood as the defining dynamic of the tale.

Regarding the *Ise*'s origins, Katagiri Yōichi has argued that the narrative emerged through a three-stage process of oral transmission, writing, and then revision that involved multiple authors and editors at the Heian court, spanning the late ninth and tenth centuries.[6] Based on an analysis of the multilayered quality of the text, Katagiri surmises the following scenario, leading to the creation of the *Ise* as we know it. First came oral *uta-gatari* (*waka* stories; what H. Richard Okada calls "poem-narrations" or "poem-talks"),[7] which described the supposed circumstances surrounding the composition of poems, most of them attributed to Ariwara no Narihira. Subsequently, the *waka* stories were written down in a form similar to a private poetry collection. This early text was then revised by one or more courtier-editors, who added supplemental comments in order to make the collection suitable for poetic instruction. The resulting text combined poetry, prose, and commentary in a way that established a new genre, the *uta monogatari* (poem-tale). Katagiri's scenario is convincing and has come to be widely accepted, but in fact the exact origins of the *Ise* remain obscure and will continue to be the topic of ongoing study and speculation. Suffice it to say that by the time Fujiwara no Teika compiled his 125-episode version of the text early in the thirteenth century, the *Ise* had achieved its status as one of the two literary classics (along with the *Kokinshū*) that were considered to be indispensable to the education of any self-respecting person of the time with a claim to cultural and literary sophistication.

Historically, one of the persistent approaches to the *Ise* has been to read it as a biographical account of the life of Ariwara no Narihira. Jin'ichi Konishi goes so far as to call the *Ise* a "factual" narrative, and that is not far from the mark in the sense that the text claims the status of truth not accorded to the frankly fictional writing of tale *(monogatari)* literature.[8] Over the years numerous scholars, beginning with Keichū (1640–1701) in his commentary on the *Ise* called the *Seigo okudan,* written in about 1692, have challenged the wisdom of reading the text as a biography. They advocate instead looking at the hero as essentially a fictional figure produced by a collective literary imagination at the Heian court. We will be taking this nonbiographical approach and at the same time will keep in mind that the historical Narihira, however elusive that construct might be, is at work in shaping the particulars of the *Ise*'s fictional hero. H. Richard Okada has expressed the problem of balancing fiction against biography in interpreting the figure of Narihira in these terms:

> Time and again the collection thwarts, even as it invites, attempts at finding historical correspondences, those politically intertextual positions of its historical, pretextual figures, and adds suggestive complications. What we have is a text that can be, as it most often has been, read under the shadow of a "life" of Narihira even though . . . it presents a continual refraction from biographical plenitude. Yet . . . we cannot simply dismiss out of hand the *Ise* biographical gesture.[9]

The *Ise*'s portraits of male friendship contain numerous such biographical gestures. The hero's friend in episodes 16 and 38 is identified by name as Ki no Aritsune, a nobleman thought to have been the historical Narihira's father-in-law. In episodes 82, 83, and 85, the hero is identified as the Director of the Bureau of Horses, Right Division *(migi no uma no kami),* one of the court titles held by the historical Narihira. His companion in the episodes is Prince Koretaka, whom the historical Narihira served. But these episodes make sense only as a literary invention, not as true accounts of the historical Narihira's friendships. To understand the way fact and fiction work together to produce the figure of the hero of the *Ise,* it is necessary to consider the origins of what Konishi calls the "myth of Narihira."[10]

During the late ninth and early tenth centuries when the *Ise* took shape as a text, the Fujiwara clan had been increasingly successful in dominating other powerful families at court, a fact the latter much resented. One of the pivotal moments in the establishment of the Fujiwara hegemony occurred when, in 866, Fujiwara no Yoshifusa (804–872) contrived to have himself appointed regent *(sesshō),* ostensibly to provide his young grandson, Emperor Seiwa (r. 858–876), with advice and guidance. It was the first time that a man who was not of imperial birth had assumed the regency, and it established the pattern of child-emperors dominated by Fujiwara Regents whereby the Northern House was able to exercise virtually complete control over the throne until the end of the eleventh century. Emperor Seiwa figures importantly in the *Tale of Ise* in several contexts. It was he who eclipsed Prince Koretaka, who appears as the object of the hero's friendship in episodes 82, 83, and 85. Prince Koretaka was the first and favorite son of Emperor Montoku and seemed destined for the throne until the future Emperor Seiwa, another of Montoku's sons, was unexpectedly named Crown Prince in 850. Prince Koretaka's eclipse can be explained by the fact that the victorious Seiwa's mother was a daughter of Fujiwara no Yoshifusa, whereas the unsuccessful Prince Koretaka's mother was a member of the Ki family and a sister of Ki no Aritsune. Aritsune likewise figures prominently as a figure of friendship in episodes 16, 38, and 46. The underlying presence of these events in fictionalized form in the *Ise* suggests that as time passed and the major courtier families found themselves overshadowed by the Fujiwara clan, their perceptions of the origins of Fujiwara domination may have focused on the sequence of events beginning in 858, when the future Emperor Seiwa was named Crown Prince, and ending in 866, when his grandfather Yoshifusa was named Regent. Because Narihira served Prince Koretaka and was likely married to a daughter of Ki no Aritsune, he became a suitable figure around whom to build the image of a disenfranchised courtier. Narihira's productivity and skill as a poet also made him an ideal candidate for transformation into a mythic figure.

The myth of Narihira was highly political in nature, as Michele Marra has argued: "[In] the *Ise Monogatari,* we see that the compilers' act of writing was motivated by their desire to express a profound political dissatisfaction with the dictatorial government of the Fujiwara."[11] In other words, a fictional Narihira who had suffered the disappointment of political setback in his court career became the hero of the tale, and this hero embodied a form of counter-Fujiwara ideology.[12] But it would be a mistake to reduce the Narihira myth to nothing more than an ideological icon, for it embodies a more personal lesson about court life, which is that a courtier must "step back from the realm of politics in order to realize the true meaning of reality."[13] The dramatic advancement of Fujiwara hegemony that occurred in the Seiwa reign inspired in future generations of politically marginalized Heian noblemen a comforting myth of nobility-in-defeat that found expression in the Narihira figure of the *Ise*. Nevertheless, the tale managed to go beyond its original political purposes and become a deeply personal work through its exploration of erotic adventure and friendship as expressions of the male courtier's dual need for intimacy. As Tsukahara Tetsuo argues in his 1988 study of the *Ise,* "The Heian nobility, bound by a bureaucratic system and forced to forfeit its humanity, was able to realize its humanity outside the bounds of the logic of a political system. If erotic adventure represented the recuperation of humanity between the sexes, then [male] friendship represented the recuperation of humanity between members of the same sex."[14]

The *Ise* begins with an episode recounting the young hero's coming-of-age and simultaneous sexual awakening and then continues with five episodes describing his erotic exploits in the capital with a high-ranking woman who is forbidden to him, presumed to be Emperor Seiwa's future Empress, Fujiwara no Takaiko (Empress Nijō). The affair ends in their separation, due in large part to a Fujiwara intervention that worked to reserve Takaiko for her future role as an imperial consort and the mother of an emperor. From that perspective, the hero's non-imperial status makes him an unsuitable partner for the woman. The opening lines of episodes 1 through 6 show just how exclusive is the focus on erotic adventure in the tale's opening episodes.[15]

> Episode 1: Once a man, having attained his majority and possessing an estate at the village of Kasuga near Nara, the [former] capital, went hunting [there]. In that village lived some very young and beautiful sisters. This man had been stealthily looking [at them] through a hole in the fence.
>
> Episode 2: Once there was a man. At the time when the capital of Nara had been left, but in this capital the houses of the people had not been properly arranged, there lived a lady in the western part of the capital. That lady outshone the other women of [her] time. [The qualities of her] heart were even surpassing [the beauty of] her features.
>
> Episode 3: Once there was a man. Intending to send a thing called *hijiki-mo* to a lady with whom he had fallen in love, [he composed the following poem].
>
> Episode 4: Once there was a person in East Gojō who lived in the Western Pavilion [of the Palace] where the Empress Dowager had taken her abode. A man, who at first had no specific intentions but [afterward] was infatuated [with her], visited her . . .[16]
>
> Episode 5: Once there was a man. He [often] went very secretly to [a lady who lived in] the neighborhood of East Gojō.

Episode 6: Once there was a man. For [many] years he continued to court a lady he would not be able to make his own. At last he eloped with her and went [away with her] while it was very dark.

Then, in episode 7, the trajectory of erotic adventure is suddenly interrupted. At work here is an aesthetic of sequencing that requires a change of subject and mood in order to achieve the desired literary texture. This particular sequencing of the *Ise*'s episodes is found in Teika's version. It is not known whether Teika invented the rupture represented by episode 7 or simply appreciated the effect of the sequencing invented by someone else with a hand in shaping the text. Whichever the case, the four episodes beginning with episode 7 and continuing with episodes 8, 9, and 11 turn away from erotic adventure and instead treat the topic of male friendship. The three episodes begin a longer and discrete sequence that ends with episode 15, known as the Journey to the East *(azuma yuki* or *azuma kudari).* The sequence does not describe the hero's journey in the normal sense of his departure from the capital, his progress, and his arrival at a destination. Instead, the sequence of episodes merely suggests a journey by placing the hero in, or on the way to, the eastern provinces. Being away from the capital elicits in the heart of the courtier the emotions of nostalgia, dislocation, and loss. The sequence recounts several separate departures, describes the hero's thoughts of home while on the road, and celebrates his erotic adventures with women in the East (Azuma, specifically the provinces of Musashi and Michinoku). These episodes place the hero far from the old and new capitals that are at the heart of events in episodes 1 through 6, moving him now into a new environment on the periphery of the court. With the change of location comes the introduction of male friendship, suggesting that the possibility of friendship exists in relation to dislocation from the capital and release from its erotic prerogatives and pressures. Erotic adventure quickly reasserts itself in the sequence once the hero reaches his destination, where he is pursued in episodes 10 and 12–15 by a variety of provincial women, all of whom are smitten by his courtly ways. Thus it is only in transit to the East that male friendship comes to the fore. Male friendship seems to emerge and flourish in the interstice between discrete locales, the capital at one end and the hero's destination in the East at the other. If point of departure and point of arrival are ruled by erotic adventure, then male friendship rules the undomesticated realm in between, a realm characterized by fluidity, no fixed abode, the absence of women, and the presence of male traveling companions.

Episode 7 is transitional between erotic adventure and male friendship. Its placement suggests that in order to encounter his friends, the hero must first abandon women and make himself utterly alone. The appearance of friendship in episodes 8, 9, and 11 is interpreted in the reader's mind retrospectively in relation to the isolation of episode 7. The opening lines of episodes 7 through 15 convey a sense of the way friendship is introduced in the tale:

> Episode 7: Once there was a man. Tired of living in the capital he went to Azuma.
>
> Episode 8: Once there was a man. (He certainly will have been tired of living in the capital.) With the intention of going in the direction of Azuma to look for a dwelling place [there] he went [away] together with one or two companions.
>
> Episode 9: Once there was a man. That man regarded himself as a useless person and did not want to live in the capital [anymore]. He went [away] in the direction of Azuma with the intention to seek a province where he could dwell. He traveled together with one or two men who had been his friends for a very long time.
>
> Episode 10: Once a man wandered as far as the Province of Musashi. And [there] he courted a girl who lived in that province.
>
> Episode 11: Once a man, when going to Azuma, sent word to his friends while he was on his way.
>
> Episode 12: Once there was a man. He eloped with the daughter of someone and took [her] to the plain of Musashi.
>
> Episode 13: Once a man in [the Province of] Musashi wrote to a lady in the capital.
>
> Episode 14: Once a man had been traveling aimlessly to the Province of Michi. A woman there—(she will certainly have thought a man from the capital especially attractive)—was deeply in love with him.
>
> Episode 15: Once [a man] often visited the wife of a man who was of no importance whatsoever in Michinoku.

It is in episodes 8, 9, and 11 of the Journey to the East sequence that the words *tomo* and *tomodachi* (friend) and *tomodachi-domo* (friends) first appear in the text of the *Ise.* Episodes 8 and 9 repeat the phrase, *tomo to suru hito, hitori futari shite yukikeri* ("he traveled together with one or two men who had been his friends"). The Chinese graph for "friend" is used in episode 9, but in episode 8 the word is written in syllabic script and is thus ambiguous in meaning, suggesting either "friend" or the homophonous "companion," which is how Vos translates it. Episode 11 contains the phrase *tomodachi-domo ni, michi yori iiokosekeru* ("sent word to his friends while he was on his way"). In episodes 8 and 9, it is the friend or friends who accompany the hero; in episode 11, it is the hero who sends word to his friends back in the capital. These three episodes begin the process of posing friendship in relation to erotic adventure in the tale.

Commentators have suggested that the Journey to the East is in fact a form of self-imposed exile from the capital, motivated by the hero's politically dangerous liaison with Takaiko, the future Empress Nijō. Friendship thus seems to emerge into prominence initially in a context of the negative political repercussions of erotic adventure, suggesting that the political perils of connection with women open the text to the possibility, and even necessity, of male friendship.

Aritsune and the Paradigm of the Intimate Friend

Episode 16 in the *Ise* begins the process of developing the first of the tale's two models of male friendship, the paradigm of the Intimate Friend. The opening lines of episode 16, in Vos' translation, describe the man's noble character: "Once there was a man called Ki no Aritsune. Serving under three succeeding Emperors he rose in the world, but, since later the world and the times had changed, he fell behind the other men of the time. As to his character, he had a noble heart and he loved distinction—thus he was different from other people." Unlike the earlier episodes (8, 9, and 11), which introduced the word *tomo* in a general context of male companionship, episode 16 introduces a specific individual, Aritsune, who is befriended by the hero of the tale. The poetic exchange between the men is occasioned by the decision of Aritsune's wife to leave and become a nun. Her decision provides, in turn, a motive for the deepening of friendship between the men.

Aritsune composes this poem and sends it to the hero of the tale:

te o orite aimishi koto o kazoureba tō to iitsutsu yotsu wa henikeri
When I count / the years we lived together / on my fingers, / saying ten / four [times:—so many years] we have passed [together].

Aritsune's initial poem elicits his friend's immediate sympathy, expressed in the hero's reply:

> toshi dani mo tō tote yotsu wa henikeru o ikutabi kimi o tanomikinuran
> *Just years / —saying ten four [times]— / [forty] you have passed [together], / but how many times / would she have come relying upon you?*

The poem is accompanied by a set of beautiful robes for Aritsune to bestow on his departing wife as a farewell gift. The episode then records two poems by Aritsune, expressing his heartfelt gratitude for the hero's gift.

> kore ya kono ama no hagoromo mube shi koso kimi ga mikeshi tatematsurikere
> *[Is] this, I wonder, / that heavenly robe of feathers, / [now intended] for a nun? / It is certainly no wonder / that you wore [it] / as your garment.*

> aki ya kuru tsuyu ya magau to omou made aru wa namida no furu ni zo arikeru
> *[My sleeves] were [so wet] / that I asked myself:— / is fall approaching / and is dew being mixed [with my tears]? . . . / It was nothing but the falling of my tears.*

Aritsune's response emphasizes for us the extraordinary value he places upon his friend's sympathy. It is through the figure of Aritsune that the reader experiences the impact and significance of the hero's friendship, and yet Aritsune is not the central figure of the episode. That honor falls to the friend who brings Aritsune comfort.

Tsukahara Tetsuo argues that episode 16 is important in the context of the unfolding narrative of the *Ise* for the way it redirects the conceptual thrust of the tale: "It stands in opposition to Episodes 1 through 15. That is, in contrast to the earlier treatment of the theme of love affairs between men and women, [Episode 16] takes up the theme of male friendship."[17] Tsukahara notes several other special characteristics of episode 16, all of them related to friendship. First, whereas several previous episodes are read in relation to each other and reflect thematically upon each other (episodes 1 and 2, 3 and 6, 7 and 15, for example), episode 16 stands in isolation, resisting integration with any of the episodes that come before it. Second, episode 16 is unique in that it opens by identifying Aritsune by name. Finally, the episode introduces for the first time a poetic exchange between characters in the episode.[18] According to Tsukahara, a close analysis of the episode is crucial not only for understanding what male friendship means but also for understanding how the sequence of episodes in the *Ise* gives coherence to the tale.

Tsukahara's first point is the absolute independence of episode 16 from everything that comes before it in the tale. As argued earlier, however, there is some preparation for episode 16's introduction of the theme of male friendship in the earlier episodes depicting male friends who travel together to the East. For example, the word *tomo* appears in episodes 8 and 9, and *tomodachi-domo* in episode 11, so that when the word *tomodachi* finally appears in episode 16, the reader has been primed for the episode. The thematic break with erotic adventure thus begins with episodes 8, 9, and 11 and is therefore less abrupt than Tsukahara describes it, for the word *tomodachi* itself links episode 16 to the three earlier episodes. Nevertheless, Tsukahara's point that episode 16 represents the first full-fledged treatment of friendship in the tale is well taken. Previously, the friends of episodes 8, 9, and 11 were present only to produce a context of male camaraderie, and what occurred within that context was not directly related to the issue of friendship. But in episode 16 the central point is to depict devoted friendship between the hero and Aritsune. In that sense, the episode is a major departure from any that came before.

The introduction of Aritsune by name is another remarkable feature of the episode, discussed by numerous scholars. In previous episodes, the male hero and his women have always remained anonymous. When they are identified, it is usually at the end of the episode in an interpretive editorial comment, as in episodes 3, 5, and 6, which allude to Empress Nijō, and in episode 6, which names the Empress' two brothers in an aside. Only in episode 4 does a story begin by identifying a woman, but the identification is indirect to the point of being evasive: "Once there was a person in East Gojō who lived in the Western Pavilion [of the Palace] where the Empress Dowager had taken her abode."[19] Not until episode 5 does the reader surmise that the woman in question is the future Empress Nijō, and then only because of the interpretive editorial comment. We can agree, then, with Tsukahara that episode 16 is extraordinary in the unfolding sequence of episodes in the *Ise* because it identifies a character by name. The effect of this naming is to personalize the hero's friendship, in explicit contrast to the impersonal quality of the earlier episodes that focused on erotic adventure.

Related to this point is a final distinction that Tsukahara makes between episode 16 and earlier episodes. He calls episodes 1 through 15 "directional episodes" *(shikō shōdan),* because erotic adventure between a man—the hero of the tale—and a woman in these episodes is "unidirectional"; that is, the feelings are not depicted as mutual or reciprocal. Episodes 1 through 6, Tsukahara identifies as episodes of the capital region *(kinai shōdan),* and in these episodes the man is the subject and the woman he pursues is the object of pursuit. The configuration is reversed, according to Tsukahara, in the episodes that take place in the East *(azuma-yuki shōdan),* where the provincial woman is the subject who pursues the man—the hero of the tale.[20] Tsukahara argues that in both configurations of erotic adventure, in the capital and in the East, there is a lack of reciprocity and mutuality between the man and the women. He further argues that episode 16, with its focus on friendship between men, is the first episode to convey a sense of reciprocity and mutuality in affection. "In other words," Tsukahara concludes, "in terms of choice of topic and the approach to their configuration, the directional episodes and the friendship episode [*yūjō shōdan,* episode 16] stand in a relationship of opposition to one another."[21] The reciprocity and mutuality of the men's friendship in episode 16 is conveyed structurally by means of a poetic exchange. Aritsune sends an initial poem of lament to the male hero of the tale, who responds with a poem and a gift, and the episode concludes with Aritsune's grateful poems in reply. This is the first proper poetic exchange in the *Ise,* and Tsukahara argues that it is evidence of a reciprocity and mutuality in male friendship that is foreign to the depiction of erotic adventure between women and men so far in the tale.[22]

It is tempting to contrast the failure of affection between Aritsune and his wife in episode 16 with the success of the men's friendship, but Yura Takuo warns against making too much of the failure of conjugal love in the episode. He argues, "There is no evidence that Aritsune's affections turned to distaste for her [despite her decision to go away]. There is only a sense of deeply human grief, and the power of Aritsune's poem lies in the fact that it expresses only this feeling [of grief, not resentment]."[23] In Yura's view, the episode downplays the rupture between husband and wife in order to direct the reader's attention to the more interesting issue of Aritsune's lingering attachment to his wife of many years as she prepares to leave him. Through what Yura calls a certain "clumsiness in the flow of language"[24] that is unlike any other episode in the *Ise,* episode 16 conveys viscerally the intensity of Aritsune's agony, which drives him to seek solace from his male friend.

The hero's responding poem and gift seem to galvanize Aritsune and lift him from despair. The hero empathizes with Aritsune's plight as he and his wife go their separate ways and responds to the lingering affection Aritsune expressed for her in his initial poem. As Yura describes it,

> The phrase "how many times she must have come relying upon you" is composed in sympathy with the feelings of the wife, and at the same time is directed at Aritsune to comfort and encourage him. It is [the expression of] Narihira's friendship. The fact that it comes with a gift of robes is what makes Aritsune weep tears of joy. Regardless of the past state of affairs between Aritsune and his wife, [Aritsune's initial poem expresses how] he now feels intensely the regret of her loss as she sets off to become a nun. We might say that the effect of Narihira's poem, composed in sympathy with the wife's feelings, is to crystallize [Aritsune's] feelings of deepest sadness and regret about those forty years.[25]

Aritsune's responding poems express his delight with the robes, for he can now present his wife with a proper gift of parting. He compliments his friend's sensitivity in the first poem by calling the garments a "heavenly robe of feathers" *(ama no hagoromo),* and in the second poem he depicts himself weeping tears of joy. This first portrait of friendship in episode 16 shows the hero of the tale bringing comfort to Aritsune in his grief.

The relationship between the hero and Aritsune is extended in another direction in episode 38. This is the second episode that develops the friendship between the hero of the *Ise* and Ki no Aritsune as a model of courtly male friendship. Because it is brief, the entire episode is given here in Vos' translation.

> Once [a man] went to the place of Ki no Aritsune, but, as [Aritsune]—having gone out on an excursion—came [back] late, [he did not meet him], [but] composed [the following poem] and sent [it to him]:
>
> kimi ni yori omoinarainu yo no naka no hito wa kore o ya koi to iuran
> *Thanks to you / I have learned / [what longing means]. / The people of [this] world, I suppose, / will call this love?*
>
> [Aritsune] return[ed the following poem]:
>
> narawaneba yo no hitogoto ni nani o ka mo koi to wa iu to toishi ware shi mo
> *What? I who, / as I had no experience, / asked everyone in [this] world: / "Oh!, what do you call love?" / [would have taught you?]*

In episode 38, the friendship of the *Ise* hero and Aritsune is once again introduced in a highly personal way, with a reference to Aritsune by name.[26] Commentators have struggled over the years with the problem of how best to interpret the episode, for the language is so compressed that even some of its most basic elements are virtually impossible to decipher. In fact, the extent of ellipsis is quite radical even by the *Ise*'s already highly elliptical standards. Gone is the formulaic opening "Once there was a man" *(mukashi otoko arikeri).* Instead, the episode begins with the words "once" *(mukashi)* and "when [I] went" *ikitaru ni,* giving the effect of a firsthand account.[27] The expected verb form would be *ikitarikeru ni,* signaling that the story is being reported secondhand. Most mystifying is the problem of logistics. Did the hero send the poem from Aritsune's house to Aritsune at another location, or did he go home and send it to Aritsune's house after Aritsune had returned home? Alternatively, did the men spend the night in conversation after Aritsune's late return, and was the poem then sent to Aritsune the following morning after the hero returned to his own home? In that case, the poem might be construed as a parody of a "morning-after" *(kinuginu)* poem sent from a nobleman to his female lover after a night spent together.[28] The compressed and suggestive nature of the language of the narrative makes it impossible to clarify even such basic questions. One of the effects of such ambiguity is to deflect the reader's attention from the episode's plot and direct it instead to the poems themselves.

The question posed by the hero in his opening poem hints at confusion about his powerful feelings for Aritsune. The hero asks, in effect, whether the longing *(koi)* he felt for Aritsune in his absence is the same as the longing a man has for a woman or a woman has for a man. Katagiri et al. state, "[Despite the erotic language,] it is a poem sent from a man to a man. The poem does not mean that [Narihira] has never known love [*koi*]. It shows that he is feeling a deep love [*omoi*] similar to the longing [*koi*] between a man and a woman."[29] Katagiri et al. acknowledge that the poem is a confession of *koi,* or longing, by the hero for his friend, but they hesitate to take the avowal as overtly erotic and instead understand it to be the expression of a feeling of deep emotion "similar to the longing between a man and a woman."

Both *koi* (longing) and *omoi* (love) were commonly used to describe a man's feelings for another man in the *waka* poetic tradition.[30] There are, for example, three such poems in the *Kokinshū,* whose development is roughly contemporaneous with the *Ise*'s early transformation from an oral tradition of *waka* stories to a written text. Poem 399, by Ōshikōchi no Mitsune and quoted earlier in chapter 1, appears in the volume of poems "On Parting."

> Poem 399: Composed on parting from Prince Kanemi after first conversing with him.
>
> wakaruredo ureshiku mo aru ka koyoi yori ai minu yori nani o koimashi

although we part / I am filled with happiness / for now I wonder / whom I might have thought I loved / before we two met tonight
Ōshikōchi no Mitsune[31]

Like the exchange between the *Ise* hero and Aritsune, poem 399 uses the word *koi* (longing for someone who is absent) to express the sentiment of love in the translation.

In *Kokinshū* poems 978 and 979, "On Miscellaneous Topics," however, the word *omoi* (feelings of love, contrasted to the longing of *koi*) is used instead to convey the feelings shared by the two men. The exchange reads:

Poem 978: Composed when Muneoka no Ōyori, who had come to the capital from the northern provinces, saw the snow falling and said, "I remember the snow piling up like this."

kimi ga omoi yuki to tsumoraba tanomarezu haru yori nochi wa araji to omoeba
If your thoughts of me / "gather thick as snow" I should / not rely on them / for once spring has come I know / the drifts will vanish from sight.
Ōshikōchi no Mitsune

Poem 979: Reply.

kimi o nomi omoi koshiji no shira yama wa itsu ka wa yuki no kiyuru toki aru
As I walked along / the road to Koshi I thought / only of you when / do the snows ever disappear / on glistening Shira Mountain.
Muneoka no Ōyori[32]

Some commentators have suggested that the avowal of feelings of love *(koi* and *omoi)* between men observed in the *Kokinshū* poems should be understood as being little more than a formulaic "literary affectation" *(bungaku-teki kyoshoku)* that derives originally from Chinese poetic practice.[33] The same approach has been taken to episode 38 in the *Ise,* with commentators suggesting that the exchange records a stylized wordplay reflecting courtly manners and is not a statement of unusual depth of feeling between the men. Yura quotes one commentary, for example, that argues, "It was perfectly normal in this historical period for two men to express their everyday feelings for each other in terms of longing [*koi*]; and because it was taken as a sign of sensitivity and the ability to discern sorrow [*aware*], this episode should be understood as a product of the author's desire to make Narihira and Aritsune appear that way."[34] Yura counters this assessment with one of his own:

> The reason I am not satisfied with this explanation hinges on its suggestion that the relationship between the hero (Narihira) and Aritsune is simply one example among many of a widespread general phenomenon. Within the *Ise,* the relationship between the hero (Narihira) and Aritsune is indeed that of father-in-law and son-in-law, but emotionally it far surpasses that. I detect in the relationship between these two men, who are only ten or so years apart in age, a certain sincerely human connection and heart-to-heart communication [*kokoro no kayoiai*]. Even in their day, it was not a normal emotional state [between men].[35]

How commentators interpret Aritsune's answering poem depends very much on whether or not they feel that it is possible for the longing expressed in the hero's poem to be reciprocated by Aritsune. Many commentators reject such a possibility and choose to read the hero's poem as a confession of longing made in jest and Aritsune's response as a denial of the feelings the hero confesses for him. Namba Hiroshi, for example, interprets Aritsune's poem this way: "Since I have never experienced longing [*koi*], I asked repeatedly what it is the world calls longing, so it is extraordinary [*igai*] that you should tell me that I could have caused you to experience feelings of longing."[36] Vos' translation is consistent with such an approach: "What? I who, as I had no experience, asked everyone in [this] world: 'Oh!, what do you call love?' [would have taught you?]."[37] According to this interpretation Aritsune expresses shock, either real or feigned, at the hero's confession of longing for him and wonders what it might have to do with their relationship. This reading of Aritsune's poem affirms the view that the longing known as *koi* belongs only in erotic adventure and must be excluded from the realm of friendship. Helen McCullough's translation follows a similar interpretive line: "How should I have taught you? I who through ignorance have constantly asked others what love might be?"[38] McCullough's note about the first poem suggests that the hero's confession of love was made in jest because "Ki no Aritsune was Narihira's friend and father-in-law; also, the element of humor in the exchange hinges on the first poet's reputation as a gallant."[39] The idea that the poem is a humorous expression of longing for Aritsune does not necessarily negate it as an expression of intimacy, however. One scholar recognizes that the humor in the poem might itself be a product of the intimacy of affection between the men: "[Episode 38] is amusing, truly an exchange of poems that could only take place between two men who had trusted each other completely" *(makoto ni yurushiatta naka de nomi yaritori dekiru uta ni natteite, hohoemashii).*[40] According to this view, the hero's confession of longing for Aritsune, though perhaps made in jest, still gives evidence that the hero trusted Aritsune not to be repulsed by his confession.

Another school of thought regarding the interpretation of Aritsune's replying poem sees it as reciprocating the hero's feelings. This reading seems to have originated with the medieval poet Sōgi in the *Shōmon shō* (1477) and the *Yamaguchi ki* (ca. 1489) and was reiterated and thereby given credence by Kamo no Mabuchi in his commentary on the *Ise,* called *Ko-i* (1753; Ancient meanings): "I had asked everyone 'what is this thing called longing,' but because I longed for you, I, too, now know what longing is."[41] Sōgi's interpretation opens the episode to the full implications of the hero's use of the word *koi,* that the men's friendship is a form of love. Sōgi's willingness to entertain the possibility of friendship as a form of love was no doubt linked to his understanding of the explicitly sexual relations possible between men in his fifteenth-century cultural milieu. In Sōgi's mind, and in the minds of many readers of the *Ise* in later generations, it would have seemed only natural that the longing for his friend expressed in the hero's poem in episode 38 should have a physical dimension, and that it be acknowledged and reciprocated by Aritsune.

Episode 46 is the last in the sequence of three episodes that contribute to establishing the paradigm of the Intimate Friend in the *Ise.* While Aritsune does not appear by name in the brief narrative, the episode is traditionally associated with him, most notably in Sōgi's *Yamaguchi ki,* because of the way the character of its central figure resonates with the character of Aritsune described in episodes 16 and 38. Yura Takuo argues that equating the friend in episode 46 with Aritsune is misguided:

> Before worrying about who [the friend] is modeled after in this episode, it is important that the reader understand first that the *Tale of Ise* treats this form of affection [i.e., friendship] as something significant. That is to say, [the episode suggests that] there was a group of several friends in addition to Aritsune around the hero of the *Ise* with whom he shared his deepest feelings [*kokoro o kawashi-atteiru tomo*] in this manner, and the man [in this episode] is but one of them.[42]

Nevertheless, I would argue that there is some undeniable internal logic that links episodes 16, 38, and 46 to the figure of Aritsune. The brief episode is presented here in its entirety, as translated by Vos.

> Once a man had a very intimate friend. Not leaving each other for a moment, they were very fond of each other. But [one day the friend] went to another province and, deploring this very much, they parted. In a letter which [the friend] sent after some time he said: "What an amazingly [long] time has passed while we were unable to meet each other! I am worrying very much lest you might have forgotten [me]. [For] it seems that the hearts of the people of [this] world are, indeed, apt to forget when they are separated." Hence [the man] composed [a poem] and sent [it to him]:
>
> me karu to mo omōenaku ni wasuraruru toki shi nakereba omokage ni tatsu
>
> *It does not even seem [to me] / that we are separated, / but, as there is not a moment / that [you] are forgotten,— / [your] image is [always before my eyes].*

Episode 46 opens with a phrase that is hauntingly beautiful in the original: *mukashi otoko ito uruwashiki tomo arikeri* ("Once a man had a very intimate friend"). The episode describes what happens when close friends are forced by circumstances to separate; the one who must leave expresses the fear that he will be forgotten by the one who remains behind. Despite the episode's extreme brevity—it is a mere six lines in the original, including the poem—episode 46 holds a special place in any description of male friendship in the *Ise.*[43] Its significance lies in the directness of its avowal of affection between the two male friends. Many commentators have perceived an unusual intensity of expression in both poem and prose portions of the episode that is suggestive of extraordinary intimacy, as if the confession of longing in episode 38 were now fully reciprocated in the friendship. The powerful sense of intimacy that the episode conveys seems to pivot on the adjective *uruwashiki* (translated by Vos as "intimate").[44] In the Heian period, the word *uruwashi* was used to refer to a particularly Chinese aesthetic of beauty that was linked to courtly characteristics such as refinement, elegance, and nobility. Takeoka notes that the word *uruwashi* "is remarkable in that it is always used to describe beauty that is perceived visually" *(shikaku ni eizuru bi).*[45] In Episode 46, *uruwashi* is usually taken as a description of the hero's feelings for his friend ("intimate"), but I think that the word could also be understood in this context as a description of the friend's looks and physical bearing. The *uruwashiki tomo* is literally a handsome friend, and it is the friend's beauty as well as his noble character that inspire the hero's intimacy with him.

The visual sense is central to episode 46. The episode begins with the statement that the hero of the *Ise* had an intimate friend, the word *uruwashi* referring to his visual appeal; and it concludes with the hero's assurances that though he can no longer "see" him, his friend is ever present in his mind's eye. The episode addresses the contradiction inherent in the visual when it is applied to male friendship: the friend fears that he will be forgotten because he is not seen, and the hero assures him that he is always present in his heart and will therefore be remembered. Not unlike Bo Ju-yi's poems of absence and remembrance in *Poems to Sing,* the separation of male friends serves as a catalyst to move them beyond reliance on the visual into a transcendent realm in which their bond relies on a symbolic vision of the heart. Episode 46 is moving to readers because it creates a moment of insight into what men long for in friendship. We observe the hero growing from a lower plane of visible experience to a higher one of invisible experience, and we see the distant friend take comfort in the assurance that he is, though unseen, yet loved.[46] The hope of transcendence is perhaps nowhere more fully formulated in the *Ise* than in this episode.

To better comprehend how the episode articulates transcending the visual, it is necessary to consider how the word *omokage* (image of a figure or face) in the poem functions in relation to the phrase "out of sight" *(me karureba)* in the narrative portion of the text. Recall that the hero's friend is afraid that he will be forgotten because the two men have not met face-to-face for such a long time, as if seeing and being seen were necessary to their intimacy. The hero assures his friend, however, that he cannot even conceive of him as gone away, for the friend is always there before him as a recalled figure *(omokage ni tatsu). Omokage* is the absent person that lingers in the mind's eye. It is thus an abstraction of the actual face *(kao,* or *men)* that is viewed with the eyes. The seeing of the absent person is a function not of the eyes, then, but of the heart. In essence, in a moment of loneliness, the intimate friend now in a distant province asks if their friendship is based on a visual system in which when someone is out of sight, he is forgotten. The lonely friend calls such forgetting a characteristic of "the hearts of people of [this] world" *(yo no naka no hito no kokoro).* In the diction of Japanese court poetry, "the world" *(yo no naka)* frequently designates something even more specific, namely, erotic relations between men and women. If we interpolate this extended sense of the phrase, the distant friend's inquiry can be taken to pose an implicit question contrasting erotic love and male friendship. In reply, the hero of the *Ise* assures his friend that their intimacy is of a different order. He denies the necessity to see or be seen in order to maintain their friendship and assures him that he always holds the image of his absent friend in his mind's eye. It is as if memory can conjure physical substance.

Despite the hero's assurances of friendship's transcendence, the unhappy fact shadowing the episode is that the mind cannot conjure the physical. The episode is poignant because the intimate friend instinctively understands that the hero's words, no matter how skillfully employed or deeply felt, cannot overcome the reality of their separation. The hero of episode 46 wants to be with his distant friend as much as the friend wants to be with him, but their former physical proximity is no longer possible. Now only memories of the other's physical presence can sustain their affection. The friends remain separated, like friends parted by death, and no artifice of language is adequate to express or erase the bitterness of that fact. The poet's avowal of affection to his distant friend carries echoes of grief along with its message of love. What episode 46 conveys so effectively for the first time in the *Ise* is an ideal of friendship that precisely reflects the spirit of friendship articulated by Bo Ju-yi in *Poems to Sing:* namely, that the truest friend is not the one present before you, but the absent friend for whom you long in your heart.

All told, the Aritsune episodes (16, 38, and 46) in the *Ise* constitute an effort to convey in the Japanese language many of the aspects of male friendship familiar to the Heian court from their appreciation of Chinese verse. At the same time, the episodes show evidence that the parameters of male friendship are expanding into new emotional territory that is opened up by the use of Yamato language. It is significant that the word "friend" *(tomo)* appears in each of the Aritsune episodes, for that fact in itself suggests that the episodes owe a debt to "interpretive reading" of Chinese verses in Yamato speech. Just as the graph for "friend" appears in Chinese verses, the graph for "friend" appears explicitly in these episodes. In terms of their content, the episodes also owe a debt to the male courtier's appreciation of Chinese verse. The Aritsune episodes focus on a moment when friendship is realized, that is, through receipt of a gift (episode 16) or through separation (episode 46), much as we found in the Chinese verses on friendship from *Poems to Sing.* Episode 38, however, brings male friendship into new territory by exploring the nature of "longing" *(koi),* a Yamato word whose nuances appear to expand the emotional possibilities between male friends. The *waka* on karmic bonds that begins with the phrase *kimi to ware* ("you and I") in *Poems to Sing* represents a similar expansion of the parameters of male friendship but through opposite means: it brings a Japanese poem of frustrated love into the realm of male friendship on the basis of a rhetorical structure found in Chinese verse. Both the *Ise* and *Poems to Sing* encapsulate a roughly contemporaneous poetics of male friendship, but with different purposes and trajectories.

Koretaka and the Paradigm of the Imperial Prince

The *Tale of Ise* is highly innovative in its treatment of male friendship in another series of episodes, episodes 82, 83, and 85, which revolve around the figure of a deposed Prince, Koretaka. The three episodes form a discrete sequence that is among the longest and most complex in the tale, rivaled in importance only by the sequences about the future Empress Nijō (Fujiwara no Takaiko) in episodes 2 through 6 and the Ise no Saigū (Ise Shrine Virgin) in episodes 69 though 71. In terms of content and language, the Koretaka episodes appear to owe little to the "interpretive reading" of Chinese verse. For example, the graph for "friend" *(tomo)* is nowhere to be found in them. Nevertheless, all three episodes have been recognized by generations of readers as constituting perhaps the most moving account of friendship in the *Ise,* albeit of an entirely different variety from the paradigm of the Intimate Friend observed in episodes 16, 38, and 46. In the Koretaka episodes, the text creates in the Japanese language a depiction of male friendship that largely sheds the elements of Chinese form and content that accrued to the earlier Aritsune episodes. The Koretaka episodes invent a narrative of male friendship in the Japanese language that pretends little knowledge of Chinese verse.

The first of the Koretaka episodes (episode 82) identifies the hero of the *Ise* by his title, Director of the Bureau of Horses, Right Division *(migi no uma no kami),* an official title that, as we noted earlier, belonged to the historical Narihira. The episode revolves around the hero's hunting excursion with an Imperial Prince, named Koretaka in the text. Recall that the historical Prince Koretaka was the eldest son of Emperor Montoku by his favorite consort, Ki no Shizuko, who was the sister of Aritsune. As Narihira is thought to have been married to a daughter of Aritsune, the participants in episode 82 might be viewed as being bound together in a matrix of familial ties. In the fictional world of the *Ise,* however, biography recedes into the background and seems to be of little relevance to the portrait of male friendship depicted in the episode. For the purposes of the narrative, Koretaka is simply an Imperial Prince, and Narihira is a nobleman in his service.

Unlike the intimate friendship of equals found in the Aritsune episodes, the friendship between the hero and the Prince in the Koretaka episodes is hierarchical and the men are of decidedly unequal status. The Prince is throughout the sequence the object of the hero's devotion, befitting his exalted station. The gap in status between the hero and the Prince dramatically affects the language and the mood of the sequence. Deference is shown discursively to the Princely figure by the use of honorifics, and their use signals in turn the inferior status of the hero. The hero's affection for the Prince is cast in terms of a subject's affection for his lord, and his devoted service to the Prince helps define the hero as a loyal courtier and subject. Part of the beauty of the Koretaka episodes is that, despite the gap in rank between the two men, the text succeeds in producing a sense of great intimacy between them. It is this quality of intimacy that has captured the imaginations of readers of the *Ise* throughout the ages, to the extent that, as one source puts it, "[Narihira's] friendship with the ill-starred Prince Koretaka became a pattern of friendship."[47]

Episode 82 celebrates the pleasures of a spring outing with the Prince in the company of other male courtiers. Ostensibly a hunting excursion, the men are more interested in the elegant pursuits of drinking wine and composing poetry. The narrative recalls the context of male camaraderie found in the earliest episodes of the *Ise,* in the account of the Journey to the East. Episode 82 is structured around three pairs of poems, the first pair about cherry blossoms, the second pair about the legend of the Weaver Maid and Cow Herd, and the third pair about the moon. The pair of poems on cherry blossoms consists of an initial poem by Narihira and a responding poem by an unidentified member of the Imperial Prince's party.

> yo no naka ni taete sakura no nakariseba haru no kokoro wa nodokekaramashi
> *If there would be / no cherry-blossoms at all / in the world, [one's] heart in spring / would be peaceful.*
> Director of the Bureau of Horses (Narihira)

> chireba koso itodo sakura wa medetakere ukiyo ni nani ka hisashikarubeki
> *Just because they are scattered, / they are all the more dear [to us]— / the cherry-blossoms, / [for] in this fleeting world / what will exist a long time?*

The second pair of poems is about the Weaver Maid and the Cowherd, a theme related to the midsummer festival of Tanabata, celebrated on the seventh day of the seventh month each year. Narihira composes the initial poem in response to the Prince's command: "Hand me the wine-cup after reciting a poem on the subject that we, having hunted at Katano, have come in the neighborhood of Amanogawa." The Prince is deeply impressed with Narihira's poem, but he must rely on Ki no Aritsune to compose his responding poem for him.

karikurashi tanabatatsume ni yado karamu ama no kawara ni ware wa kinikeri
Having hunted all day long, / let me pass the night / at the Weaver Maid's! / [For] I have come / to the bank of the River of Heaven.
DIRECTOR OF THE BUREAU OF HORSES (NARIHIRA)

hitotose ni hitotabi kimasu kimi mateba yado kasu hito mo araji to zo omou
As she was waiting for [her] lord / who comes only once / a year, / I think there will be no other man / to whom she will give a lodging.
KI NO ARITSUNE

The final pair of poems begins again with a poem by Narihira. He is moved to compose it when the Prince decides to retire for the night, just as the moon is about to set. Once again, Ki no Aritsune responds with a poem in the Prince's stead.

akanaku ni madaki mo tsuki no kakururu ka yama no ha nigete irezu mo aranan
Is the moon already / hiding herself / while I am not [yet] tired of [gazing at her]? / I should like the mountain-ridge to recede / and not let [her] go down!
DIRECTOR OF THE BUREAU OF HORSES (NARIHIRA)

oshinabete mine mo taira ni narinanamu yama no ha nakuba tsuki mo iraji o
would that / everywhere / the mountain-tops had become flat! [For], if there were no ridges, / the moon would also not hide herself.
KI NO ARITSUNE

Seasonally, the poetic themes represent a movement from spring to summer to fall. The locus of activity, however, is restricted to the spring hunting excursion, divided between the actual hunt outside the Prince's palace and the subsequent revelry within the palace. The aura of intimacy between the Imperial Prince and the hero is created by phrases such as "he always *(tsune ni)* took along a man who was the Director of the Bureau of Horses." Despite the honorifics that elevate the Prince, there is an explicit attempt to eliminate the hierarchy of rank by means of poetry, expressed in the phrase "all [members of the party]—high and low alike—composed poems" *(kami naka shimo mina uta yomikeri)*. Japanese court poetry does not make use of honorifics, and thus it possesses an inherent egalitarianism that is exploited here in the text. As Mark Morris has noted,

> For all its aesthetic limitations, or rather because of its limitations, [*waka*] was one form of language that an empress and her servant might exchange with relative freedom. It provided a special, less restrictive socio-aesthetic idiolect that allowed a kind of expression and communication between sites of unequal power that speech might inhibit or forbid. This freedom within restrictions of the poetic code was no doubt one of the most pleasurable aspects of composing *waka* for the individual and was itself an important social function.[48]

Nevertheless, prose conventions affect the way *waka* function when they are embedded in a poem-tale. Though the Imperial Prince speaks in the narrative, no verses by him are recorded. This is one way in which the text defers to the Prince and signals his exalted status. In each case when the hero initiates a poem, the responding poem is composed by a surrogate. In the first case the surrogate is not identified, but in the second and third cases it is Aritsune. The poems are presented as an exchange between the hero of the *Ise* and his Prince, even though the exchange is mediated by Aritsune.

Jin'ichi Konishi's critique of "implicitness" *(naikōsei)* in the *Ise* suggests a way to interpret the Prince's poetic silence and also helps explain several dimensions of the portrait of male friendship in episode 82.[49] "Implicitness—a preference for sorrow over joy, stillness over motion, and the feminine over the masculine—is an important characteristic of Japanese literature. . . . An awareness of the value of implicitness probably arose during the period when the Narihira figure within oral *waka* stories—the epitome of disappointed amorousness—took shape as a character."[50] In each case in episode 82, the hero of the *Ise* occupies positions that might be described as subverting the value of implicitness. The first poem—about how pleasant spring would be if cherry blossoms didn't exist to remind us of its passing—suggests the possibility of a spring untinged by sadness. Against this suggestion of unbridled joy, the responding poem reasserts the value of implicitness: it is precisely because cherry blossoms remind us of spring's passing that we celebrate them. "Sorrow" asserts itself over "joy" in the poetic exchange.

Likewise, in his poem about lodging with the Weaver Maid, the hero boldly expresses a desire to spend the night in the mythical maiden's chambers on the "River of Heaven" (the Milky Way galaxy). As Vos notes, "The poem is an allusion to the well-known legend of the star Vega (the Weaving Maid) in Lyra and the star Altair (the Herdsman) in Aquila who are permitted to meet each other once a year, on the 7th day of the 7th month. On this night the Weaving Maid crosses the River of Heaven, *Amanogawa* (the Milky Way), over a bridge made by magpies extending their wings."[51] The poem is dynamic, metaphorically advocating the Prince's conquest of the celestial realm. Ki no Aritsune's surrogate response rejects such a possibility with its insistence that the Weaver Maid would never open her lodgings to anyone but her lord *(kimi),* the Cow Herd. Aritsune's articulation of the Weaver Maid's refusal to receive the Prince asserts "stillness" over the hero's desire for "motion."

The hero's final poem metaphorically equates the Prince with the moon itself by linking the Prince's retiring for the night to the setting of the moon. In his surrogate response, Aritsune affirms the conceit of the hero's poem that the hills should fall so that the moon might never set in the sky. The moon has distinctly feminine associations, linking the Prince once again to Konishi's sense of implicitness, in which the feminine is valued over the masculine. The Prince's practice of silence, represented by his use of a surrogate in the responding verses, further places his persona in the realm of the implicit and the feminine.

Through the integration of values of implicitness and explicitness, a new dimension of male friendship emerges here in the *Ise.* Unlike the egalitarian directness of the Intimate Friend paradigm observed in episodes 16, 38, and 46, what we see here in episode 82 is a hierarchical relationship between male subject and male lord that mimics gender binarism and asserts the precedence of the feminine. The aesthetic of implicitness, including (in Konishi's formulation) a preference for sorrow, stillness, and the feminine, is not subverted by the hero's explicitness, but affirmed by it. In a sense, the "explicitness" of his poems, and their insistence on joy, movement, and the masculine, are elements that must be asserted if the value of implicitness is to be recognized at all, for it can become apparent only in relation to its binary opposite.

The significance of this formulation of male friendship in episode 82 is to show that, in certain cases, friendship between men is achieved through a manipulation of the status gap that exists between them in ways that echo gender differences. A man who is lower in a hierarchical structure encounters a man who is his superior within that structure, and the man who occupies the lower position asserts explicit attributes of joy, movement, and masculinity against the man in the higher position, who counters by asserting the values of implicitness (sorrow, stillness, the feminine). This pseudo-gendered exchange joins both men in a bond of friendship.[52] The uneven hierarchical relationship momentarily balances itself through the playful enactment of binary pairs, countering joy with sorrow, movement with stillness, the masculine with the feminine; and it is this pairing that stabilizes the bond between them. Symbolically, the man of higher status—the Imperial Prince—has the wisdom of age (an implicit quality), while the man of lower status—the Director of the Bureau of Horses—has the vigor of youth (one of the qualities of explicitness).[53] Their respective qualities of maturity and youth further constitute a pairing that binds the men in friendship.

Put another way, the hierarchical difference between the hero and the Prince in episode 82 constitutes the basis for the friendship between them. Male friendship as seen in the Intimate Friend sequence of episodes 16, 38, and 46 is a product of mutual affection and attraction between equals, but in episode 82 it arises from the interplay of socially defined male and female qualities that, by drawing on metaphors of gender, serves to balance a potentially divisive hierarchical relationship between men and turn it into a relationship of a matched pair. The interplay of explicitness and implicitness asserts the binary opposition and, at the same time, makes the opposition interdependent and stable. Thus the distinct realms defined socially as male and female are realigned narratively in episode 82 to produce an intimate portrait of friendship between the hero of the *Ise* and his Prince.

The depiction of friendship in episode 82 is modified and made more complex in episode 83, where we glimpse the Prince in defeat. Its closing lines have long been beloved by readers of the *Ise* as capable of "bringing a person to tears," and some scholars even speculate that the beauty of the writing suggests that it was authored by none other than the master and champion of Japanese prose, Ki no Tsurayuki himself.[54] The poignancy of the episode rests on the way the impatient hero (Director of the Bureau of Horses), who is eager to abandon the Prince and return to the capital after a hunting excursion to Minase, is transformed into a devoted friend who desires only to remain at the Prince's side. It is given here complete, in Vos' translation.

> Once Prince Koretaka, who regularly visited Minase [once a year], was [there] for his usual hunting. In his *suite* served an old man who was Director of the Bureau of Horses. After several days [of hunting] he returned to the Palace [in the capital]. [The old man], having accompanied him [so far], wanted to go away quickly, but [the Prince], intending to give [him] *sake* and a reward, did not allow [him] to go. This Director of the Bureau of Horses was impatient and composed [the following poem]:—
>
> makura tote kusa hikimusubu koto mo seji aki no yo to dani
> tanomarenaku ni

I will certainly not / pick grass and tie [it together], / intending [to make] a pillow [thereof],— / [This night] not being reliable / as the nights of fall. . . .[55]

The time was the end of the third month. The Prince had spent the night without going to bed.

In this way [the old man] came and served the Prince, but, unexpectedly, the Prince had become a priest. When in the first month [the old man] was coming to Ono in order to pay his respects [to the Prince], the snow was lying very high, because it was at the foot of Mt. Hie. When he had got with difficulty to [the Prince's] abode and paid his respects [to him], [the Prince], not having anything to do, was very lonely, so that he served [him] somewhat longer, and—remembering things of former times—he talked about them [to the Prince]. But all the same, though he thought: "I should like to serve [the Prince]," he was unable to do so, because he had [his] official duties and, intending to return in the evening, [he recited the following poem]:—

wasurete wa yume ka to zo omou omoiki ya yuki fumiwakete kimi o mimu to wa

When I had forgotten [your present condition], / it would be like a dream. . . .[56] */ Did I [ever] think / that I would [go to] see you, / making my way through the snow?*

Having spoken thus, he came home in tears.

In the first part of the narrative, the Prince detains the hero for the night. The hero's public duty obliges him to stay with the Prince, despite his private desire to leave. By the end of the episode, a complete reversal has occurred. It is the hero who wishes to stay, but public duty compels him to leave the Prince's side. In both cases, the hero is reluctant to serve in his official capacity and fulfill his obligations, first to the Prince and then to his office at court. In terms of his relationship to the Prince, however, the hero is transformed from a reluctant subject into a devoted companion, a friend. The hero's desire to be with the Prince is no longer motivated by office, but by affection.

The hero's transformation is occasioned by the Prince's tonsure *(shukke).* In the idiom of Heian politics, an Imperial Prince's tonsure means that he has suffered political defeat and been removed from succession to the throne. When the text tells us that the Prince has shaved his head and become a Buddhist monk, we are to understand that he has suffered a complete political defeat. The problem addressed in the episode is that the

Prince has not yet resigned himself to his fate. Having experienced the prestige and power afforded by his birth as the firstborn son of Emperor Montoku, the Prince struggles to relinquish his hopes of becoming emperor, in particular because of the ambitions of his supporters in the Ki clan. (Recall that Prince Koretaka's mother was a sister of Ki no Aritsune's.) The Prince's agony in defeat is made real through the hero's interaction with him in the text. The hero sees that the Prince is alone and preoccupied with sad thoughts, so he draws the Prince into conversation about bygone days *(inishie no koto nado omoi ide kikoekeri),* intending perhaps to comfort him. Suddenly, the past is set up in dynamic opposition to the present. This temporal rupture creates the defining structure of the episode. The emblem of the Prince's defeat, his tonsure, divides the hero's world into a "before" and an "after." The diminished present now stands in relation to a glorious past. In the first half of the episode there is no past, only the present, when the hero is impatient to be off, unaware of the terrible setback that awaits his Prince. Episode 83 suggests that when one man of lower status sees another of higher status suffer setback and defeat, it generates in him one of the most passionate forms of friendship between men, based on a sense of a shared fate that both men are impotent to alter. The passion of their friendship is a product of their shared experience of loss and their shared memories of a better time. Only when a diminished present is constructed in relation to a glorious past is this sort of passionate friendship activated between men. In the innocent present of the first half of episode 83, where the diminished past yet resides unseen, male friends never exhibit the intensity of passion that is evoked by sharing in the experience of political defeat.

When reconsidered in this light, the previous episode, episode 82, must be read as an account of the innocent present, which, through the events of the second half of episode 83, becomes transformed into a better time in the past. Episode 82, with its lighthearted camaraderie, records that the men "drank wine and told stories" *(sake nomi monogatari shite).* In episode 83, however, "telling stories" gives way to "remembering" *(omoi ide kikoekeri).* Telling tales is one of the innocent pleasures of the present, but remembering what was or what might have been is by nature one of the most painful mental processes people are subject to, for it represents a futile assertion of the human desire to recapture that which was lost. When the hero sees his Prince suffer utter defeat, it stirs in him powerful feelings of affection tinged with remorse, sorrow, and guilt. By participating with his Prince in "remembering things of former times" *(inishie no koto nado omoi ide kikoekeri),* he is in fact engaged in one of the greatest acts of friendship available to a man.

When considered in relation to each other, episodes 82 and 83 suggest that the context of a glorious past juxtaposed with a diminished present intensifies the bond between friends. Male friendship of a playful kind may exist in the innocent present, based on the enactment of a complementary binary pairing of two men of unequal status in a pseudo-gender-based relationship as seen in episode 82, but political defeat is capable of transforming friendship between men. Defeat recontextualizes the former lighthearted intimacy into one that is deeper and more passionate because it is informed by suffering.

Episode 85 serves as a coda to the events of episode 83 and suggests in the long-term what might be a fitting outcome for the friendship between the hero and his Prince. Vos' translation is given here.

> Once there was a man. The lord whom he had served since [his] boyhood had become a priest. In the first month [of every year] he visited [his former lord] without fail. As he served at Court, he could not visit [him] frequently, but [when he could] he did so without any change in [his] former feelings.
>
> [Once] the people who had formerly served him, both laymen and the priests, assembled in a large number, and, saying: "It is New Year, so it is a special occasion," [the lord] gave [them] *sake*. The snow fell as if [someone was] pouring [it] out and did not stop all day. All got drunk and there were poems on the theme "I have been snowed in." As [somebody] recited:—
>
> omoedomo mi o shi wakeneba mekare senu yuki no tsumoru zo
> waga kokoro naru
> *Although I am fond [of you], / I [can]not split [my] body. / Therefore the*
> *accumulation of snow / which does not stop / is just what I want—*
>
> the Prince admired [his poem] very much and, taking off his garb, gave [it to the poet].

In episode 85, we see the friendship of the hero and his Prince several years after the events of episode 83. The image of snow is consistent in both episodes, although its function differs. In the earlier episode, the hero battles his way through drifts of snow to pay his respects to the Prince in the New Year and departs by nightfall, having composed a poem expressing his deep sorrow at being forced to witness the unhappy plight of the tonsured Prince in seclusion in the hills. By contrast, episode 85 depicts the delight of the hero who finds himself snowed in at the Prince's palace. The pleasure that the hero finds in the company of the Prince is palpable in the poem, and serves to illustrate the prose phrase earlier in the episode that describes the hero's continued devotion ("without any change in [his] former feelings") to the Prince. The hero's feelings of longing are apparent in the poem when he expresses the desire to remain at the Prince's side. The hero cannot be in two places at once, both at court and with his Prince, and the heavy snowfall solves the dilemma by allowing him to remain with the Prince as he wishes. The tonsured Prince's bestowing of his robe on the hero proves that the hero's affection communicated itself powerfully in the poem and signals the Prince's utmost affection and esteem for the hero. It is with good reason that the hero's devotion to the ill-starred Prince became a "pattern of friendship" in Japanese culture.

What links the paradigms of friendship found in the Aritsune and Koretaka episodes in the *Ise* are common rhetorical modes that either affirm friendship or bring solace to the friend. In episode 16, the hero's gift of a set of robes comforts a grieving Aritsune, whose wife prepares to leave him; in episode 38, the hero affirms his feelings of longing for Aritsune; and in episode 46, the hero's poem consoles his intimate friend with the assurance that he will not be forgotten. Likewise, in the Koretaka sequence, episode 82 affirms a friendship, mediated in part by Aritsune, between Narihira and the Prince that is based on a socially gendered binarism in which the hero plays masculine qualities of explicitness against the Prince's feminine implicitness. In episodes 83 and 85, Narihira commiserates with the defeated Prince and comforts him with his presence.

Through these modes of avowing friendship and comforting the friend, the *Ise* constructs a sense of how friendship deepens in the course of the episodes. Episode 16 shows the hero giving a gift to Aritsune, then moves to episode 38 where the hero confesses his longing for Aritsune, and culminates in episode 46 when the hero assures his distant friend that his image is always in his mind's eye. Likewise, episode 82 moves from a simple pairing of two friends, the hero and his Prince, to the events of the following episodes, political defeat in episode 83 and a life lived in seclusion in episode 85, which deepen the bond of friendship between them. The sequences illustrate that separation of male friends caused by political defeat at court, as in episodes 46, 83, and 85, only cements the bond between them, and that male friendship offers a hope of transcendence in the face of suffering.[57]

The *Ise*'s final statement on male friendship may be found in the concluding episodes of Teika's version of the text, found in episodes 124 and 125. Episode 124 shows the hero alone and friendless, and episode 125 is understood to be Narihira's death poem.

Episode 124. What thoughts on what occasion, do you suppose, prompted a man to compose this poem?

omou koto iwade zo tada ni yaminu beki ware to hitoshiki hito shinakereba

It will be best / to keep silent / and not say what I think, / for there is no other / who shares my feelings.

Episode 125. Once a man was taken ill. Sensing the approach of death, he recited,

tsui ni yuku michi to wa kanete kikishikado kinō kyō to wa omowazarishi o

This road, / I have long been told, / man travels in the end— / yet I had not thought to go / yesterday or today.[58]

The hero's sense of abandonment in the penultimate episode can be interpreted as a comment on male friendship. The companionship and comfort of friends offer him the hope of transcending his sorrows, but in the end that hope is betrayed because friends, too, are subject to loss through death. When the prose preface to the poem asks the question "What thoughts on what occasion, do you suppose, prompted a man to compose this poem?" our answer must surely be that the hero has experienced the death of a like-minded friend who "shares [his] feelings" *(ware to hitoshiki hito).* The profound truth of friendship's loss, avoided in the paradigms of the Intimate Friend and the Imperial Prince, comes to the surface here because it prepares the hero for his own encounter with death in the final episode.

The *Tale of Heichū*

The *Tale of Heichū* presents a vision of courtly male friendship that differs in several interesting ways from that found in the *Ise.* The first major difference is that the hero of the *Heichū* is the recipient of friendship and does not befriend or comfort others as the *Ise* hero did. Another distinguishing factor is that the *Ise* hero's friendships exhibit a mutuality that is to a great extent lacking from his attempts at intimacy with women, and the friendships are not subject to the vagaries of erotic love. The *Ise* thereby suggests that the pleasures of a courtier's erotic adventures with women are destined to fade, but that his friendships with men will endure. In the *Heichū,* by contrast, both erotic adventure and male friendship are depicted as being equally frail and subject to the fickleness of the human heart. Finally, the

Heichū articulates the possibility of friendships between women, thus abandoning the assumption in the *Ise* that the subject of friendship is always male. All of this is not to imply that friendship in the *Heichū* is completely inconsistent with friendship in the *Ise.* Rather, the parameters of friendship differ because of the text's differing assumptions regarding who can be the subject of friendship. These assumptions revolve around questions of gender and the sex of the subject and object of friendship. Because women can be friends in the *Heichū,* Taira no Sadabumi (or Heichū, the Taira Captain) ends up being a very different sort of hero from the figure of Narihira in the *Ise,* especially in relation to the literary ideal that the hero should both love women and be a friend of men. In short, the hero of the *Ise* reflects the masculine subjectivity of Chinese verse, whereas the hero of the *Heichū* reflects a combined masculine and feminine, or interpenetrating, subjectivity that acknowledges the presence of women as subjects in Japanese narrative. To explore these points, it is necessary to study in detail how male friendships and female friendships work in several of episodes of the *Heichū.* The episodes most important to our understanding of the poetics of male friendship are episodes 1, 5, 14, 21, and 25.

Episode 1 opens with the explosive line "Long ago, two men courted one woman." We immediately note that the three-poled structure of male rivalry contrasts with the two-poled structure of male friendship. As episode 1 unfolds, we soon learn that the hero of the *Heichū* has won the lady's affection, even though his rival outranks him. The higher-ranking man then slanders the hero to the Emperor, making the hero's continued service at court difficult. At the urging of the rival, the Emperor dismisses the hero from his official position for neglecting his post. Distressed by the setback, the hero resolves to quit the world of the court and become a monk *(shukke).* His parents, predictably, urge patience and work behind the scenes for his official reinstatement. Unable to act on his resolve to take the tonsure, the hero composes a pair of poems expressing his grief. It is at this point in the narrative, when the hero is most in need of comfort, that three interventions by male friends occur. The first and third interventions are by groups of friends *(tomodachi-domo),* who pay the hero a visit at his residence. The second intervention is by an individual friend *(tomodachi)* who does not visit but exchanges poems offstage with the hero.

In the first case, a group of male friends gathers at the *Heichū* hero's mansion where he entertains them with wine. They, in turn, distract him with an elegant musical performance on stringed instruments. The climax of the visitation scene occurs when the hero composes a poem, telling his friends that, for the moment at least, he has forgotten his sorrows, thanks to their comforting presence. The friends are deeply affected by the poem and continue their musical performance until morning. Here the narrative makes clear that the role of male friendship is to provide solace to a courtier in the face of his political setback. This is reminiscent, of course, of the comforting role played by the hero in the *Ise,* but there is one crucial difference: the hero of the *Heichū* is placed in the exalted position of receiving comfort. The heroes of the *Ise* and the *Heichū* can thus be understood to perform opposite roles in the enactment of friendship; the hero of the *Ise* befriends, whereas the hero of the *Heichū* is befriended.

The second intervention of male friendship in episode 1 involves a poetic exchange between the hero and his male friend *(tomodachi).* One night the hero gazes alone at the moon, feeling wretched and forlorn, and his thoughts turn to a friend who "understood the ways of this melancholy world." Thinking that this friend may be similarly sleepless and alone, he sends off a poem comparing the flow of his tears to the "river of heaven" *(ama no kawa),* the Milky Way, in the night sky. As it turns out, the friend was also lying sleepless, and he receives the poem with great excitement *(ito okashimite).* When he writes his reply, he expands on the metaphor of the Milky Way as a "river of tears" and indicates that he understands the intensity of the hero's anguish. The exchange of poems is given here in Susan Videen's translation:

> The next evening the moon shone with an extraordinary beauty. His mind filled with countless recollections, Heichū slipped out onto the verandah, where he sat gazing at the sky. Meanwhile, as night deepened, the wind began to blow most mournfully. When sad memories grew too painful to be borne alone, Heichū's thoughts turned to a friend who understood the ways of this melancholy world. "I wonder whether he, too, is awake and gazing at the moon?" he thought and sent this verse:
>
> nagekitsutsu sora naru tsuki o nagamureba namida zo ama mo kawa to nagaruru
>
> *As I gaze unseeing / on a moon as empty / as the sky, / I grieve, my teardrops flowing / as Heaven's Starry Stream.*
>
> It had been quite by chance that Heichū thought to send his friend this verse, but like Heichū he was up and gazing intently on the moon. Immensely intrigued to have a message brought at such a moment, he replied:
>
> ama no kawa / kimi ga namida no / mizu naraba / iro koto nite ya / ochitagiruramu
>
> *If Heaven's Starry Stream / flows with the waters / of your tears / wondrous must its color be / as it cascades and foams!*[59]

The exchange suggests a synchronicity of feeling between the two men in multiple ways: not only is the friend indeed awake and gazing at the moon as the hero imagines him to be, but he even professes to be able to see the intensity of the hero's tears in the Milky Way. This one-on-one synchronicity epitomizes the ideal of the Intimate Friend in courtly male friendship, with the sole distinction that the hero of the *Heichū* receives the avowal of friendship, while the hero of the *Ise* gives the avowal. This distinction informs every aspect of the depiction of male friendship in the two works.

The third intervention of male friends in episode 1 is similar to the first, except that the narrative indicates that this time the visit is from a different group of friends *(koto tomodachi-domo).* A poem by one of the friends expresses sympathy for the hero's suffering caused by his removal from court office, to which the hero replies with a poem asserting his innocence and expressing regret for allowing himself to succumb to the treachery of the rival whose false reports to the Emperor led to the hero's unjust dismissal. He next addresses a pair of poems of complaint and grief to women, and one of the poems, to an attendant of the mother of the Emperor, proves to be effective; for we learn that, through the good offices of the Emperor's mother—as it turns out, a distant relative of the hero—the Emperor relents and restores the hero to court with a promotion in rank.

This depiction certainly places the *Heichū* hero in a different relation to political power from that occupied by the hero in the *Ise.* The hero is denied access to political power in the *Ise,* and this denial serves as the impetus for his search for alternative forms of power through erotic adventure and male friendship. If we admit the element of Narihira's biography that underlies the *Ise,* the figure of the hero could be said to reflect, in some shadowy form, the subject positions of the disenfranchised Ki and Ariwara families. In the *Heichū,* by contrast, political power seems familial and accessible, reflecting an implicit alliance with the position of the Fujiwara's dominant Northern House. It was not unusual in the Heian period for a young emperor to be subject to the directives of his Fujiwara-born mother, who might plausibly put in a good word for a nobleman bemoaning his demotion.

Compared with the narrative complexity of episode 1, episode 5 is a short and highly focused depiction of male friendship, similar to episode 46 in the *Ise.* Episode 5 opens with a description of a forlorn scene: the hero sits in his chambers on the first day of the New Year, gazing out at a heavy rainstorm. This is a classic image of a man sunk in despondent thought. Given that court promotions are announced in the New Year, we can assume that the hero's sense of despondence is related to failure to receive a hoped-for promotion in rank. Into this gloomy scene comes a poem from the hero's friend *(tomodachi),* bemoaning the unfruitful passage of years. Videen's translation of episode 5 follows:

> On New Year's Day a heavy rain was falling. Heichū was staring absently at the downpour, quite absorbed in his own melancholy reflections, when this verse arrived from a friend:
>
> harusame ni furikawariyuku toshitsuki no toshi no tsumori ya oi ni naruramu
>
> *Spring showers mark / the old year's passage to the new / as months and years go by— / with each raindrop, with each year / does old age not come down on me?*
>
> Afterwards, when he had not heard from his friend for quite some time, Heichū sent a verse of his own:
>
> kimi ga omoi ima wa ikura ni wakureba ka ware ni nokori no sukunakaruramu
>
> *Can it be because / there are so many now to claim / their portion of your love / that what is left for me / seems no more than a pittance?*
>
> His friend replied:
>
> toshigoto ni nageki no kazu wa souredomo tare ni ka wakemu futagokoro nashi
>
> *Though every passing year / adds to the number of my woes, / who else could there be / to claim a portion of my love? / Singlehearted I remain!*

One oddity of this sequence is that the friend's initial poem is not coupled with a responding poem from the hero. This represents a distinct departure from the *Ise* in two ways: first, expressions of friendship normally come from the hero in the *Ise;* and second, such expressions are normally met with the friend's or his surrogate's responding poem. Clearly, the *Heichū* creates a different sort of hero, one who does not initiate the avowal of friendship and does not respond to it either. When the hero finally does write to his friend, after an unspecified interval of time has elapsed, it is to make an accusation of neglect. The hero's poem questions the friend's love *(omoi)* for him because of his failure to come for a visit: *Can it be because there are so many now to claim their portion of your love that what is left for me seems no more than a pittance?*[60] It is a poem that might be sent by a jealous lover, and indeed the poem can plausibly be read as a woman's accusation of infidelity addressed to her male lover. The reply from the friend is unequivocal: *Who else could there be to claim a portion of my love? Singlehearted I remain!*[61] The final line, *futagokoro nashi,* reassures the hero in the clearest possible terms that the friendship is as strong as ever. *Futagokoro* (traitor's heart) is the word generally used in the *waka* poetic vocabulary to describe betrayal in love, and its appearance here in the context of an avowal of friendship is unusual. It suggests that the hero in episode 5 has similar—and perhaps similarly unrealistic—expectations of his friend that a woman might have for her lover, namely, his exclusive love *(omoi).*

On the basis of episode 5 in the *Heichū,* it is possible to reconsider the three interventions of male friendship discussed earlier in episode 1 as actually representing two distinct forms of friendship. One type (seen in the first and third instances) comforts the grieving courtier through reassurances received from a band of like-minded men, called *tomodachi-domo.* This type is reminiscent of the early episodes of male camaraderie in the *Ise* that served as a prelude to the Aritsune episodes. The other type, seen in the second pair of poems about the Milky Way in episode 1, involves the presence of an individual friend, called a *tomodachi,* with whom the hero shares an intimate friendship that excludes other men. Episode 1 provides examples of both types of friendship, with comrades and with an intimate friend, while episode 5 focuses exclusively on the figure of the Intimate Friend, albeit from an exalted stance as the recipient of friendship.

Episode 14 is a typical account of friendship involving a group of comrades *(tomodachi-domo).* In this case, the hero and his friends have gone on a spring excursion to view the cherry blossoms, a quintessential courtly endeavor. As in episode 82 in the *Ise,* the camaraderie generates an elegant rivalry in poetic composition, here on the theme of "the pain of turning home again before wearying of the flowers." The hero is the first to recite his poem, and since it is the only poem of the group to be recorded, the narrative makes the hero the winner of the poetry competition. The poem conjures erotic adventure in the context of male camaraderie through the image of the *ominaeshi,* or lady flower: *Why hurry home when blossoms still invite? Far better to spend the night camped in a field where throngs of lady flowers dance.*[62] The poem makes male-female erotic adventure its pretext, but its context (a group of male friends spending the night camping out) asserts male friendship in the absence of women. Eliminated in person from the context of male camaraderie, "women" are reduced to being present only in the form of a graph used to write the word *ominaeshi.* Among the episodes on friendship in the *Heichū,* episode 14 is noteworthy for the way it juxtaposes erotic adventure and male friendship in a single episode, much like episode 82 in the *Ise*'s sequence involving Prince Koretaka. The difference, of course, is that the episode in the *Heichū* consists of a single poem and thus chooses to focus on the hero in isolation, without developing his character as a friend who comforts and responds as observed in the *Ise*.

Episode 14 helps clarify another characteristic of friendship in the *Heichū*, namely, the way it tends to depict the intersection of male friendship and sexual rivalry. In episode 1, we saw how the rivalry between two male courtiers for a lady led to political setback for the hero and inspired his male friends to comfort him. Another episode, episode 17, depicts the hero in a new relationship with a woman, but when he goes to visit her one night he discovers to his chagrin that a priest, hiding in a thick patch of plume grass, is also courting her. The hero expresses sympathy for his rival's plight: "I have not been coming here that long myself. For all I know, he may have been her lover from the first! And even if he did come after me, what difference does that make now? How monstrous! How the gossips' tongues will wag with the scandal of it all! Just because of that heartless woman!"[63] The woman is heartless because of her willingness to accept the attentions of both men at once, and the humiliated hero breaks off further contact with her in a final poem: *Do you rustle so, waving to your very tips before each gust of wind, trying to decide, plume grass, which way you'll finally bend?*[64] While male friendship is not overtly present in the narrative, the hero's willingness to point the finger of blame at the faithless woman instead of his rival indicates a double standard that condones freedom for men and not for women.

Episode 34 depicts a similar but far more complex rivalry between the hero and a high-ranking male courtier. Again, the judgment against the woman is harsh. The narrative begins with the hero's discovery that his female lover is corresponding with a man of much higher rank than he, and he soon suspects that the man has replaced him. The three-poled structure of the dilemma places the narrative firmly in the realm of rivalry, not friendship. Feeling betrayed, the hero nevertheless confronts neither his rival nor the woman. Early one morning, on his way home from another woman's house where he has spent the night (the narrative makes no comment about the double standard at work here), the hero stops at the first woman's gate. There he watches her usher out his rival. He confronts her about what he has seen with an accusatory poem. She is flustered that the hero should appear at such an unlikely hour, and her protests of innocence ring hollow because of what he has just observed. The narrative describes his decision to abandon her forever. If the narrative were to end here, the story would be little more than a conventional account of love gone wrong, but the episode ends with a twist. The concluding lines tell us that the high-ranking rival hears a rumor that the woman had been seen in the company of Heichū Assuming that she has betrayed him, he, too, abandons her. Such are the consequences for the woman when the hero and his rival discover that she has a traitor's heart *(futagokoro).*

Despite the harsh judgment against women who are the object of male rivalries in these episodes, we find in other episodes of the *Heichū* a narrative space for conceptualizing and enacting female friendship. Episode 16 is the first time that the word friend *(tomodachi)* is used in relation to two women. What sort of possibilities does friendship between women open up in the text? The narrative recounts that the hero has become enamored of a woman who is the friend *(tomodachi nite)* of a woman with whom he is intimate. From the perspective of the hero, the three-poled structure of the narrative presents the hero with a tempting choice, not rivalry as seen earlier in episodes 1 and 17. Out of deference to the first woman, the hero hesitates to approach the new woman until he learns that the first woman is revealing embarrassing things about him to her friend. Counting that as a betrayal, the hero abandons the first woman and succeeds in courting her friend. The remainder of the narrative is taken up by an exchange of poems between the hero and his new lover after their first night together. In the episode, the fact that the two women are friends presents the hero with a dilemma, but this dilemma resolves itself when he learns that the first woman is telling lies about him. There is no indication in the text that the hero's new lover hesitated to link herself to him in deference to her friendship with the other woman. The narrative focuses on the hero's feelings that result from his erotic involvement with two women who are friends, but it ignores the feelings of the female friends. For that reason, we might conclude that the *Heichū* depicts female friends not as the subject of narrative but as a mere pretext for the text's exploration of the male hero's erotic adventure.

Episode 23 also narrates a story of female friends. In this case, again, the arrival of the female lover's beautiful female friend presents an amorous opportunity to the hero. In contrast to episode 16, here the first woman disappears from the narrative after the opening line, and the hero shows no deference to her feelings at all. While the woman's female friend seems to resist the hero's advances, the resistance is purely for appearance's sake and is not motivated by concern for the feelings of the hero's original lover. The woman's friend encourages the hero's advances with a poem and soon spends a night with him. The episode's concluding line, "One wonders what happened afterwards,"[65] seems directed at the unanswered question of how this affair played out in the emotions of the first woman, betrayed as she was by both male lover and female friend.[66]

In contrast to episodes 16 and 23, which introduce an individual female friend of a female figure in each narrative, there is a much longer episode, episode 25, in which a group of female friends take center stage in the action of the story. The women are ladies-in-waiting at court and have made a pilgrimage by oxcart from the capital to Shiga. They are delighted to have the companionship of the hero, who happens to join them on the way. Unfortunately, he is obligated to leave Shiga and stay elsewhere that night in order to avoid a directional taboo. Before he leaves, he promises to inquire after the ladies when he gets back to the capital, and to that end he asks where their rooms are located in the imperial palace and who their servants are. In this way, he is sure to locate them after their return. When the hero parts from the ladies, both sides seem eager to renew the acquaintance back at the capital.

Upon the ladies' return from the pilgrimage to Shiga, they tell their friends *(tomodachi-domo)* at the palace all about the excursion and the interesting man they met there. By chance, one of the friends was a former lover of the hero's. When she realizes that the man the ladies met in Shiga is her former lover, she proceeds to denounce him for his fickle ways. Unaware of this turn of events, the hero tries to contact the women as agreed, but the ladies refuse his letters. At this juncture, the hero turns for help to a man the text calls "as good as a friend" *(tomodachi mekitaru ga)*. It is an interesting phrase, suggesting perhaps that the "friend" was not a nobleman who could be considered worthy of being called a friend, but a man of lower rank with whom the hero was nevertheless on intimate terms. In a poem to the man, the hero expresses his frustration at being rejected by the ladies. When the man comforts Heichū with the words, "I know just how you feel,"[67] the narrative for the first time calls the man a friend *(tomodachi)*.

The hero again meets up with the ladies-in-waiting one day when they are out on another excursion. They resist his advances, but the episode concludes with the intriguing possibility that one of the ladies went on to establish a relationship with the hero, despite the warnings of her female friend. In general, the *Heichū* highlights the power of erotic adventure to subvert female friendship, suggesting that the bond of friendship between women is secondary to the bond of erotic adventure between man and woman. This is directly opposite to the *Ise*'s conclusion about male friendship, that the bond of friendship lingers long after erotic adventure has faded.

In another episode, episode 27, female friendship appears in an entirely new light when a young woman's female friend acts as her intermediary in an amorous affair with the hero. The narrative describes a very high-placed lady whose romantic longings are frustrated by her vigilant mother. In desperation, the young lady turns for help to a kinswoman *(shizoku),* who is referred to thereafter twice in the narrative as her friend. The word occurs once in the phrase "the woman who is the friend" *(tomodachi no onna),* in contrast to "the woman who is the mother" *(haha no onna),* and later simply as friend *(tomodachi).* The friend arranges to distract the mother by playing the koto one moonlit night, thus allowing the hero to pay his first visit to the lady. The cautious mother is not completely taken in by the ruse and soon chases the hero, barefoot, out of her house. The mother banishes the so-called friend from the house for her betrayal and, to the hero's utter disappointment, gives her daughter in marriage to another man. What makes episode 27 unusual is the way the kinswoman is depicted as performing an act of friendship that is intended to help the young lady satisfy her amorous desires. The kinswoman is clearly not an object suitable for the hero's amorous attention, perhaps due to her age, and her role in the narrative is limited to facilitating the romance of the girl and the hero. In that sense, the kinswoman is a different kind of female friend from the ones observed in other episodes, because she does not compete for, or become an object of, the hero's affection.

ULTIMATELY, THE *ISE* and the *Heichū* can be understood to provide two competing visions of friendship in Heian court literature. The *Ise*'s depiction of male friendship appealed to court literati of later ages almost certainly because of the way it framed friendship as a masculine experience that complemented a man's experience of erotic adventure. It also captured the truth that friends may bring companionship and comfort but are nevertheless subject to loss through death. The hope of transcendence is thus betrayed, consistent with the final poem on the death of a friend in *Poems to Sing,* by Fujiwara no Okikaze (early tenth century), which may have been written contemporaneously with the *Ise.* As a result of these qualities, the *Ise* would remain the quintessential and authoritative literary statement of courtly male friendship long after the Heian period had come to an end. As we shall see, the legacy of the *Heichū*'s formulation of male friendship, which revolved around male sexual rivalry and female friendship, would lie elsewhere: in the prose narratives being produced by middle-ranking women of great literary attainment in the mid-Heian court.

Chapter 3

Poetic Sequences in the *Kagerō Diary*

The *Kagerō nikki* (Kagerō diary) is a poetic narrative written in the fashion of a memoir that covers a twenty-one-year period from 954 to 974 in the marriage of a noblewoman of the Heian court. Its author is known variously as Lady Kagerō, after her text, or as Michitsuna's Mother (Michitsuna no haha, ca. 936–995), after her son, Fujiwara no Michitsuna. She was the daughter of Fujiwara no Tomoyasu (d. 977), from a minor branch of the Fujiwara clan. The text is narrated in the first person, apart from a brief introduction narrated in the third person. The diary opens with a description of the woman's poetic courtship by an unnamed man and their subsequent marriage. The man was Fujiwara no Kaneie (929–990), the eldest son of the clan's dominant Northern House, who was in his mid-twenties at the time. The woman he courted is thought to have been about age eighteen at the time of her marriage and was reputed to be one of the great beauties of her day. She had already acquired a formidable reputation as a poet. Her poetic skill is amply reflected in the *Kagerō,* which records her verses along with a substantial percentage of Kaneie's and their son's. In fact, scholars have argued that the *Kagerō* probably served as a sort of "private poetry collection" *(shika shū)* whose existence greatly enhanced Kaneie's prestige at court and her own.[1] Kaneie would ultimately go on to become chieftain of the Fujiwara clan and Regent to the Emperor and was without question one of the most capable leaders the Northern House was to produce.

The *Kagerō* has been described as one long complaint about the state of the author's marriage to Kaneie. Readers today may respond to her narrative with sympathy if they feel that the author is justified in blaming Kaneie for his neglect, or with impatience if they feel that she is clinging to a failed marriage that she should more wisely have abandoned. In general, men and women of the court had a remarkable degree of freedom in choosing to remain with a marriage partner or lover. It was common for Heian noblemen to have more than one wife, and Lady Kagerō knew that Kaneie was already married when she and her family accepted his proposal of marriage. In fact, there is evidence that they considered the match a stroke of remarkable good fortune and that Tomoyasu, Lady Kagerō's father, benefited from the marriage in terms of his postings as a provincial governor. Kaneie's first wife, Tokihime, bore him several sons and daughters, all remarkably gifted, and as a result she came to be acknowledged as his principal wife. Lady Kagerō would bear one son, Michitsuna, and this son's success at court never matched that of his brothers.

In the final section of the *Kagerō,* the author expresses the wish that she had borne a daughter. This wish probably reflects Lady Kagerō's knowledge that a daughter would have enhanced her standing with Kaneie by providing him with a useful political tool, for daughters of Fujiwara regents commonly became consorts to the emperor and thereby strengthened the Fujiwara's grip on the imperial institution. Lady Kagerō's status would have been greatly enhanced had she borne a daughter who became empress, but it was Tokihime instead who produced the future empresses. Lady Kagerō's wish for a daughter is granted only indirectly, when Kaneie asks her to oversee the upbringing of a girl who is the product of a liaison with another woman. The narrator reveals that Lady Kagerō took considerable pleasure from caring for this adopted daughter. The *Kagerō* concludes with a record of the courtship poetry of the author's son, Michitsuna. Within the frame of a story about a noblewoman's marriage, the *Kagerō* preserves the poetic production of three people: the author, Kaneie, and Michitsuna. The text is thus a complex work that has the quality of a personal poetry collection coupled with an autobiography or memoir. The resulting poetic diary has been widely admired as an honest depiction of the inner life of a noblewoman, and it probably represents the earliest such text in the history of Japanese literature.

At one point in the *Kagerō,* its author depicts the friendship of Kaneie and an Imperial Prince Minamoto no Noriakira (924–?). The section consists of their exchange of three sequences of poems, titled *natsuhiki no ito* (Summer-spun thread), *nururu koiji* (Muddy path of love), and *nagaame no koro* (Season of long rains).[2] Narrating many years after the fact, in a section of the text covering events from the Second Year of Tentoku (958) to the Second Year of Ōwa (962), the author recollects the first major crisis of her marriage, which was precipitated by Kaneie's relationship with a lady known as "the Machi Alley woman" *(machi no koji no onna).*[3] The narrator is contemptuous of the woman and describes the jealousy and deep depression the affair causes her. To communicate her resentment to her husband, she strikes upon the unusual idea of writing him a "long poem" *(chōka).* "Long poems" had by this time fallen into disuse in favor of the more familiar "short poem" *(tanka)* that we now generally think of as representative of Japanese court poetry. Male courtiers had a means of expressing themselves at length in poetic writing through Chinese verse, but women's poetic production was generally confined to this shorter *tanka* form. The author's resorting to an archaic and extended mode of expression was her only way of voicing a long complaint in poetic language. Her long poem accuses Kaneie of neglect, and in it she pleas for an apology and his admission that his neglect of her is unjustified. Kaneie responds with a long poem of his own, but it does not contain the apology she seeks. Instead, he tells her that her jealous nature has driven him into the arms of another woman. Their son, Michitsuna, is clearly on their minds as they subsequently parry short poems back and forth about the merits of going their separate ways or reconciling. At length, the narrator concludes fatalistically that she must resign herself to marital unhappiness.

At exactly this juncture in the narrative, an event occurs that has unexpected benefits for the narrator's marriage: Kaneie is promoted to the fourth rank within the court hierarchy, and as a result the narrator begins to see more of him. This occurred in 962, when Kaneie was thirty-four years old, the author was about twenty-six, and their son, Michitsuna, was eight.[4] It was an important promotion, and with it Kaneie acquired both enhanced prestige and further sources of income. The promotion was accompanied, however, by Kaneie's assignment to an undesirable official post, Vice-Minister of War *(hyōbu no tayū)*. Although representing an advancement in the court hierarchy, the position itself held no interest for Kaneie because it conferred little actual power. Edward Seidensticker notes that "the War Ministry apparently was not popular with elegant Heian gentlemen."[5] Perhaps more distasteful than any military associations of the office was the inconsequential nature of its duties, amounting to little more than "choosing and rehearsing contestants for the Court's archery matches."[6] The narrative describes how Kaneie ignored his official duties and devoted himself instead to his own projects. What made the period a happy one from the perspective of the narrator was that Kaneie's newfound leisure allowed him to spend more time with her, "two or three days at a time" *(futsuka mika nado ari)*.[7]

Sequence 1: Summer-Spun Thread

As Vice-Minister of War, Kaneie was obliged to report to his superior, Minister of War *(hyōbukyō no miya)* Minamoto no Noriakira, a son of Emperor

Daigo (885–930) and five years Kaneie's senior. Sonja Arntzen states of Noriakira, "He was noted as a man of elegant tastes, being skilled in the composition of Chinese poetry and the playing of the *koto.* He was not, however, in the first circles of power as is indicated by his posting in the unpopular War Ministry."[8] The three sequences of poetic exchanges between Noriakira and Kaneie occurred during a two-month period in 962 when Lady Kagerō was staying with Kaneie at her father's house, and they represent the text's most in-depth depiction of male friendship. These three poetic sequences show the narrator interjecting herself into the friendship between the men in some very interesting ways.

The first sequence takes place just before the narrator's move to her father's house. The exchange is initiated by Prince Noriakira with a poem to Kaneie. Keeping in mind that the entire six-poem sequence hinges on Kaneie's neglect of his official post, the first poem opens with Prince Noriakira making an elegant inquiry of Kaneie about his absence from the War Ministry, couched in the language of male friendship. The translations of the poems are by Helen McCullough.[9]

> [1] midare ito no tsukasa hitotsu ni narite shi mo kuru koto no nado taenitaruramu
>
> *Now that our duties / join us like random threads / ordered on a skein, / why should it be, I wonder, / that the spinning has ceased?*

This initial poem expresses the Prince's hope of friendship with Kaneie, since fate has brought the two men together in the same office, but it also suggests the possibility of betrayal of that hope. The Prince's expression of uneasiness is reminiscent of the Intimate Friend in episode 46 of the *Ise,* who worried that he might be forgotten because he was unseen. It also echoes the hero's accusation in episode 5 of the *Heichū* that his friend has betrayed his love by consorting with other friends. As we might expect based on the rhetoric of male friendship observed in those episodes, Kaneie responds with an avowal of his devotion to the Prince. He first asserts how pained he is that the Prince might doubt his attentiveness, and he then affirms his hope of sharing an ongoing bond with Noriakira, based on their shared positions in the War Ministry.

> [2] tayu to ieba ito zo kanashiki kimi ni yori onaji tsukasa ni kuru kai mo naku
>
> *It is very sad / to hear talk of breaking off. / I shall have gained nothing / by changing to the office / where I hoped to be with you.*

Prince Noriakira replies immediately in a way that shows sympathy with Kaneie's reasons for neglecting his duties. He accomplishes this by alluding to Kaneie's reputation for amorousness: Kaneie is neglectful of the Prince because he is busy "spinning thread in summer" *(natsuhiki no ito),* a reference to Kaneie's pursuit of erotic adventures with women.

> [3] natsuhiki no ito kotowari ya futame mime yoriariku ma ni hodo no furu ka mo
> *It is as natural / as to spin thread in summer: / time is bound to pass / while one goes around calling / on two or three different wives.*

This sympathetic poem seems to embolden Kaneie to become more open with the Prince, judging from his reply. In this next poem, Kaneie turns from his earlier avowal of devotion to admitting his lack of devotion. The excuse for his neglect is the sheer quantity of "summer-spun thread" he is busy gathering:

> [4] nanahakari ari mo koso sure natsuhiki no itoma ya wa naki hitome futame ni
> *The number, I fear, / may total seven or more. / I would not lack time / were it merely a question / of one or two* me *of thread.*

Perhaps Kaneie has gone too far in admitting his neglect of the Prince, for he now risks appearing over-inclined to erotic adventure and thus as less of a "friend of men" than he ought to be. The Prince acknowledges this imbalance in his reply, which takes the form of a poem of farewell:

> [5] kimi to ware nao shiraito no ika ni shite ukifushi nakute taemu to zo omou
> *Let the two of us / agree to go separate ways / with feelings intact: let our relations be as smooth / as cleanly twisted white thread.*

The poem establishes the two-poled structure of male friendship with the phrase *kimi to ware,* translated here as "the two of us." The Prince expresses his feeling that Kaneie's entanglements with women are competing with the demands of their friendship, and since Kaneie appears to be more interested in being a "lover of women" (as attested in the preceding poem), Prince Noriakira has no choice but to conclude that he is less inclined to be a "friend of men." In response to the Prince's expression of disappointment in their prospects of friendship, Kaneie in the sixth and final poem in the sequence adroitly reverses course and expresses once again his devotion to the Prince in this remarkable poem:

> [6] yo o fu tomo chigiri okiteshi naka yori wa itodo yuyushiki koto mo miyuramu
>
> *A man and his wife / may go their separate ways / after many years, / but no such painful breach need part / one comrade from another.*

The final phrase in Kaneie's poem—*no such painful breach need part one comrade from another*—asserts that the pleasures of erotic adventure with women are fleeting in contrast to male friendship, which can be counted on to last. This value judgment was implied earlier in the *Ise,* episode 46, when the Intimate Friend expressed this fear: "I am worrying very much lest you might have forgotten [me]. [For] it seems that the hearts of the people of [this] world are, indeed, apt to forget when they are separated." As noted then, "the hearts of the people of [this] world" *(yo no naka no hito no kokoro)* could be taken to refer to erotic relations between men and women, exactly as the phrase does here in Kaneie's poem. The conceit articulated in both texts is that male friendship allows a man to experience unwavering devotion from his friend in a way that erotic adventure with a woman cannot. Similarly, Kaneie's use of the word *chigiri* ("vow") in his final poem recalls the anonymous *waka* in *Poems to Sing,* poem 738: *You and I—what promises* [or *vows*] *must we have made in a former life? How I would like to know!* Both poems imply that the vow of friendship between men is not susceptible to betrayal or change of heart and thus transcends the vagaries of human frailty and time. Finally, if we compare Prince Noriakira and Kaneie in this section of the *Kagerō* to the heroes of the *Ise* and the *Heichū,* it becomes clear that Kaneie is behaving more like the hero in the *Ise* who befriends and avows his steadfastness, and less like the hero of the *Heichū* who was befriended by others. Prince Noriakira enjoys in turn exalted status as the befriended one who receives the reassurance and devotion of Kaneie.

In sum, the *Kagerō*'s author has created a poetic dialogue in the Summer-Spun Thread sequence in which her husband comes out looking quite dashing, as an *Ise*-like hero who possesses the double persona of "lover of women" and "friend of men." Because Prince Noriakira speaks for himself and not through a surrogate, as Prince Koretaka was depicted in the *Ise* episodes, we might conclude that the *Kagerō* depicts its Prince as an Intimate Friend of Kaneie's, not unlike the episodes in the *Ise* where Aritsune speaks for himself in an intimate dialogue with the hero.[10]

Arntzen expresses perplexity at the author's equanimity in recording this exchange of poems between the men, particularly because the poems allude to Kaneie's numerous love affairs, which have been so vexing to her—especially his recent affair with the woman of the Machi Alley. One way to explain the author's stance toward the material here is to imagine her as an artist in this section who is writing a fictional narrative or tale *(monogatari),* not a truthful account of her own feelings of jealousy as would be expected in a more naively factual autobiography or memoir.[11] Attuned to the ways in which she can create an idealized image of her husband, she devises a depiction of male friendship to make him the hero of her narrative. Thus, in her act of writing, Lady Kagerō achieves a mastery of the man that eluded her in their married life.

The female narrator's presence in the scene introduces another dimension to our discussion of male friendship. The poetic exchange between Kaneie and Prince Noriakira is hardly a one-on-one exchange between the two men in an enclosed masculine realm, of the sort observed in *Poems to Sing,* the *Ise*'s Intimate Friend and Imperial Prince episodes, or the *Heichū*'s episode 5. The *Kagerō* embeds the exchange within the feminine realm of the narrator's marriage, and the author/narrator is thus present in the male friendship on at least three complex and interpenetrating levels: as observer, as participant, and as creator of the poetic exchange. As Arntzen has noted: "Probably one of the reasons Kaneie wanted to have Michitsuna's Mother for a wife was her skill in poetry composition. He may actually have expected her not only to help him with the composition of poems for occasions like this interaction with the prince, but also to be the collector for his poems, creating just such a record as [this one]."[12] What this poetic exchange between Kaneie and Prince Noriakira makes clear is that Lady Kagerō was far more than a mechanical collector of her husband's poems and was in fact a skilled writer capable of conceptualizing in her narrative a potential role for women as observers, participants, and even creators of male friendship. The *Kagerō* is perhaps the first Heian text to put forth a female perspective on male friendship. In the author's hands, the diary becomes a textual space in which the feminine depiction of male friendship (where women are observers, participants, and creators of friendships between men) coexists with a masculine depiction of male friendship that had previously excluded feminine perspectives.

It is interesting to consider Edward Seidensticker's interpretation of the Summer-Spun Thread sequence—found in his translation of the *Kagerō,* titled *The Gossamer Years*—in order to see how male friendship is conveyed there. Note that Seidensticker reverses roles and calls Kaneie "the Prince" and Noriakira "the Minister" in the translation:

> The Minister, his superior, sent over a poem asking why the Prince never came to the office: [1] *"Threads in the same skein. Why then do they not meet?"* The Prince replied: [2] *"How sad to be told that being of the same skein should mean so little."* The Minister followed with a second poem, pursuing the silk-reeling figure: [3] *"It is proper to take in silk while the summer is high; and while we are tending to our two and three strands, the time somehow slips by."*
>
> [4] *"And is one's time to be taken up by a poor two and three strands?"* the Prince replied. *"Count mine rather as the seven white skeins of the old song."*
>
> The Minister promptly apologized for underestimating the range of the Prince's activities, and added a poem to his letter: [5] *"Let us part without rancor, you and I, to pursue these white threads."* He was in penance, he said, and could write no more.
>
> The Prince answered: [6] *"But as the years go by, unpleasantness will arise from those white threads."*[13]

In Seidensticker's rendition, War Minister Noriakira expresses resentment for Kaneie's neglect of him *(Threads in the same skein. Why then do they not meet?)* in the opening poem, and this is followed by Kaneie's reply suggesting that he desires that Noriakira recognize his true devotion *(How sad to be told that being of the same skein should mean so little).* This interpretation seems to be at odds with the actual dynamics of the poetic exchange. As noted earlier, Kaneie responds to Noriakira's lament that their ties might be broken with a pronouncement of his devotion to Noriakira. The proper dynamic involves the Prince seeking and then receiving assurances of his friend's devotion.

In the next exchange of poems, Seidensticker conveys a sense of camaraderie between Noriakira and Kaneie with his rendering of poem 3, *It is proper to take in silk while the summer is high; and while we are tending to our two and three strands, the time somehow slips by.* Noriakira's sympathy for Kaneie is then based on the conceit that both men are busy pursuing love affairs, the "two or three strands" of silk in the poem. To this, Seidensticker has Kaneie boasting, *And is one's time to be taken up by a poor two and three strands? Count mine rather as the seven white skeins of the old song.* As discussed earlier, such boastfulness is perfectly plausible in a man such as Kaneie and has the effect of convincing Prince Noriakira that Kaneie's interest lies not in a friendship with him but elsewhere.

In the final exchange of poems in the sequence, Seidensticker renders poem 5 by Noriakira as, *Let us part without rancor, you and I, to pursue these white threads.* This would seem to indicate that Prince Noriakira's sentiments align perfectly with Kaneie's and that both men would rather pursue their separate erotic adventures than a mutual friendship. Regarding poem 5, Seidensticker states in a note, "The Minister's poem seems to have homosexual overtones, or perhaps it is to be considered only a conventional flourish. Another possible explanation is that Kaneie's poems are really the author's, and the Minister knows it."[14] In other words, according to Seidensticker's rendering, Noriakira is propositioning either Kaneie or the author/narrator, Kaneie's wife. The note does not clarify which words in the poem convey Noriakira's sexual interest in Kaneie, or alternatively in Kaneie's wife, if Noriakira is indeed addressing her in his poem. If we consider the meaning of the poem within a context of courtly male friendship, the two-poled structure of "you and I" is the closest Prince Noriakira's poem comes to proposing a one-on-one relationship between the men, but it should probably be understood as referring to the hope of friendship between them, consistent with the use of "you and I" observed in *Poems to Sing*. When Prince Noriakira offers to terminate his friendship with Kaneie in the poem, he is calculating that he will receive assurances of Kaneie's devotion in response. As we have seen, Kaneie responds with exactly this sort of avowal of friendship. Seidensticker renders poem 6 rather cryptically, however: *But as the years go by, unpleasantness will arise from those white threads.* In a note, Seidensticker tries to clarify some of the poem's implications: "Hence a relationship between two men is more secure? This is no better than a guess at what Kaneie's poem might mean. It revolves around the word *yuyushii,* which has two very nearly opposite meanings. If the alternative possibility is taken, then Kaneie might be saying, in answer to the Minister's rather odd poem, that he prefers the company of a lady."[15]

If, as Seidensticker's translation suggests, poem 5 was a sexual proposition by Prince Noriakira to Kaneie, then poem 6 is either Kaneie's acceptance of that proposition ("a relationship between two men is more secure") or a rejection of it on the basis that he has a preference for women (the entangling "white threads"). If, on the other hand, we choose to understand this scene as the *Kagerō* author's narration of courtly male friendship, then Kaneie's response comparing the durability of male friendship with the frailty of the bond between men and women must be understood not as an expression of sexual preference but as a means to assure Noriakira that he intends to remain his friend.

The dynamic of male friendship communicates itself in clearer terms in Arntzen's translation of the same passage, which follows. Note that in Arntzen's rendition the identity of the men is implied through terms of respect that show deference toward the Prince; Noriakira is referred to as "his Highness, the prince" and Kaneie as "my husband."

One day, there comes this missive from his Highness, the prince, who was in charge of the ministry toward which my husband did not feel attracted:

[1] midare i no tsukasa hitotsu ni narite shimo kuru koto no nado tae ni taruramu

Like scattered threads / wound onto a single spool, / we ended up in the / same office, yet it seems that / you would like to break those ties.

His respectful reply:

[2] tayu to ieba ito zo kanashiki kimi ni yori onaji tsukasa ni kuru kahi mo naku

When you say "break ties," / how sad it makes me feel! / There is nothing to do / but be wound together on / the same spool of office.

A response comes back right away:

[3] natsuhiki no ito kotowari ya futa me mi me yori ariku ma ni hodo no furu ka mo

Traveling around / to gather summer-spun thread / for two skeins, three skeins, / I understand perfectly / how the time passes away.

His respectful reply:

[4] nana bakari ari mo koso sure natsu hiki no itoma ya ha naki hito me futa me ni

As numerous as / seven are the skeins I have / of summer-spun thread. / How could I say I had no / time were there only one or two?

Again, from the prince:

[5] kimi to ware naho shira ito no ika ni shite uki fushi nakute taemu to zo omofu

With so many threads / entangling you, as for you and me, / in the end, perhaps we / had best cut our ties while we / still can with no hard feelings.

"Two or three women would really be too few but as I have probably already overstepped the bounds of propriety, I shall stop here."

His respectful reply:

[6] yo wo futomo chigiri okiteshi naka yori ha itodo yuyushiki koto mo miyuramu

With time's passage / vows between men and women / may unravel, / but could we ever see such / an awful thing between us?

Arntzen's translation suggests a plausible reading of the passage as a depiction of courtly male friendship. The initial poem by Prince Noriakira suggests a hope for friendly intimacy with Kaneie, and Kaneie's response establishes grounds for friendship between them on the basis of their paired assignment as Minister and Vice-Minister at the War Ministry. Prince Noriakira in essence accuses Kaneie of insincerity in poem 3, since Kaneie seems to have more important things to do ("traveling around to gather summer-spun thread") than appearing at his post. Kaneie's excuse (the quantity of summer-spun thread he is busy gathering) can be understood as an apology of sorts, but Prince Noriakira does not accept it and instead suggests a break between the men. The intent of this threat is to summon a statement of commitment from Kaneie. Kaneie responds appropriately, in the sixth and final poem in the sequence, with a statement of utter devotion to the Prince: *Vows between men and women may unravel, but could we ever see such an awful thing between us?* The durability of friendship between the men is thus affirmed.

Sequence 2: The Muddy Path of Love

The *Kagerō* continues with another sequence of poems between Prince Noriakira and Kaneie, this time sent from a different location. Lady Kagerō has moved to her father's house to avoid a directional taboo, and Kaneie joins her there. We learn that Prince Noriakira's estate is adjacent to theirs, and their new proximity inspires the Prince to communicate once again with Kaneie. This time the exchange consists of an odd number of poems; the aborted ending occurs when Kaneie refuses to reply to the Prince's fifth poem. Once again the translations of the poems are McCullough's.[16]

> [1] tsurezure no nagame no uchi ni sosoguramu koto no suji koso okashikarikere
>
> *Bored and disheartened / by these interminable rains, / I have found amusement / in observing the furor / where there seems to be a leak.*

Although not apparent in translation, Prince Noriakira seems to be paying an artful compliment to his neighbors on the beauty of the koto music emanating from their house in this initial poem. According to Kawaguchi Hisao, linking the sound of rain to the sound of the koto was a poetic convention: "In the midst of the tedium of this endless rain, how charming to hear the flowing tone of the *koto*."[17] There is a pun in the phrase *"koto no suji,"* meaning either "the flowing tone of the *koto*" or "the flow of events *(koto)*." This pun gives the poem its secondary meaning as a reference to the commotion caused by the leaking roof. In Kawaguchi's reading, the poem is primarily an elegant note of appreciation to Kaneie for the beauty of his wife's playing, which the Prince feels is the one pleasant diversion on this otherwise dreary day.

Interestingly, the text introduces the narrator's assessment of the poem prior to citing the poem itself, calling it "maddening" *(mono-kuruhoshiki).* This is frequently taken to mean that the Prince's poem is "mad" or inappropriate, but Kawaguchi suggests a revisionist reading that takes the word to be a description of the narrator's own feelings of embarrassment (feelings that may have been shared by Kaneie): "There was a commotion when the roof leaked, and we were greatly embarrassed that [the Prince] noticed it."[18] Another possibility, related to Noriakira's reference to the narrator's musical performance, is that the narrator was vexed that the Prince should have overheard her and for that reason found his poem maddening. Prince Noriakira had a reputation himself as a skilled player of the koto, and although his musical skills are not mentioned in the *Kagerō* itself, the Prince's complement would probably have indicated to Heian readers that Lady Kagerō was a musician of considerable skill.

In any case, the narrator and Kaneie are certainly flattered to receive the Prince's poem, and the narrator's assertion that she found the Prince's poem "maddening" is probably best understood as a comment on her own state of mind, not a criticism of the poem. That the narrator's fine koto caught the Prince's ear makes the narrator unusually important in this scene, because the narrator casts herself as the inspiration for the Prince's renewed interest in her husband. The subject of the sequence is friendship between two noblemen, but the female narrator revels in her role as the instrument that summons the male friend to her husband's side. As the exchange unfolds, we see that the *Kagerō*'s author is deliberately creating a central role for her female narrator in her depiction of Kaneie's experience of male friendship.

> [2] izuko ni mo nagame no sosoku koro nareba yo ni furu hito wa nodokekaraji o
>
> *Since this is a time / of general commotion / as the long rains cause leaks, / the exceptional man alone / may boast of a tranquil heart.*

While again it is not apparent in translation, Kaneie's reply communicates to Noriakira his sense that both men have suffered political setback by their posting to the War Ministry:[19] "Hardships are everywhere these days, and no one who has seen his fortunes decline can rest easy." Kaneie's sympathy with Noriakira is based on their shared fates. Their lack of success at court becomes a bond between them, couched here in the language of male friendship.

Poem 3 is Noriakira's reply, and it picks up on the statement in poem 2 that "no one . . . can rest easy."

> [3] ame no shita sawagu koro shi mo ōmizu ni tare mo koiji ni nurezarame ya wa
> *Since this is a time / when continual rains cause / general commotion, / everyone's robes must be drenched / by mud from the flooding waters.*

Prince Noriakira's poem points to the existence of political turmoil: *ame no shita* is both "under [rainy] skies" and "under heaven" *(tenka),* suggesting the realm of the imperial court. In the midst of this flood—of rain, of political turmoil—the Prince suggests that no one's reputation escapes getting "muddied." The word *koiji* ("muddy," or "the path of love") is used this way later in the *Kagerō* in a long poem *(chōka)* that the narrator sends to Kaneie's sister, whose husband and sons have been banished from the capital: "Still sadder, the muddy paths *(koiji)* / down which they must tread, / the beloved children each / reaping his own fate. . . ."[20] Here, Noriakira's poem expresses the sense that both men are "muddied," their reputations sullied by being relegated to the margins of power in the War Ministry. This is what binds the Prince to Kaneie in friendship.

If Kaneie's response to the Prince's poem were to follow the spirit of the *Ise*'s depictions of courtier-princes who suffered political setbacks such as Aritsune and Koretaka, it would build upon Noriakira's attempt to establish a common ground between them on the basis of their frustrated ambitions and seek to comfort him. Instead, Kaneie's reply in poem 4 seems to deny that there might be any sympathy between them.

> [4] yo to tomo ni katsu miru hito no koiji o mo hosu ma araji to omoi koso yare
> *There must be no time / for his muddy robes to dry— / that gentleman / who never ceases to roam / from one brief love to another.*

Through a pun on *yo* (meaning "world" and "night"), the poem has two overlapping meanings: "for a man who is active in the world, there is no time for the mud to dry" (i.e., the muddied reputation does not stick); and "for a man who pursues love each night in these constant rains, there is no time for his robes to dry." Kaneie's poem challenges Noriakira's assertion of his own insignificance in the court hierarchy, pointing out that Noriakira is in fact not marginalized at all but active at court and therefore more fully integrated into the center of state power than Kaneie is. It implies that the Prince has not experienced a true political setback and therefore Kaneie will not even attempt to comfort him. To judge from the harshness of Noriakira's reply, the Prince was angered by Kaneie's failure to sympathize as a friend.

> [5] shika mo inu kimi zo nururamu tsune ni sumu tokoro ni wa mada koiji dani nashi
>
> *You are the one / whose robes are drenched by your failure / to stay as I stay. / Mud has yet to stain a man / who keeps always to the same place.*

The Prince seems to be saying in poem 5 that he is indeed a defeated man, for he has given up both his worldly ambitions and his pursuit of erotic adventure. In fact, he argues, it is Kaneie whose ambitions and interest in amorous pursuits remain very much alive. Prince Noriakira is accusing Kaneie of insincerity in their friendship and at the same time expressing his fears that Kaneie's ambitions will deepen the Prince's sense of his own defeat instead of bringing him hope of transcending it.

The exchange of five poems concludes with an enigmatic phrase that has baffled interpreters of the *Kagerō* text: *sa mo keshikaranu onsama kana nado iitsutsu moroton ni miru.* The last part of the phrase is clear enough. *Moroton ni miru* means that the narrator and Kaneie looked at the Prince's poem together. This in itself is more significant than it may at first seem. As Arntzen describes in a note, drawing on Shinozuka's interpretation of the sentence, "There are only a few places in the diary where [the narrator] notes explicitly that they did something together. They mark places of exceptional intimacy and harmony."[21] What is more difficult to decipher is their reaction to the poem, *sa mo keshikaranu onsama kana.* Seidensticker translates this phrase, "We read this last poem together, and thought him something of a rogue."[22] Arntzen renders it, "As we looked at this together, he said something like, 'How outrageous of him.'"[23] Clearly, Noriakira's reply offended Kaneie's sensibilities. In a note, Kawaguchi Hisao interprets the phrase to mean, "How dare he [Noriakira] say such a thing."[24] Kaneie must have realized here that his last poem to Noriakira had the effect of upsetting the trajectory of their friendship. If we read this scene as a literary enactment of male friendship, then poem 5 ruptures the bond of friendship that has been developing between the noblemen, because it fails to satisfy the Prince's desire for comfort and transcendence. The poem signals the termination of their poetic exchange in this sequence.

In terms of the author's larger purposes in the *Kagerō,* more significant than the rupture in the men's friendship is the glimpse of intimacy between husband and wife that lingers at the end of the scene, when the narrator and her husband look at the poem together *(moroton ni miru)*. This narrative juncture represents a bold inversion. The earlier sequence on Summer-Spun Thread ended with Kaneie's poem announcing the durability of male friendship in comparison with erotic adventure, but the Muddy Path of Love sequence ends here with a breakdown in the men's poetic exchange and a subtle affirmation of the conjugal bond between the narrator and Kaneie. The author masterfully disrupts the masculine poetics of male friendship to create a feminine counterpoetic, illustrating with subtlety and skill that male friendship is in fact fragile and that its failure may lead to heightened intimacy between a man and a woman. Far from providing Prince Noriakira with hope of transcending the disappointment of his post in the Ministry of War, his friendship with Kaneie becomes a pretext, in its failure, for the renewal of the narrator's romantic hopes.

The following is Seidensticker's rendering of the Muddy Path of Love sequence in English. This translation interprets the poetic exchange in overwhelmingly sexual terms. Once again, in a reversal, Kaneie is referred to as "the Prince" in the translation, and Noriakira as "the Minister."

> Toward the end of the Fifth Month the Prince and I moved to my father's house (he was still away in the provinces) to begin a forty-five-day penance.
>
> The Minister was staying at a neighboring estate. We were all kept inside by heavy rains which lasted on into the following month, and the house, rather a poor one, had a leaky roof. At the height of our distress, the Minister sent over a poem that struck us as rather perverse: [1] *"The long, dreary rains—but the sound of the dripping is pleasant."*
>
> And we replied: [2] *"How, submerged in this long rain, could a person find time for such wit?"*
>
> "Right your are," he wrote again. [3] *"And who, among those who travel the mud-spattered way, does not get his sleeves wet in this disturbing downpour?"*
>
> And the Prince returned: [4] *"And those who regularly follow the muddy path have few nights to dry their sleeves."*
>
> The Minister came back again: [5] *"It is you, the irregular, whose sleeves should be wet; where one stays regularly there is no worry about the muddy way."*
>
> We read this last poem together, and thought him something of a rogue.[25]

In Seidensticker's rendering, Noriakira's initial poem is an inquiry into how they are faring in the rainy weather, but the poem strikes the narrator and her husband as "rather perverse" because it appears to make light of their soggy situation. The translation of the poem *(The long, dreary rains—but the sound of the dripping is pleasant)* captures the spirit of the original, discovering a pleasant sound in the midst of dreariness, but without any reference to koto music. The clever rejoinder sent by Kaneie and the narrator takes the Minister to task for indulging in wittiness at their expense *(How, submerged in this long rain, could a person find time for such wit?).* Their reply shows an easygoing willingness to tease the Prince that perhaps goes beyond the intentions of the original. The Minister's replying poem continues the rain-soaked metaphor: *And who, among those who travel the mud-spattered way, does not get his sleeves wet in this disturbing downpour?* As explained in a note, the poem makes a general observation about love: that those who love inevitably shed tears of heartbreak and regret. The note explains the meaning of the phrase "mud-spattered way" in these terms: "*Koiji,* 'muddy way' and 'way of love' (suggesting unrequited love). Wet sleeves of course indicate tears. Hence, 'who among those traveling the way of love does not weep?'"[26] Kaneie's reply seems to flatter Noriakira for the vast extent of his erotic adventures: *And those who regularly follow the muddy path have few nights to dry their sleeves.* Kaneie's implication is that a man who loves widely, such as Noriakira, has even more cause for tears. Up to this point, the exchange seems rather innocuous, even hackneyed, as both parties develop clever responses to each other's poems, employing similar motifs and images that resonate with each other. Poem 5, however, appears to overstep some boundary in the decorum the men have been observing. The Minister's poem harshly reprimands Kaneie, as a note suggests, for his "unfaithfulness" in failing to report to his ministerial post regularly. Seidensticker's translation indicates that both the narrator and Kaneie were taken aback by this poem (we "thought him something of a rogue"), to the extent that they sent no replying poem, but the exact source of their discomfort remains unclear.

Arntzen's rendering of the Muddy Path of Love sequence conveys a somewhat different trajectory of emotions. Here, "the prince" indicates Prince Noriakira, as it should.

> Around that time, somewhat after the twentieth of the fifth month, in avoidance of a forty-five day period of abstinence, I moved into my absent father's residence, which was only separated by a hedge from the residence of the prince. Extending into the sixth month, the rain poured down ferociously and we were all cooped up on account of it. Since the house is

quite run down, we had a big commotion dealing with the rain leaking in. Noticing this, the prince deigned to send over this message that was quite mad:

[1] tsuredzure no nagame no uchi ni soso kuramu koto no sudji koso okashikarikere

With nothing to do, / one stares out at the long rain, / yet over at your place / there seems to be such a flurry / of activity, how very charming.

His respectful reply:

[2] idzuko ni mo nagame no sosoku koro nareba yo ni furu hito ha nodokekaraji wo

Since everywhere / a flurry of activity pours on / us with the long rains, / there must be no one in the world / who can take it easy.

Again, he deigned to correspond, "So you can't take it easy?"

[3] ame no shita sawagu koro shimo ohomidzu ni tare mo kohidji nurezarame ya ha

An unsettled time indeed, / for all under these rainy skies, / in the midst of this flood, / who has not been drenched / on the muddy path of love?

His respectful reply:

[4] yo to tomo ni katsu miru hito no kohidji wo mo hosu yo araji to omohi koso are

You who with the night / visit one after another / on love's muddy path, / I imagine there is never / a time when your lovers' tears dry.

And again from the prince:

[5] shikamo winu kimi zo nururamu tsune ni sumu tokoro ni ha mada kohidji dani nashi

It is not like that, / you are the one damp with tears, / for me who lives / in the same place, always, / there are no muddy paths of love.

As we looked at this together, he said something like, "How outrageous of him."[27]

According to Arntzen, the first poem contrasts the Prince's tedium ("nothing to do") with the flurry of activity next door ("how very charming"), without a hint of the musical dimension of the overheard koto. Arntzen takes Kaneie's reply in poem 2 as a straightforward statement of the discomfort Kaneie is experiencing due to the continuing heavy rains. Poems 3, 4, and 5 pursue the imagery of wetness and its associations with erotic adventure. At the end of the Muddy Path of Love sequence, however, the cause of Kaneie's outrage over the Prince's reply is mystifying. Arntzen attempts to explain it in these terms:

> *He said something like, "How outrageous of him"*—It is difficult to know what Kaneie means by this remark. Perhaps he is remarking on the crazy turn the poetic exchange has taken. Having started with joking about the problems with a leaky roof, the prince's bantering has led to an exchange where male and female speaking positions have become blurred. The prince's last poem is particularly ambiguous. It may be taken as a reproach of Kaneie for not visiting, which would mean that the prince is assuming a feminine persona. Yet, the first line speaks of Kaneie as the one "damp with tears," which in association with the previous poem would put Kaneie in the feminine position of waiting for the prince.[28]

How might the blurring of "male and female speaking positions" explain Kaneie's outrage at the culmination of this poetic sequence? If we recall the Imperial Prince sequence in the *Ise,* the interplay of feminine and masculine roles served to connect the hero and Prince Koretaka in a symbolic male-female pairing. There the Prince occupied the feminine realm throughout the exchange. In the *Kagerō*'s Muddy Path of Love sequence, the way in which Prince Noriakira's final poem reproaches Kaneie for his failure to visit is consistent with the Prince's occupying a feminine position, for in *waka* poetics it is the man's prerogative to visit his lover and the woman's fate to await him. What does it mean for the Prince to assert that it is Kaneie who is "damp with tears"? If this scene is a depiction of male friendship, then it may be more appropriate to read "the muddy path" *(koiji)* as a metaphor for political disappointment instead of disappointment in love. Arntzen's speculation that the Prince's poem "may be taken as a reproach of Kaneie for not visiting" indicates that the Prince desires closer intimacy with Kaneie than Kaneie is prepared to give. The discrepancy between the two men's expectations regarding their friendship gives rise to the hurt tone of the Prince's poem and to Kaneie's outrage. This breakdown of friendship, in turn, serves the author's purposes in showing her narrator's renewed intimacy with her husband.

Sequence 3: Season of Long Rains

The narrative continues during another period of heavy rain with a third and final sequence of poems. It begins when a poem from Noriakira arrives in Kaneie's absence. It appears that Kaneie has taken advantage of a break in the rain to go out on an excursion. The author refers to Kaneie's destination that day as "the usual place [he] goes back-and-forth to" *(rei no kayoi-*

dokoro), taken as a reference to the house of his principal wife, Tokihime. The author uses the same word "usual" *(rei no)* in reference to a letter from Prince Noriakira, "there was the usual letter [from the Prince]" *(rei no onfumi ari).*[29] The parallel use of *rei no* "usual" is intriguing here, for it suggests a regularity in Kaneie's contact over time with Tokihime, his principal wife, and with the Prince, his male friend, that the author presents as being similarly intimate and predictable. While friendship was paired with erotic adventure in the *Ise* as a form of masculine intimacy more durable than the intimacy between the sexes, in this sequence of the *Kagerō* male friendship is paired as complementary to marriage. When the narrator states *amama ni, rei no kayoidokoro ni monoshitaru hi, rei no onfumi ari* ("During a lull in the rain, on a day when [Kaneie] went to the usual place [he] goes back-and-forth to, there was the usual letter [from the Prince])," it suggests two kinds of regular, daily forms of intimacy that constitute Kaneie's personal world in the text. From the narrator's perspective, the friendship with the Prince is far less threatening because she occupies a central role in it as audience and participant. The author is outside the domestic world Kaneie shares with his principal wife, Tokihime, at "the usual place [he] goes back-and-forth to," but she fully integrates herself into his masculine world of friendship and goes on to develop it further in the sequence.

The Prince's messenger delivers his poem even though he knows Kaneie is absent from home.

> [1] tokonatsu ni koishiki koto ya nagusamu to kimi ga kakio ni oru to shirazu ya
> *Are you not aware / of how I have lingered / beside your hedge, / hoping to comfort a heart / ever longing to see you?*[30]

The phrase "soothe my longing" *(koishiki koto ya nagusamu)* can be understood in two different senses, as a reference to the longing between a man and a woman or to the longing of a man for his absent male friend. At the level of diction, this poem can be read as either a love poem or a poem of male friendship. The Prince may in fact be exploiting this ambiguity. The poem is followed by a prose phrase "since it is useless, [I humbly] take my leave" *(kainakereba makarinuru).* Again, the poet's despair ("it is useless") can be understood in terms of his dashed hopes for either love or friendship. Presumably, if this were an expression of love, the narrator might have hesitated to show it to Kaneie upon his return, but this is not the case. She shows it to her husband without hesitation, and he reads it with equanimity, suggesting perhaps that she thought of it as a poem of male friendship. In this regard, it is interesting to consider Arntzen's analysis of the passage that appears in a note to the translation:

> Since the prince's poem and note could easily be interpreted as an amorous advance, it is interesting that she does not hide it from her husband. Moreover, although the correspondence that follows is characterized by ambiguity and indirection, it is nonetheless evident that the prince is not upset to think that Kaneie might have seen the poem, nor is Kaneie disturbed to have seen it. In a conversation about this passage, Akiyama Ken remarked that Kaneie was likely flattered to have the prince show an interest in his wife. Her stock goes up, as it were, since she is desired by a member of the royal family. Of course, this good humor might have evaporated had the flirtation exceeded the realm of play.[31]

In contrast to this reading of the Prince's poem as an amorous advance, albeit in the realm of play, an equally plausible possibility is that all parties understood this poem within a context of male friendship. The Prince's poetic confession of feelings for the recipient of the poem is not an amorous advance directed at Lady Kagerō but a confession of his desire for Kaneie's friendship. In the context of the rupture between the men that ended the Muddy Path of Love sequence immediately before this, the Prince's first poem seems conciliatory and designed to reopen the channels of communication between the men.

When Kaneie sees the Prince's letter two days later, he feels that too much time has elapsed to send a replying poem. He decides simply to send a letter inquiring after the Prince with the line, "Recently, we have not had the honor of your communication" (*kono goro wa, ōsegoto n [mo] naki koto).* The Prince sends this poem in reply:

> [2] mizu masari ura mo nagisa no koro nareba chidori no ato o fumi wa madou ka
>
> *It is the season / when ever-rising waters / make the shore disappear: / that must be why the plover / finds no place to leave its track.*[32]

The Prince seems perplexed that Kaneie's letter ignores his conciliatory poem of longing. The Prince employs two puns in his reply that allow him to convey his deeper meaning within a poem that is innocuous on its surface. The first gloss is, *It is the season when the tide is full, and the bay [covers] the strand; did my footsteps therefore go astray, following the traces of a plover's footsteps, I wonder?* The second gloss hinges on puns on *ura mo nagisa* (the bay and strand) and the embedded *ura mo naki* (no ulterior motive) and *fumi* (footstep or letter): *I have been honest with you; did my letter somehow go astray, I wonder?* The poem is followed by a prose comment, "As such appears to be the case, it is unfair of you to resent [my failure to write]" *(to koso mitsure, urami tamau ga warinasa).* The Prince's reply also says that Kaneie promised in his letter to pay the Prince a personal visit, for it concludes, "[You wrote] 'yourself', [but] is it true [that you will be visiting me]?" *(mizukara to aru wa makoto ka).*

The narrator then comments that the Prince's reply was written in *onna-de,* "woman's hand." This is taken to mean that the Prince is writing in *hiragana* (syllabic script) developed from Chinese characters for the purpose of writing the vernacular language phonetically. The question that has vexed interpreters of the passage is, why was this script worthy of comment? The answer to this question hinges on how the following line, *otoko no te nite koso kurushikere,* is interpreted. *Otoko no te* refers to the style in which Kaneie wrote his reply, the "man's hand," which employed Chinese characters in angular, less cursive form than found in the "woman's hand." The phrase can be interpreted as either hypothetical ("how difficult, or inappropriate, it would have been if [Kaneie's reply] had been written in man's hand)" or speculative ("it was surely difficult, or inappropriate, that [Kaneie] wrote in man's hand)." To further complicate interpretation is this question: from whose perspective is the man's hand difficult or inappropriate? Is it from the perspective of the narrator, of Kaneie, or of the Prince? Theories abound, but ultimately there may be no definitive reading of the passage. Arntzen, who translated the entire text and is no doubt intimately familiar with its many vexing passages, notes, "This is one of the most difficult passages to decipher in the diary."[33]

Nevertheless, as is usually the case, attempts to decipher the passage are informed by the reader's prior conception about what is going on in the passage. If we read the exchange in which this passage appears as an enactment of courtly male friendship, then how might we best interpret the enigmatic reference here to "woman's hand" and "man's hand"?

First, it is useful to summarize the various ways the passage has been interpreted, beginning with Edward Seidensticker's translation, as follows:

> The Minister [Noriakira] answered: "'*The water rises and the strand disappears; is the plover lost in the rain?*'—I think my letter must have gone

> astray, and it is hardly fair of you to suggest that I have not written. May I really expect to see you?" It was written in a lady's hand, something of a relief—a man's hand could have been so difficult.
>
> The Prince [Kaneie] sent a return poem: *"To find those lost tracks, we must wait for the waves to recede—but that too will be hard."*[34]

Regarding the line "May I really expect to see you?" Seidensticker notes, "This sentence indicates that Kaneie has promised to call, although there is no such suggestion in Kaneie's letter."[35] Another note explains that "written in a lady's hand" means the Prince's letter was written "in straight *kana,*" presumably using phonetic script and without any Chinese graphs. It follows that the female narrator is the one expressing relief that the poem is written in simple *kana* script, because Chinese would have been too difficult for her to decipher.

By contrast, Arntzen's reading of the passage suggests that Kaneie's reply was written in "man's hand" and therefore stood in opposition to the Prince's use of "woman's hand." Seidensticker takes the word *kurushikere* to be a hypothetical reference to the preceding poem by the Prince from the narrator's perspective as a woman ("If the prince had written his letter in man's hand, that could have been so difficult for me *as a woman*"). Arntzen, on the other hand, takes *kurushikere* to be a speculative reference to the following poem by Kaneie from the Prince's perspective ("Though it must have seemed [to the Prince] graceless to do so, we wrote our reply in man's hand"). Arntzen's translation of the passage follows:

> The prince deigned to send this in response:
>
> [2] mizu masari ura mo nagisa no koro nareba chidori no ato wo fumi ha madofu ka
>
> *The water is high, / no beach welcomes the plover's tracks, / your felicity leaves / no room for my approach, I / wonder, did my letter go astray?*
>
> "This is what I have been thinking. Your complaint of no news is misplaced. Is it true that I shall hear from you yourself?" This was written in "woman's hand." Though it seemed graceless to reply in "man's hand":
>
> [3] ura gakure miru koto kataki ato naraba shihohi wo matamu karaki waza kana
>
> *If hidden on the / beach, those tracks are hard to see, / it seems we must wait / until the tide dries even though / a bitter thing it will be.*[36]

In a note, Arntzen elaborates on her interpretation of the passage in these words:

> The three participants are playing a cat-and-mouse game with each other. The fact that Kaneie and the author ignore the prince's poem about the pinks has puzzled him. He is trying to find out whether Kaneie saw the poem or not. When he says, "Is it true I shall hear from you yourself?" in the context of the communication between the two men alone, he may mean that he expects a personal visit from Kaneie. In the context of the communication involving the three of them, he may be looking for a direct response from the author. After all, his sending the poem about the pinks may simply have been to acquire a poem of hers in her own hand just for the fun of it.
>
> This brings us to the matter of "hands," which further complicates this passage. Why does the author specifically mention that the prince wrote in "woman's hand" and their response was in "man's hand"? "Woman's hand" was the name for the cursive style of writing Japanese that was preferred by women. It was not written exclusively by women, however, since it was a mark of courtliness for a man to be able to write it fluently. "Man's hand" refers to a stiffer writing style in which the graphs are closer to the square forms of Chinese characters.
>
> The prince's choice to write in woman's hand could be construed as a display of his elegance, or as an indication that his correspondence is meant for the author as well as Kaneie. Or, if his previous letter had been written in woman's hand, he may be simply being consistent so as not to arouse suspicion. Whatever the prince's motives in the choice of hands, Kaneie's response in man's hand has the effect of bringing the communication solidly back into the "man's world" again.[37]

Arntzen's discussion of the passage raises several important concepts that, with some modification, prove useful for producing a reading of the passage as an enactment of courtly male friendship. First, she identifies the passage as being embedded in two contexts, "the context of the communication between the two men alone" and "the context of the communication involving the three of them." From the perspective of depicting male friendship, two processes are occurring simultaneously at the intersection of these two contexts. First, the men are communicating directly (man-to-man) about their relationship as friends; second, the female narrator serves as a mediator in the friendship between the Prince and Kaneie and thus plays an important role in the intimacy between them. The question of "hands" serves a purpose similar to that in the sequence in the *Ise* between Prince Koretaka and the hero, in that the Imperial Prince (in this case Noriakira) is associated with the feminine by the authorial comment that he writes in "woman's hand." In opposition to the gender associations of the Prince's feminine mode of writing, Kaneie responds in "man's hand," which, as Arntzen notes, is an assertion of the masculine realm. If we understand this dynamic in terms of the *Ise*'s Princely paradigm of male friendship, then what we see emerging in this sequence of the *Kagerō* is an image of Kaneie as a courtly hero who, by asserting explicit qualities against implicit ones, creates a pseudogendered pairing of male friends, consistent with the heroic figure of Narihira in relation to Prince Koretaka in the *Ise.* Kaneie momentarily becomes the hero of a poem-tale through the depiction of his interactions with Prince Noriakira in this section of the *Kagerō,* and it is no accident that the heroic depiction coincides with a period of heightened intimacy between Kaneie and the narrator.

Kaneie's replying poem in McCullough's translation reads: [3] *If the plover's tracks / be hidden on the shore, / impossible to see, / I must suffer the suspense / of waiting for the ebbtide.*[38] Seidensticker renders the same poem this way: *To find those lost tracks, we must wait for the waves to recede—but that too will be hard.*[39] According to Kawaguchi Hisao, there is a pun in this poem on miru, "seaweed" or "see," so that the opening lines can be glossed as "seaweed hidden on the strand" or "[it is] hard to discern [because it is] hidden on the strand." Furthermore, the poem concludes with the word *karaki* (salty, difficult to bear), which is related in poetic diction to *shio* (tide, salt).[40] The poem establishes a problem and its solution: "If the traces are hard to discern hidden on the strand, [then] let us wait for the tide to ebb, though [waiting is] hard to bear." In short, Kaneie seems to be putting off meeting with the Prince until another time.

Whether we assume that Kaneie's answering poem is written in man's hand or not, how does Prince Noriakira respond to it? This is McCullough's translation:[41]

> [4] ura mo naku fumi yaru ato o watatsuumi no shio no hiru ma mo nani ni ka wa semu
>
> *It would be pointless / to wait for the ebbtide / on the boundless sea, / merely to search for tracks / where there is no shore to be found.*

The Prince's reaction suggests that he has given up the idea of meeting Kaneie, and that he suspects Kaneie is putting him off because he may have misunderstood the Prince's intentions. The poem reads, in Arntzen's translation, "'*In those tracks there was / nothing to keep us apart, / on the open sea, / what need is there to wait for / the tide to dry to see the shore.*' Or so I think; I hope there has been no misunderstanding."[42] Seidensticker renders the same poem this way: "'*Wait for the waves indeed—a frank and generous poem I sent, and this is the way you taunt me!*' There is a misunderstanding here."[43] Kawaguchi identifies puns on *ura* (bay, heart) and *umi* (sea, sadness), which produce this reading: *My letter was sent without guile; it saddens me that it went astray and, moreover, has led to resentment between us. What shall I do in the interval?*[44] Kawaguchi further suggests that the phrase that concludes the sequence, *kotozama ni mo hata,* means that the Prince is afraid that Kaneie believes the initial poem to have been addressed to Kaneie's wife as a love poem, and he wants to assure Kaneie that such suspicions are unfounded.

All told, the poetic sequence Season of Long Rains sketches a vivid picture of Prince Noriakira eager to pursue a friendship with Kaneie, and Kaneie reacting ambiguously to his advances. The sequences dwindle from six poems to five and, finally, to four, as if to reflect the dwindling fortunes of the friendship between the two men. While the poems pose many enigmas to reader and scholar alike, the key to their interpretation lies in our understanding of the ways a nobleman's desire for courtly male friendship was being enacted in this mid-Heian text.

The poetic sequences of Summer-Spun Thread, the Muddy Path of Love, and the Season of Long Rains are followed later in the text by two short vignettes involving the same three actors (Prince, Kaneie, and narrator), and each vignette can be understood to serve as a coda to the preceding poetic exchanges, reintroducing and in some ways resolving the tensions raised in them. The first vignette contains a poetic fragment by the Prince. The poem is apparently incomplete as a result of lost or damaged pages in the original. It is followed by a single poem by Kaneie (written most likely with the assistance of the narrator). The second vignette contains a single poem by the Prince.

The last poetic sequence, called the Season of Long Rains, is followed by a prose section in which the narrator describes a summer excursion with Kaneie to a mountain temple. There she tries to recuperate from a persistent cough, which she attributes to a malign spirit. A sense of renewed intimacy between Kaneie and the narrator emerges most explicitly in the passage when they observe preparations at the temple for celebrating the midsummer Bon Festival: "Looking out I see a procession of servants hurrying to bring offerings, carrying them in the oddest of ways, some on their shoulders, some balanced on their heads, watching this together, we find it so engaging and laugh."[45] The significant phrase again is *moroton ni mite,* "watching together," indicating the physical and emotional proximity between the two. Kawaguchi Hisao calls the scene a "memorable description reminiscent of a tableau in an ancient picture scroll."[46] Autumn and winter pass uneventfully, and in the New Year, Kaneie is removed from the Ministry of War and reinstated to a position that allows him once again to serve the Emperor directly at court. The passage is transitional, carrying the narrative to the next poetic moment in the text. It also links the Prince's last communication to Kaneie to his next. Unfortunately, the Prince's poem is lost and we thus can achieve only an incomplete picture of the author's intentions for the scene. The passage begins, "It was the day of the Kamo Purification Rites in the fourth month, when the prince from before graces us with this letter, 'If you are going to view the event, I would like to ride in your carriage.'"[47]

Seidensticker and Arntzen present two diametrically opposing versions of what follows. Seidensticker takes the scene as a description of a carriage ride shared by the Prince and Kaneie alone, while Arntzen believes that the narrator is present with them in the carriage. If, following Seidensticker, we assume that Kaneie and the Prince are riding together in the carriage, then the scene shows that the sometimes troubled attempt in the earlier three sequences to establish their friendship has ended in success. On the other hand, if we follow Arntzen and assume that the narrator is with the men in their carriage, the scene illustrates in concrete terms the central role she has played all along in enabling the friendship. Both readings are plausible, and neither can be refuted conclusively. At best, only a fragmentary reading of the scene is possible. To picture Kaneie alone with the Prince is more consistent with the *Ise*'s two-poled model of intimate male friendship, and it contributes to Kaneie's qualities as the hero of a poem-tale. On the other hand, injecting the female narrator into the scene resolves issues raised in the second poetic sequence, the Muddy Path of Love, by reconciling here the hero's dual personae of "lover of women" and "friend of men." Readers of the text may choose between imagining the men alone together in the carriage, in a two-poled configuration, or joined by the female narrator, in a three-poled configuration, one reflecting male interiority and the masculine experience of friendship, the other reflecting female observation of men and the female experience of intermediacy in male friendship.

Seidensticker's translation of the carriage scene reads as follows:

> On the day of the purification for the Kamo Festival the Minister [Noriakira] sent a letter suggesting that, if the Prince [Kaneie] was going to the ceremony, perhaps they could ride together. Included was a poem: "*My*

> *years . . .*" He was, it seemed, not at his usual residence, and the Prince [Kaneie] went first to the side street where we supposed him to be, and, as he came out, sent this over to him: *"Spring has been unduly late here to the south of your street, but now at length, we meet it."* The two of them went off together.[48]

Arntzen's version is in many ways more literal, but apart from that literalness it also suggests a very different role for the author-narrator in the scene.

> It was the day of the Kamo Purification Rites in the fourth month, when the prince from before graces us with this letter, "If you are going to view the event, I would like to ride in your carriage." In the margin, he had also written a little poem that began *"This year for me . . .* [missing text]." The prince had not lately been at his villa next door. We thought he was off visiting a place near Machi no Koji, and inquiring about this we were told, "Yes, he is here." Requesting an inkstone, he wrote this:
>
> kimi ga kono machi no minami ni tomi ni osoki haru ni ha ima zo tadzune mawireru
>
> *Just as a late spring / quickly visits you in the / south of this city, / I have come as fast as I could / to attend you and here I am.*
>
> Thus it came about that we went out together.[49]

Regarding the concluding line of the translation, Arntzen remarks in a note, "The original contains the phrase *morotomo ni,* "together," which the author uses very sparingly to indicate times when she felt a particular sense of intimacy with Kaneie. In this case, she is not only together with Kaneie but also with the prince. This experience would have been a very unusual one for her."[50] In any case, the tenor of Kaneie's poem to the Prince is warm and untainted by the resistance and miscommunication that threatened the earlier sequences between the men. In all, the passage suggests that harmonious relations exist between the men, and the narrator implies that her services as go-between have contributed to their friendship.

The final prose coda about Prince Noriakira concludes with a particularly agreeable poem about pampas grass. In many ways, the passage acts as a *waka* story that describes the circumstances of a poem's composition, like those found in the *Ise* or the *Heichū.* The *Kagerō*'s narrator mentions an earlier visit to the Prince's garden that had occurred the previous year, but no such visit is recorded in the diary. This has led Kawaguchi to suspect that pages are missing from the text, but I prefer to interpret the sudden recollection of earlier events not as a sign of factual inconsistency, but as a sign of the author's literary shaping or fictionalizing of personal experience into a poem-tale in the *Kagerō*. She invents a prose setting for the poem—from her memory, or from her imagination—that is "recalled" in the text to serve her artistic needs. Her goal again appears to be to make Kaneie the hero of a poem-tale through the record of her husband's poetic communication with a Prince.

In Arntzen's translation, the Prince's poem reads, *When it flowers, / it beckons people off the road, / my garden's pampas grass; / thus your special wish for it, / and my special digging efforts.*[51] Seidensticker takes the final line *horu ga wari nasa* to indicate the Prince's reluctance to dig up and part with the grasses: *How it pains me to dig up grasses which, when they put out their plumes, will beckon pleasant guests.*[52] Whatever the exact reading, the poem clearly is based on a *Kokinshū* poem by Ariwara no Muneyama, number 243: *are they the flowing / sleeves of the autumn grasses / in the ripening fields / the waving tassels appear / to be beckoning to us now.*[53] McCullough's translation reads: *That miscanthus plumes / should resemble sleeves of girls / beckoning glad-faced— / Is it because they are sleeves / of bushes in autumn fields?*[54] The narrator's response to the Prince's poem is *ito okashū mo,* "how very charming/ clever," followed by a confession that she has forgotten how they replied to the Prince. She also expresses her sense of the unreliability of her memory, and this serves to excuse a leap in the narrative to summer the following year.

The narrator notices at that time a cooling in her husband's feelings, and following a scene that elaborates on her fears for her marriage, she suffers the devastating death of her mother. Thus the sequence on friendship between Prince Noriakira and Kaneie is bracketed before and after by scenes expressing the author's bitterest disappointment with her husband, preceded by an exchange of long poems instigated by her husband's relations with the woman of the Machi Alley, and followed by her mother's death and her increased estrangement from Kaneie. The three poetic sequences involving the friendship of Kaneie and the Prince represent a rare interlude of extended harmony between husband and wife in the *Kagerō*. Discursively, that harmony is a product of the central role played by the narrator in Kaneie's on-again, off-again friendship with Noriakira. The *Kagerō* succeeds in making Kaneie the hero of an embedded poem-tale as a lover of women and a friend of men, much like the hero of the *Ise,* but it does something entirely new when it makes its female narrator essential to her husband's experience of friendship with the Prince. In addition to giving her female narrator a role in her depiction of male friendship, the author of the *Kagerō* also devises a counterpoetic in which the failure of male friendship serves to bring greater intimacy to the hero and his wife.

Depicting Female Friendship

The three extended poetic sequences between Kaneie and the Prince resonate with the masculine perspective on male friendship articulated in the *Ise,* and elsewhere in the *Kagerō* we discover its author extending into new territory the *Heichū*'s depictions of female friendships. As we have seen, when female friends appear in the *Heichū,* they serve predominantly to create a triangular structure that presents the hero with a choice of lovers. The issue of actual friendship between women is embryonic at best, and female subjectivity remains largely undeveloped. The text of the *Kagerō,* on the other hand, contains several poetic sequences that may be construed as enactments of friendship between the narrator and her female friends. Arntzen discusses this issue in the introduction to her translation, *The Kagerō Diary,* and traces the idea of female friendship in a section titled "The Author and the People around Her."

> Other people of importance in the author's circle were female friends. Although she does not name most of them, there is quite a number. She goes on several excursions and pilgrimages with unnamed female friends. When she secludes herself during her retreat, she is visited by a woman who comes to scold her and ends up in tears with her. She carries on a correspondence with many friends. Her long poem for the wife of Minamoto Takaakira and subsequent correspondence with her is some of the most touching writing in the work. However, it is her friendship with Kaneie's sister, Tōshi, or Lady Jōganden as she is referred to most often in the diary, that is one of the highlights in her life. She first had the occasion to get to know Tōshi when they were temporarily sharing one of Kaneie's houses. Friendship with Tōshi was as close as the author ever got to the glamour of the court. Tōshi had been married to an imperial prince who died young. Then she was involved in an affair with the emperor Murakami. Emperor Murakami's principal consort was Tōshi's and Kaneie's elder sister, Anshi. Tōshi was in the habit of visiting her elder sister at court, and it was during one of those visits that the emperor became enamored of her. Anshi turned a blind eye to a couple of meetings but then asserted her authority and ended the affair. . . . When Anshi died, however, Emperor Murakami quickly summoned Tōshi to his side. They did not have long together, because a mere three years later, Murakami died. It is shortly after Mura-

> kami's death that Tōshi comes to share the same house with the author. They form a friendship that lasts throughout the period recorded by the diary.[55]

Arntzen mentions three settings of female friendship in the *Kagerō* that are worth considering in detail in relation to the episodes depicting male friendship: her excursions with female friends, her correspondence with the wife of banished Minister Minamoto no Takaakira, and her extended friendship with her husband's sister, Tōshi. The excursions and pilgrimages with female friends resemble the *Ise*'s and *Heichū*'s episodes that depict the hero's camaraderie with groups of male friends. Similarly, the *Kagerō* contains several scenes of travel between the narrator's residence in the capital and her destination at a temple when she is accompanied by female friends. In most cases, the narrator initiates the pilgrimages as an escape from her husband's neglect. Ostensibly at least, she leaves domestic life behind in order to find spiritual comfort. Thus female companionship comes to the fore in the *Kagerō* in conjunction with a journey occasioned by the breakdown of relations between husband and wife, not unlike the Journey to the East of the hero in the *Ise*. It is possible to discern a heroic aspect to the author's self-depiction that resonates with the figure of the *Ise* hero, surrounded by one or two male friends as he journeys into exile. The same heroic self-depiction can be found in more lighthearted excursions to shrines and such for sightseeing, which create a setting of female camaraderie not unlike the male camaraderie celebrated in certain episodes in the *Ise* and the *Heichū*.

The narrator's record of her correspondence with the wife of Minamoto no Takaakira is especially interesting when considered in light of the *Ise*'s depiction of male friendship. Takaakira was a son of Emperor Daigo and the brother of Prince Noriakira, Kaneie's "friend" in the poetic sequences discussed earlier. He was at the center of one of the major political upheavals at the mid-Heian court known as the Anna Incident—it took place in 969, the second year of the Anna Era. The Anna Incident illustrates the ferocity of Fujiwara domination of the imperial court. Takaakira was in the powerful position of Minister of the Left at the time, but he ended up banished from the capital because he made an ambitious move: he gave his daughter in marriage to Prince Tamehira, who was the reigning Emperor Murakami's favorite son and reputed heir. The marriage represented a serious threat to the Fujiwara method of marriage politics whereby Fujiwara Regents exercised total control of the imperial institution. Although Takaakira was married to a sister of Kaneie's, and Prince Tamehira was Kaneie's nephew (Tamehira's mother, Anshi, was Kaneie's full sister), the familial ties did not make them immune from Fujiwara attack. As Arntzen describes it,

> Takaakira's marrying his daughter to Tamehira brought him into direct competition with the main Fujiwara family, whose goal was always to have the reigning emperor's principal consort be a Fujiwara woman. When Emperor Murakami died in 967, his second son succeeded to the throne as Emperor Reizei, but a year later, Tamehira was passed over for designation as crown prince in favor of the fifth son, who was a mere child of nine years old. As *Eiga monogatari* puts it succinctly, Tamehira "lost the throne when he married Takaakira's daughter."
>
> The chagrin of Takaakira about this was apparent to all. As a way to put his political ambitions completely out of the way, charges that he was plotting to overthrow the current emperor [Reizei] were leveled against him, and he was exiled to Kyushu as provisional governor-general of Dazaifu. To see one of their own in such a high position be brought so low shocked all members of the aristocracy.[56]

After Takaakira's banishment from the capital, his wife immediately renounced court society by taking the tonsure and becoming a nun *(shukke)*. To add to her tragedy, three days later the palace where she and Takaakira had lived was burned to the ground, probably on Kaneie's orders, and she was forced to move to another residence. The complicity of Kaneie, her own half-brother, in bringing the charges of treason against her husband and then burning down their palace would not have escaped the woman.

It was in response to this extraordinary political event that the narrator of the *Kagerō* took up her brush and wrote another long poem *(chōka)*, this time expressing her deepest sympathy to the woman. She attached a short poem *(tanka)* at the end. The translations here are Arntzen's.

> yado mireba yomogi no kado mo sashinagara arubeki mono to omohikemu ya zo
>
> *Seeing your dwelling / with mugwort now blocking the / gate, so desolate, / how could anyone have dreamed / that it would have come to this?*

The narrator hesitates to send the poems, however, because she seems to understand the central role Kaneie has played in orchestrating Takaakira's political demise, and she fears that Takaakira's wife might think her perverse for daring to express her sympathy.[57] Finally, at the urging of others, the narrator agrees to send the poem, but she instructs the messenger to say that it is from the woman's brother in Tōnomine. Takaakira's wife eventually learns the true identity of the sender and makes a reply, but it goes astray. Hearing this, the narrator sends another poem.

> yama biko no kotahe ari to kikinagara ato naki sora wo tadzune wabinuru
> *Although I have heard / there was a response from / the mountain echo, / troubled, I have searched the / traceless skies to no avail.*

After a lengthy interval that strikes the narrator as strange, she at last receives the lady's reply.

> fuku kaze ni tsukete mono omofu ama no taku shiho no keburi ha tadzune idezu ya
> *To the blowing wind, / were attached her melancholy thoughts, / did they not reach you, / smoke from the brine fires kindled / by the sister of the sea?*

To this, the narrator replies respectfully.

> aruru ura ni shiho no keburi ha tachi keredo konata ni kahesu kaze zo nakarishi
> *From the rough wild shore, / the smoke from the brine fires / rose up . . . but / alas there was no wind / to carry it hither.*

The sequence of four poems, beginning with the narrator's "long poem," is designed to comfort a woman whose husband has suffered political defeat, and thus it parallels the way male friends compose poems of comfort in the *Ise* and the *Heichū*. When the narrator of the *Kagerō* is depicted as reaching across the brutal political divisions in the family to comfort her husband's grieving sister, the scene resonates deeply with earlier depictions of male friendship in which the ability to befriend is elevated to the level of a heroic virtue.

The *Kagerō* narrator's ability to befriend was apparent earlier in her correspondence with Tōshi, Kaneie's younger sister. The first exchange of poetry between them is occasioned by the death of Emperor Murakami (r. 946–967). Tōshi became his consort in 964, and the narrator writes to comfort her in her loss.

> yo no naka wo hakanaki mono to misasagi no umoruru yama ni nagekuramu yo zo

This world's frailty, / such have you seen in the scene / of his interment, / by that Misasagi mountain, / how you must have been lamenting.

In her reply to the narrator, the grieving consort seems to be addressing the spirit of the departed Emperor.

okureji to uki misasagi ni omohi iru kokoro ha shide no yama ni ya aruramu
"I shan't be long, my lord" / at heart, this sorrowful self / dwells on Misasagi / and is it not already with you / on the mountain crossing to death?

Kaneie was placed in charge of Crown Prince Reizei's household, and when Reizei became Emperor upon Murakami's death, Kaneie enjoyed rapid promotions in the court hierarchy, first to middle captain and then to third rank. With these promotions came important duties at court that kept Kaneie increasingly busy. He therefore provided Lady Kagerō with a nearby residence so that he could visit her more easily. Shortly after, his sister Tōshi joined her in another part of the same mansion, and this proximity led to a fruitful period of poetic exchanges between the narrator and former Imperial Consort. The first of these exchanges occurs at the New Year in 968 and is called the Fabricated Woodsman. The narrator sends a figure of a woodsman bearing a load of New Year's treats to Tōshi and, with it, a poem that confesses, in a pun, her desire to meet. Kawaguchi Hisao interprets the "desire to meet" in the two poems as the women's desire to meet each other. Around one leg she has tied a knot that looks like a swollen cyst, *koi,* which Arntzen translates as "wen":

kata kohi ya kurushikaruramu yamagatsu no afuko nashi to ha mienu mono kara
Pity the poor woodsman / with a wen on one leg as painful / as one-sided love. / Yet it isn't as though he hasn't / a yoke nor we time to meet.

A pun on the word *kata koi* ("cyst on one leg" or "unrequited longing") expresses the narrator's longing to meet, and the Consort reciprocates with an avowal of the same desire. She returns the same figure carrying a load of dried seaweed and has attached to the other leg an even larger cyst fashioned of wood. The narrator discovers a poem with it.

yamagatsu no afu ko machi idete kurabureba kohi masari keru kata mo arikeri

Finally the time comes / for the poor woodsman to meet / his beloved, when we / compare wens and swollen love, / this side is surely the largest.

Arntzen comments in a note, "Even in this playful exchange, it is evident that the language of poetic discourse for expressing friendship between women is not different at all from the language for romantic love between men and women."[58]

If we compare Seidensticker's rendering, however, we see that the "desire to meet" is taken more generally, as a reference to the women's desire to meet with a male lover, not with each other. This interpretation of course undermines the reading of the passage as an enactment of friendship between the women. Numerous poems and episodes about male friendship in the *Ise,* the *Heichū,* and the *Kokinshū* make use of the words "longing" *(koi)* and "yearning" *(omoi),* even though they are more commonly associated with erotic love. If we follow Kawaguchi's interpretation, as Arntzen does, we discover in the sequence of the Fabricated Woodsman that "longing" is being used to describe the desire of two women for each other's friendship.

Another exchange between the women, the Letter Gone Astray, occurred when a letter from Kaneie intended for his sister Tōshi, the former Consort, was mistakenly delivered to the narrator. The incident led to an exchange of two poems that allowed the women to display their tactfulness to each other and also highlighted their common link with Kaneie. Shortly afterward, the Consort was obligated to leave Kaneie's house and serve at the imperial palace in her new status as parental guardian to the Crown Prince, her nephew Morihira, who would succeed his brother, Emperor Reizei, the following year and ascend to the throne as the Emperor En'yū (r. 969–984). On the eve of her departure, the text records a brief meeting between the two women: "as far as we are informed in the diary, this is the first and last time the ladies meet face to face."[59] Certainly male friends were more mobile and could expect to meet each other more frequently than this in the course of their courtly friendships. That the friendship between the women is mediated almost entirely by poetry makes it a product of discursive contact, not physical. As such, it resembles the long-distance male friendships of Chinese verse in *Poems to Sing* and the poems addressing absent friends in the *Ise* and the *Heichū.* The meeting between the ladies is frustratingly brief, for no sooner does the narrator arrive for her visit with the Consort than they hear Kaneie's voice. The narrator prefers to ignore his summons, but the Consort urges her to go: "It sounds as though it is his bedtime; no doubt he'll get cranky. Better be quick," to which the narrator replies, "You would think he could do without a nanny by this time." As

Arntzen notes, "There is something charming about these two women sharing a joke that characterizes this powerful man as a small, petulant child."[60] The scene again highlights the way in which Kaneie serves as the common link that binds the women together. The three-poled structure of friendship is utilized here to show two women linked by a man: Tōshi (Kaneie's sister, the former Consort) and Lady Kagerō, Kaneie's wife.

The next poetic exchange between the narrator and the consort is called Far Side of the River. The sequence consists of six poems, the number in the *Kagerō* that constitutes a complete and uninterrupted cycle of poems. It occurs at a point in the narrative one year after Emperor Murakami's death, when his former consort, Tōshi, is finally able to set aside her robes of mourning. She is free at this juncture to leave the palace and rejoin the narrator in her house, but a series of ominous dreams prevents her from doing so. Seidensticker characterizes the ensuing passage in these terms, "The exchange of poems is in general a debate over which of the two ladies is the more forlorn," and he translates it accordingly.[61]

> In the Fifth Month came the anniversary of the Emperor's death, and the Lady Jōganden [Tōshi] again left court. She had planned to come here as before, but an unlucky dream forced her to go to the Prince's instead. There the bad dreams continued, and one very bright night in the Seventh Month, as she was searching about for some way to avoid the bad luck they augured, she sent me this poem: *"I know now how hard it is to seek through the sad autumn nights an escape from the future a dream has told of."*
>
> I answered: *"Sad indeed that must be; but just as sad to wait for a meeting that does not come."*
>
> And again from her: *"I am seized, from a dream of a meeting, with a sadness and longing that lingers on."*
>
> And my reply: *"But at least you have dreamed of a meeting; how is it when there is nothing, no word at all?"*
>
> "'No word at all'—what an unlucky thing to say," she came back in her next letter. *"I see in a dream the one I would meet, but cannot cross over to that far bank; and must you add to my ill fortune?"*
>
> And again I answered: *"That river may keep two persons apart, but is it to separate their hearts?"*

Seidensticker's reading of the passage is built on the assumption that the women are communicating poetically about their feelings for their absent men. The former Consort expresses her grief over the death of Emperor Murakami, and the narrator responds by asserting her own sense of bereavement due to Kaneie's neglect. In essence, the narrator suggests that the Consort's ties to the deceased Emperor are intact, whereas her ties to a living man, Kaneie, are broken. In this way, the narrator seeks to comfort the Consort by comparing the Consort's loss to the grief of her own disastrous marriage. Seidensticker's reading of the poetic sequence resonates to some extent with depictions of a hero who brings comfort to his male friend in enactments of courtly male friendship, transferred here to a context of friendship between two women.

Arntzen's rendering of the same poetic sequence does much more to emphasize the element of personal friendship between the women by taking the women themselves as the subject of the poems. Whereas Seidensticker observes a relational structure of two interwoven triangles in the poetic sequence ("Consort, Emperor, narrator" in poems 1, 3, and 5 and "Consort, Kaneie, narrator" in poems 2, 4, and 6), Arntzen perceives the structure as two-poled, because the women are addressing each other one-on-one, very much like the two-poled structure observed in poetic sequences in *Poems to Sing*, the *Ise*, and the *Heichū*. This is Arntzen's rendering of the scene:

> Then, in the fifth month, when her ladyship was excused from court duty on the occasion of the formal removal of mourning clothes on the first anniversary of the former emperor's passing, there was talk that she would come and stay as before; however, she complained, "I have been having bad dreams," so she ended up staying over there. Thereafter, as she kept having these ominous dreams, she apparently said, "If only there were some way to be delivered from this." Then one night in the seventh month, when the moon was very bright, she sent me this:
>
> [1] mishi yume wo shigahe wabinuru aki no yo zo negataki mono to omohi shirinuru
>
> *These long autumn nights / as I struggle to alter / the dream that I see, / now, I have understood / how hard they make it to sleep.*
>
> I replied:
>
> [2] samo koso ha chigafuru yume ha katakarame ahade hodo furu misahe uki kana
>
> *It is as you say, / to transform one's dreams is / difficult indeed, / as painful as I feel it / to live on never meeting you.*
>
> She replied immediately:
>
> [3] afu to mishi yume ni nakanaka kurasarete nagori kohishiku samenu narikeri

In a dream, I saw you / half in, half out of that dream / I am now living / so fond of the memory, / I waken not to consciousness.

And I to her again:

[4] koto tayuru utsutsu ya nani zo nakanaka ni yume ha kayohidji ari to ifu mono wo

This reality where / we are cut off each from each / why must it be so? / The dream road of which you speak / is neither here nor there.

And again from her, "What is this you say, 'cut off each from each,' how very inauspicious to speak thus":

[5] kaha to miti yukanu kokoro wo nagamureba itodo yuyushiku ihi ya ha tsubeki

Seeing the other side, / not able to cross this river / as I brood and feel blocked, / is it meet for us to speak / thus in such an ill-omened way?

My reply:

[6] wataraneba wochikata hito ni nareru mi wo kokoro bakari ha fuchise ya ha waku

Not crossing over, / we become persons apart / on opposite banks, / only in our hearts will the / depths and shallows be clear.

and so we passed the whole night.[62]

Several of the poems deserve further scrutiny from the perspective of reading this sequence as an enactment of friendship between the women. In poem 3, the consort seems to be positing a similar approach to the problem of separation found in the *Ise*'s episode 46, where the hero and his Intimate Friend lament that they must be apart. The hero of the *Ise* denies the reality of their separation when he affirms to his friend, *It does not seem [to me] that we are separated, but, as there is not a moment that [you] are forgotten,—[your] image is [always before my eyes]*. Likewise, the Imperial Consort denies her separation from the narrator by affirming her friend's presence in her dreams: *In a dream, I saw you half in, half out of that dream. I am now living so fond of the memory, I waken not to consciousness.* Kawaguchi Hisao gives this gloss for poem 3: *[In reality we are apart, but] I dreamed that we met, and the dear memory of the dream is still vivid [in my mind].*[63] The statement avowing the former consort's devotion to the narrator is constructed in very similar terms to the avowals of friendship between the two men in episode 46 of the *Ise*. By extension, we observe that the *Kagerō* makes the Imperial Consort the heroine of the exchange on the basis that she is the one who befriends, just as Kaneie befriended Prince Noriakira in the earlier Summer-Spun Thread sequence.

The resemblance to the Summer-Spun Thread sequence between Kaneie and Prince Noriakira is even more striking when we consider the narrator's replying poem 4 in relation to poem 3, and the former Consort's response in poem 5. Recall that in the first poem in the Summer-Spun Thread sequence, Noriakira suggested to Kaneie that their ties could be broken: *Like scattered threads wound onto a single spool, we ended up in the same office, yet it seems that you would like to break those ties.* Kaneie responded in poem 2 with a statement denying that any such thing could occur between them. The poem was designed to reassure Noriakira of Kaneie's devotion: *When you say "break ties," how sad it makes me feel! There is nothing to do but be wound together on the same spool of office.* The possibility of breaking the ties of friendship appears again in poems 5 and 6 in the Summer-Spun Thread sequence when Noriakira accuses Kaneie in poem 5 of neglecting their friendship, beginning with the telltale phrase *kimi to ware,* "you and I": *With so many threads entangling you, as for you and me, in the end, perhaps we had best cut our ties while we still can with no hard feelings.* Kaneie's response voices a model of devoted friendship: *With time's passage vows between men and women may unravel, but could we ever see such an awful thing between us?*

In the Far Side of the River sequence between the narrator and the former Consort Tōshi, the poetic narrative unfolds according to a very similar dynamic. The Consort sends poem 3, assuring the narrator that she is vividly present in her dreams, and the narrator responds with a poem reiterating her grief at their separation: *This reality where we are cut off each from each, why must it be so? The dream road of which you speak is neither here nor there.* Kawaguchi's gloss is *[You say we meet in your dreams, but] in reality our words are cut off from each other; how I hate it.*[64] Here the narrator is playing very much the same role assigned to Prince Noriakira in the Summer-Spun Thread sequence, suggesting that the bond of friendship is breakable. Just as Kaneie did earlier, the former Consort is here obligated to protest such a suggestion: *Seeing the other side, not able to cross this river as I brood and feel blocked, is it meet for us to speak thus in such an ill-omened way?* The heroine of the narrative has avowed that their friendship is unbreakable, and the sequence might well end on that note. Nevertheless, since the former Consort initiated the sequence, the symmetry of the exchange demands a final poem that affirms the bond of friendship between them. Her affirmation has the effect of blurring the distinction between the Consort as the one who befriends and the narrator as the one who is befriended, a distinction that never came into question in the earlier poetic sequences between Kaneie and Prince Noriakira. If both women are cast in the heroic role of befriending, that fact has profound implications for the narrator. One of the consequences if the narrator switches roles in the final poem from being the one who is befriended to being the one who befriends is that the narrator becomes a heroine of the sequence. This is consistent with the narrator's heroic self-depiction in the accounts of excursions with female companions to temples and shrines for sightseeing that can be found throughout the narrative. In Seidensticker's three-poled interpretation of Far Side of the River, the absent men (Emperor Murakami, Kaneie) haunt the poetic sequence unseen, whereas Kawaguchi and Arntzen's two-poled interpretation of the sequence has no room for such male ghosts.

Chapter 4

The Tale of Genji

"Two Cranes Flying Wing to Wing"

If there is one great friendship in the *Genji monogatari* (Tale of Genji), it is that between Genji, the hero of the tale, and Tō no Chūjō. The exposition of their friendship has a psychological complexity that far surpasses anything seen before in the literature. This complexity is possible in part because the narrative stretches across the lifetimes of the characters, thus allowing the scope of friendship to be expanded exponentially in comparison with its treatment in the brief and tightly focused genres of poetry, poem-tale, and memoir addressed thus far in this study. Many scholars of the *Genji* have noted that, in Norma Field's words, "[Genji], far from being the controlling center of the work, is as much constituted by his heroines as they are by him."[1] A similar argument should be made for the centrality of Tō no Chūjō to our understanding of who Genji is, for it is Tō no Chūjō's presence in the narrative that allows us to observe Genji's other dimension as a friend of men.

The first description of the relationship between Genji and Tō no Chūjō appears at the beginning of "Hahakigi," or the "Broom Tree" (chapter 2). Genji is about age seventeen at the time, and Tō no Chūjō a year or two older.[2] Interestingly, the noun "friend" *(tomo)* appears nowhere in the description. Instead, their youthful friendship is described with verbs and adverbs that emphasize their intimacy: they are emotionally close, behave with openhearted familiarity, study together and spend all of their free time together, are well matched in their abilities, speak informally when together, and reveal their innermost feelings to each other. This depiction of perfect openness and compatibility early in the "Broom Tree" is contradicted almost immediately in the next scene, which opens on a rainy evening at the imperial palace. Tō no Chūjō has joined Genji in his quarters, where they are quietly reading books by the light of an oil lamp. Tō no Chūjō discovers several love letters that Genji has carelessly placed in full view on a shelf and is curious to read them. Genji turns his friend's curiosity into a game in which Tō no Chūjō tries to guess the sender of each letter. The text informs us that these are the least significant of Genji's love letters; the important ones Genji has put safely away. The revelation suggests that Tō no Chūjō's discovery of the letters had not been the result of Genji's carelessness but was deliberately orchestrated by him to probe and explore his friend's love life. Genji then issues a challenge to Tō no Chūjō: if you show me your love letters, I'll show you mine. The scene is highly seductive, each man drawing the other into his world of desire. The scene also reveals a certain degree of calculation in the openness Genji allows himself with Tō no Chūjō. Such calculation on Genji's part makes for good storytelling because it suggests psychological complexity and the potential for a rift in the friendship. Norma Field has noted that "secrecy, as it is used in the *Tale of Genji,* is a medium for the development of inner awareness, of a private self that can become the matter of fiction."[3] This is especially true of secrecy in Genji's friendship with Tō no Chūjō. When Genji withholds information from his friend about his love affairs, it creates a productive tension between them that leads, inexorably, toward a deepening of the reader's sense of who Genji is and what Tō no Chūjō means to him.

Genji's challenge to Tō no Chūjō to show him his love letters in the "Broom Tree" sets the stage for the celebrated scene of the "rainy night critique of ranks" (*amayo no shina sadame,* described memorably by Field as "an elegant locker-room discussion on the varieties of women available to young aristocrats"),[4] during which two lower-ranking courtiers—a Captain of the Left Cavalry *(sa uma no kami)* and a Secretary of the Ministry of Rites *(tō shikibu no jō)*—regale Genji and Tō no Chūjō with stories of their erotic adventures. With the rainy-night scene, the friends embark on a sexual rivalry that dominates the next several chapters of the tale, covering the entire span of their youth.

The intimate friendship between Genji and Tō no Chūjō described in the "Broom Tree" is gradually transformed by their sexual rivalry in subsequent chapters, but it reemerges later in the tale, beginning in "Sakaki" (chapter 10) and culminating at the end of "Suma" (chapter 12), when Genji is living in self-imposed exile from the capital. By that time, several years have passed since the events of the "Broom Tree," and Genji is now in his mid-twenties. The reappearance of their intimate friendship in these chapters is closely tied to the political disgrace that Genji suffers. Based on our knowledge of the way courtly male friendship worked in the *Ise* and the *Heichū,* where it offered hope of transcendence to a nobleman suffering political or personal disappointment, it makes perfect sense that Genji's erotic adventures should recede into the background and his friendship with Tō no Chūjō should come to the fore when political setback is highlighted in the narrative.

The course of events that leads to Genji's exile in the coastal village of Suma begins in "Sakaki" with the death of the Emperor, Genji's father, when Genji is twenty-three years old. The court has now come under the complete domination of the Minister of the Right, whose grandson—Genji's half brother—has been placed on the throne as Emperor Suzaku. Previously, the protective influence of Genji's father, whose abdication is announced in "Aoi" (chapter 9), had countered the malevolent power of the Minister of the Right, described as "an impulsive, vindictive sort of man,"[5] but now that the former Emperor is dead, nothing prevents the Minister of the Right from exercising his whims, and he proceeds to make life exceedingly unpleasant for Genji and his faction at court. The Minister of the Left—who is the father of Tō no Chūjō and Genji's principal wife, Aoi—resigns from his court position to protest the Minister of the Right's egregious behavior, which included a refusal to extend the expected New Year's promotions to Genji and Tō no Chūjō. The resignation saddens Emperor Suzaku and alarms the more reasonable members of the court, who had relied on his steadying influence to counter the negative influence of the Minister of the Right on the realm.

Genji's political eclipse in the face of the Minister of the Right's animosity means that he and Tō no Chūjō will spend long hours in each other's company at the Sanjō mansion of the Minister of the Left. Tō no Chūjō's proximity to Genji has a predictably reinvigorating effect on their friendship. From the "Broom Tree" to this point in the narrative, erotic adventure and its concomitant sexual rivalry between the two friends had been the driving force behind movements in the plot, but from "Sakaki" onward, a perceptible shift occurs that takes Genji and Tō no Chūjō back to that earlier time in their youthful friendship described at the outset of the tale. The shift allows male friendship to displace erotic adventure and become the driving force behind plot movements, at least for a time.

In an attempt to lift their spirits, Genji and Tō no Chūjō organize a Chinese poetry rhyme contest on a rainy summer evening reminiscent of their companionship on that other rainy night years before. Genji's side performs admirably and wins the contest. Two days later, Tō no Chūjō organizes a banquet to celebrate the victory. The revelry includes singing and performances on musical instruments. The performance of one of Tō no Chūjō's young sons so pleases Genji that he removes one of his robes and presents it to the boy. All at the banquet are moved to tears by Genji's special sign of favor, and the text comments on Genji's extraordinary physical beauty that seems to draw everyone to him. The celebratory banquet scene provides a period of heightened intimacy in the friendship between Genji and Tō no Chūjō, as if preparing them for the terrible crisis they are about to confront. The Minister of the Right and his daughter Kokiden, mother of Emperor Suzaku, oppose Genji's interests at court and have long sought for a pretext to banish him. They are finally able to force him into a self-imposed exile after the Minister discovers Genji's scandalous affair with Oborozukiyo, the Minister's daughter and Kokiden's sister. Genji's departure for exile in Suma is filled with deeply felt scenes as Genji prepares to bid farewell to the many women he has loved.

More important, for our purposes, is that Genji's exile establishes the requisite framework of political setback that allows an enactment of friendship between Genji and Tō no Chūjō that is certainly the most beautifully rendered scene of courtly male friendship in the tale, and perhaps in all of Heian literature. The friendship scene in the "Suma" chapter follows closely a familiar pattern of courtly male friendship observed in the *Ise,* the *Heichū,* and the *Kagerō;* namely, the hero brings comfort to an Intimate Friend or to an Imperial Prince who has suffered political defeat, and through his friendship provides the hope of transcending the loss. The scene exhibits several of the features of male friendship observed in the other texts: the encounter between the friends is located outside of the capital; it takes place in a masculine environment defined overwhelmingly in terms of poetic imagery from Chinese verse; and women are entirely absent from the scene.

The "Suma" friendship scene begins with the exiled Genji recalling an earlier banquet held in the capital when the cherry blossoms were in bloom; he feels intensely isolated and forlorn when he realizes that he will not be part of the festivities this year. The narrative then shifts to the capital. We learn that Tō no Chūjō has somehow avoided Genji's fate and been promoted to Middle Captain of the Third Rank and given the title of Imperial Consultant *(saishō).* The narrator tells us that he is a man of noble character and is much admired at court, but that he takes little pleasure in carrying out his courtly duties without Genji and finds himself longing for him constantly *(koishū oboetamaeba).*[6] Unable to bear his intense longing, he decides to pay Genji a visit in Suma. It is a risky move, for he knows that the faction in power will punish him if they discover what he has done. The journey to Suma by horse is swift, and the moment Tō no Chūjō sees Genji, he weeps tears of joy mingled with sorrow.

The narrative goes into considerable detail describing Tō no Chūjō's response to Genji's new circumstances in Suma. Tō no Chūjō first notes the setting, which is utterly—and very stylishly—Chinese *(iwamu kata naku kara mekitari),*[7] like a Chinese hanging scroll. Tang dynasty paintings of mountain hermitages of Chinese sages would have been familiar to noblemen of the time, and the reference would have immediately conjured a vivid image in the mind of the Heian reader. At the level of diction, the text's description of the scene draws on the language of a Chinese verse by Bo Juyi; Tō no Chūjō is fascinated with the "bamboo-plaited walls [or fence], stone steps, and pine pillars" of Genji's house, if only because their rustic quality is such a contrast to the elegantly appointed chambers to which he and Genji were accustomed back in the capital. The author has created the phrase in Yamato language, "bamboo-plaited walls, stone steps, and pine pillars," out of a Chinese verse from the *Collected Works of Bo Ju-yi.*

> *[There are] five shelves, three rooms in [my] pavilion of new grass;*
> *[It has] stone steps, cinnamon-wood pillars, bamboo-plaited walls.*
> *At the south eaves [I] take in the sun, warm [under] the winter sky;*
> *At the north door [I] welcome the breeze, cool [under] the summer moon.*[8]

Since the Chinese verse would have been read in Japanese using the mode of interpretive reading *(yomi kudashi),* whereby the Chinese graphs are pronounced as Japanese words and their order modified to comply with the rules of Japanese syntax, the process of incorporating the Chinese verse into the Yamato-language narrative of the *Genji* is accomplished with relative ease. Its effect is to give a masculine, Chinese quality to the scene that the author exploits masterfully in establishing a setting for the ensuing enactment of friendship between the men.

Next, the narrative describes Tō no Chūjō's response to Genji's attire. Heian readers were attuned to the nuances of court dress, and the *Genji*'s author provides detailed descriptions of attire in order to develop characterization. In this case, Tō no Chūjō observes that Genji is dressed in what he characterizes as the style of a rustic mountaineer—a hunting cloak and trousers in shades of blue-gray and yellow-rose. The narrator suggests through Tō no Chūjō's perceptions that Genji looks pale and appears to have lost weight, but it only enhances his beauty. In short, Tō no Chūjō is dazzled by Genji's masculine good looks and cannot help but smile with pleasure. Throughout the narrative of the *Genji* there are numerous descriptions of men and women responding to Genji's physical beauty in this way, but here we have a description of Tō no Chūjō doing so for the first time.

Genji's rooms are then described in the text as Tō no Chūjō surveys them. The narrator observes that they are furnished modestly and are open to full view in a countrified manner that is unpretentious and appealing. Religious instruments used in intoning the sutras suggest to Tō no Chūjō that his friend has been diligent in his prayers. The survey is interrupted by the arrival of a group of fishermen, who have brought shellfish for Tō no Chūjō's meal. Tō no Chūjō next watches as his horses are groomed and fed, apparently an intriguing and unusual spectacle for him. The sight inspires him to break into recitation of a poem or song he knows about grazing horses, "Asukai." Alternately weeping and laughing, the two friends talk about the months that have passed since they last saw each other. Genji is overcome with emotion when Tō no Chūjō reports that the retired Minister of the Left is deeply concerned for the future of Genji's son, Yūgiri. The narrator then injects an aside to the reader: it is impossible to record the sense of their conversation, in full or in part, and so she will simply leave off. The comment suggests that there are emotional depths to the reunion between Genji and Tō no Chūjō that are best left to the reader's imagination.

As the scene continues to unfold, we next learn that the men spend the night composing letters *(fumi),* a reference to Chinese verse. As dawn approaches, Tō no Chūjō's thoughts turn to the unpleasantness that awaits him in the capital if his visit to Genji should become known. He reluctantly decides that he must set out immediately. The parting is exceedingly difficult for both men. Together they raise cups of wine and sing the words to a Chinese verse by Bo Ju-yi about the poet's farewell to his old friend Yuan Zhen. The text records one line of the Chinese verse in the *yomi kudashi* style: *Tears of drunken sorrow fill the wine cup of spring.* The original poem contains a "you and I" sequence, typical of Bo Ju-yi's poems of friendship.

> *You return to the land of Qin, taking leave of the hot frontier;*
> *I set out for Zhong Zhou, entering dampness and mist.*[9]

Genji's and Tō no Chūjō's attendants are deeply affected by the scene, weeping as they listen to the men's voices raised in unison. Each seems to have deep feelings of regret that the brief visit must end. At this point in the narrative, Genji observes geese flying in a line across the morning sky and composes a verse expressing his feelings:

> furusato o izure no haru ka yukite min urayamashiki wa kaeru karigane
> *O when will I go, in what spring, to look upon the place I was born? What envy consumes me now, watching the geese fly home!* [10]

Royall Tyler, who produced the above English translation of the poem, notes, "The motif of the departing geese (the departing friend) is from a poem in Chinese by Sugawara no Michizane."[11] In response to this expression of Genji's emotion, Tō no Chūjō struggles for words to fittingly bid his friend farewell. He continues the metaphor of a wild goose flying home:

akanaku ni kari no tokoyo o tachi wakare hana no miyako ni michi ya madowamu
With lasting regret the wild goose knows he must leave his eternal home, although he may lose the way to the City of Blossoms.[12]

Tyler notes here, "The wild goose is Tō no Chūjō, who likens Genji to the 'eternal home' of the geese."[13] The "eternal home" *(tokoyo)* in Tō no Chūjō's poem is an extraordinary image, suggesting that the men share a timeless and transcendent bond of friendship. The idea that a friend can find his eternal home only within the heart of another friend has nowhere been so movingly expressed as it is in this poetic exchange between Genji and Tō no Chūjō. When Genji expresses envy that Tō no Chūjō is able to return to the capital, though it means leaving him behind, Tō no Chūjō fittingly comforts him with an assertion of his true friendship. In the hands of the author of the *Genji,* this image of friendship's "eternal home" achieves a depth and heartfelt intensity rarely equaled in the literature.

From the sublimely lyrical, the narrative shifts next to practical matters. Tō no Chūjō has presented Genji with gifts from the capital, and Genji owes him gifts of similar value and quality in return. Genji decides to give Tō no Chūjō a splendid black horse, a gift that resonates on several literary levels with bidding farewell. For one, a black horse has a Chinese precedent as a parting gift, found in the *Han shu;* also, as Tyler notes, "a parting gift was called *uma no hanamuke,* a gift to 'turn the horse's nose toward home.'"[14] Here, Genji's gift is literally a horse taking Tō no Chūjō home to the capital. Furthermore, Genji tells Tō no Chūjō that the horse "neighs whenever the wind blows," a phrase borrowed from a poem in the Chinese anthology *Wen xuan.*[15] The weight of Chinese literary allusion charges Genji's choice of gift with masculinity and is consistent with the other Chinese elements pervading the "Suma" friendship scene.

In return for the impressive horse, Tō no Chūjō gives Genji a flute renowned for its sound. It is meant as a surrogate for Tō no Chūjō himself, "to take my place" *(katami ni shinobitamae),* he says.[16] The idea of leaving an object as a replacement of oneself is an innovative one in the depictions of courtly male friendship. In no other text addressed in this study can we find a friend who leaves an object of remembrance of this sort. The friendship scene reaches its climactic moment shortly thereafter as the sun rises, not unlike the parting of lovers at dawn after a night of lovemaking. Certainly, the timing of Tō no Chūjō's departure imbued it with a certain emotional freight that Heian readers of the text could appreciate from their own experience. Genji, filled with emotion, watches Tō no Chūjō rush off for the capital. For the moment, at least, Genji is placed metaphorically in a feminine position, reminiscent of the dynamic of the Prince Koretaka episodes in the *Ise* where the interplay of masculine and feminine allowed for a pseudogendered intimacy between the hero and his defeated Prince. Court women reading the text might have found their hearts captivated anew by this suffering hero whose position was now essentially the same as their own.

Just before the two men part, Tō no Chūjō asks Genji when they will meet again. Surely, Genji's banishment cannot last forever, he muses. To this, Genji gives a discouraging response: Judging from past history, there are very few examples of exiles who ever recover their former glory, even among the Chinese sages of the past. Genji is forced to admit that he may never set foot in the capital again. He addresses a final poem to Tō no Chūjō, this time likening his friend to a crane:

> kumo chikaku tobi kau tazu mo sora ni miyo ware wa haruhi no kumorinaki mi zo
> *You who soar aloft so very close to the clouds, O high-flying crane, look down on me from the sky, blameless as the sun in spring.*[17]

The clouds *(kumo)* refer to the court where Tō no Chūjō serves the Suzaku Emperor as his Imperial Consultant. In the poem, Genji asks only that his friend look upon him and know that he is innocent of any crime against his brother, the Emperor. Tō no Chūjō responds to this with an exquisite poem of friendship that picks up Genji's metaphor comparing his friend to a crane:

> tazu ga naki kumoi ni hitorine o zo naku tsubasa narabeshi tomo wo koitsutsu
> *Forlorn in the clouds, I lift in my solitude cries of loneliness, longing for that old, old friend I once flew with wing to wing.*[18]

The loneliness of the crane is made palpable by the poem's use of a highly sensual word, *hitorine,* "sleeping alone," which in normal poetic diction suggests a lover lying in bed at night and longing for his or her mate. In this context, *hitorine* is appropriated to convey the desolation of male friends separated from each other. The sensuality inherent in the phrase is further strengthened by the word *koitsutsu* ("longing [for someone's physical presence]") and by the poignant image of two friends (cranes) lying (or flying) side by side. The poem is one of the most sensual evocations of male friendship in all of Heian literature.

The "Suma" friendship scene concludes with some final words by Tō no Chūjō. He tells Genji that he feels honored to have been his friend and that he has but one regret: had he and Genji not let themselves become so intimate, they might have been spared the pain of today's separation. This is a common conceit in Heian court poetry, similar to the sentiment conveyed by Narihira's poem in episode 82 of the *Ise:*

> yo no naka ni taete sakura no nakariseba haru no kokoro wa nodokekaramashi
> *If there would be / no cherry-blossoms at all / in the world, [one's] heart in spring / would be peaceful.*[19]

The poem written in reply in episode 82 might have been a fitting expression of Genji's feelings in parting from Tō no Chūjō that day; he might have comforted Tō no Chūjō by telling him that their friendship had allowed him to discern the truth of human frailty in the face of the passage of time.

> chireba koso itodo sakura wa medetakere ukiyo ni nani ka hisashikarubeki
> *Just because they are scattered, / they are all the more dear [to us]— / the cherry-blossoms, / [for] in this fleeting world / what will exist a long time?*[20]

Instead, Tō no Chūjō departs from Genji in anguish, and Genji stares sorrowfully in the direction of the capital for the rest of the day. The "Suma" chapter ends a page later with an ominous dream. In it, Genji's father, the deceased former Emperor, comes to him urging him to leave this place. The dream provides a pretext for Genji's move from Suma to Akashi, where he encounters the Akashi Lady, a woman who will change his life by bearing him a daughter.

There are several notable aspects to the depiction of Tō no Chūjō's visit to Genji in Suma that illuminate how the *Genji*'s author has created for her readers a moving account of Genji as a friend of men. Perhaps foremost is the highly Chinese aura of the encounter between the two friends. The passage depicts Genji and Tō no Chūjō intoning two Chinese verses, and their poems in Japanese likewise allude to images from Chinese verse. The effect is to make Genji's place of banishment in Suma a Sinified, masculine world that excludes women and the realm of erotic adventure in order to create the necessary setting for an encounter between male friends. Another important aspect of the scene is that Tō no Chūjō is its hero, bringing comfort to Genji, the exiled Prince, while Genji seems to embody both *Ise* paradigms as an Intimate Friend and an Imperial Prince. Tō no Chūjō's heroic stature serves, as in the *Ise,* to accomplish another important purpose of the narrative: to establish Genji's exalted status. A final noteworthy aspect of the scene is its reliance on the two-poled model of male friendship. Except for the passages when fishermen visit bringing shellfish for their meal and their attendants weep as the two intone a Chinese poem together, the entire scene unfolds between Genji and Tō no Chūjō without mediation of any kind. The scene creates a literary experience of friendship that shows the sophisticated sensibility of the author and her absolute mastery of the *wakan* apparatus in depicting male friendship.

Sexual Rivalry in Male Friendship

The "Suma" friendship scene resonates nicely with the paradigms of the Intimate Friend and the Imperial Prince observed in the *Ise,* but elsewhere the author of the *Genji* dispenses with the neat division between erotic adventure and friendship that was carefully maintained in the text of the *Ise* and opts instead to show how rivalry in love creates intimacy between male friends, observed in embryonic form in several of the episodes from the *Heichū.* The depiction of Genji and Tō no Chūjō's sexual rivalry raises a question that has long concerned scholars of the *Genji,* namely, what is the proper arrangement of the tale's early chapters?[21] Especially up to "Makibashira" (chapter 31), the *Genji* has often produced in readers a sense that they are reading two different but interrelated narratives. Some chapters appear to contribute to the development of a main story, while other chapters digress and develop a parallel story that only in retrospect makes sense in relation to the primary narrative.[22] In general, the primary narrative concerns itself with Genji's royal birth and his relationship to power and personages close to the imperial court, while the secondary narrative focuses on Genji's erotic adventures and his sexual competition with Tō no Chūjō.

Some years ago, Abe Akio analyzed the problem of the *Genji*'s dual narratives in terms that have proven to be influential.[23] In essence, he used internal evidence to separate the *Genji*'s early chapters into primary and secondary narratives. He argued that the primary narrative begins with Genji's birth in "Kiritsubo" (chapter 1) and continues with Genji's discovery of Murasaki in "Wakamurasaki" (chapter 5); the birth of a son to the Imperial Consort Fujitsubo in "Momiji no Ga" (chapter 7); Genji's banishment in "Suma" and "Akashi" (chapters 12 and 13); and finally his triumphal return to the capital in "Miotsukushi" (chapter 14). The primary narrative then concludes with Genji's consolidation of power at court in chapters 17–21. According to Abe's analysis, the secondary narrative begins in the "Broom Tree," or "Hahakigi" (chapter 2) and continues in "Utsusemi" (chapter 3), "Yūgao" (chapter 4), and "Suetsumuhana" (chapter 6) and in portions of "Momiji no Ga" (chapter 7). It is partially resolved in "Yomogiu" (chapter 15) and "Sekiya" (chapter 16) and reemerges in chapters 22–31 with Genji's consolidation of political power, symbolized by his gathering of his various women into the Rokujō estate. These parallel narratives Abe divided into two groups of chapters and designated them the Kiritsubo narrative and the Broom Tree narrative.

Haruo Shirane has noted two important characteristics of the Broom Tree narrative.[24] First, he says that Genji is less idealized in it as a result of the amorous setbacks he sustains at the hands of four women—known as Utsusemi, Yūgao, Suetsumuhana, and Gen no Naishi—who make their appearance in this section of the tale. Second, Shirane notes that Tō no Chūjō plays a far more prominent dramatic role in the Broom Tree narrative. Genji's and Tō no Chūjō's youthful sexual rivalry provides the cohesive dynamic whereby the *Genji*'s author advances this portion of the tale. Her development of courtly male friendship in terms of male sexual competition allows her to incorporate into her narrative a far-reaching critique of some of the troubling aspects of Genji's pursuit of his father's Consort Fujitsubo and his rivalry with his brother Suzaku in the Kiritsubo narrative, and it also allows her to explore alternative aspects of desire to those that dominate the Kiritsubo narrative.

Because Tō no Chūjō is the eldest son and heir of the Minister of the Left, and his mother is Princess Ōmiya, Tō no Chūjō is one of the few noblemen who is Genji's equal in the tale. His standing in relation to Genji makes him the perfect narrative device, as companion and rival, to aid in the development of Genji as a fictional construct. Tō no Chūjō first enters the tale in "Kiritsubo" with the story of his marriage to a daughter of the Minister of the Right, immediately following the account of Genji's marriage to Tō no Chūjō's sister, Aoi. With the announcement of Genji's death in "Niou Miya" (chapter 42), Tō no Chūjō also passes from the tale. His passing is indicated by a single reference to "the late minister" *(ko chiji no oidono)*.[25] Their fates as characters in the tale are inextricably linked, but Tō no Chūjō's fictional existence does not serve merely to complement Genji's. Rather, Genji's primacy in the tale is itself a product of the juxtaposition with Tō no Chūjō.

Tō no Chūjō and Aoi are the only children of the Minister of the Left and Princess Ōmiya—although the minister has numerous other children by secondary wives—and they are the favorites of Genji's father, their uncle the Emperor. When Genji marries his cousin Aoi immediately after coming of age, his entry into the household of Minister of the Left is designed to shield Genji from the machinations of the Minister of the Right and Kokiden by providing Genji with powerful male backing. The Minister of the Right immediately counters the marriage by marrying his favorite daughter, the Fourth Princess, to Tō no Chūjō, thus effectively neutralizing Genji's advantage. The tenuous and unstable equilibrium in the political rivalry of the two ministers achieved at the end of "Kiritsubo" is an ongoing concern of the larger Kiritsubo narrative.

In a sense, Tō no Chūjō possesses from the start what Genji was born without: powerful male backing from his maternal side. The friendship between Tō no Chūjō and Genji is a product of this context, and Genji's connection with Tō no Chūjō arises in part from a desire to compensate for the weakness of his political position. The friendship is made complicated, however, when Tō no Chūjō marries Kokiden's sister. Kokiden was the principal Consort of Genji's father and also archenemy of Genji's late mother, and she would later prove to be the most troublesome rival of Fujitsubo, the Consort who replaced Genji's mother in the Emperor's affections and became Genji's first love. Once Tō no Chūjō marries into the household of the Minister of the Right, which is to say from the very first chapter of the tale, the friendship between Genji and Tō no Chūjō exists in a state of political tension.

When Genji challenges Tō no Chūjō to show him his love letters in the "Broom Tree," it sets the stage for the rainy-night critique of ranks. As we have seen, Genji and Tō no Chūjō are joined by two others on guard duty at the palace that early-summer evening. The Captain of the Left Cavalry and the Secretary of the Ministry of Rites are lower in rank but their elders in years, and they regale Genji and Tō no Chūjō with stories of their erotic adventures and discuss the qualities of a highborn woman that might make her a suitable marriage partner. Throughout the scene, Genji functions primarily as a listener rather than a contributor to the discussion, in keeping with his description at the beginning of the chapter as a sober and studious young man. By contrast, Tō no Chūjō is described as being a sexually adventurous young man *(sukigamashiki adabito nari)*.[26] Tō no Chūjō's role in the scene is to question the Captain and the Secretary about their erotic adventures and thereby draw out their sometimes implausible stories.

Scholars have frequently noted that the rainy-night critique of ranks foreshadows and frames many of the emotional and sexual encounters that follow in Genji's life. Genji learns two things that night. He realizes for the first time the erotic appeal of noblewomen of the lower ranks, a group he had previously thought unworthy of his attention. He also arrives at the conviction that one peerless woman—understood to be Fujitsubo, his father's Consort—possesses none of the faults his companions have discovered in other women. This dual lesson establishes a motive for the unfolding of Genji's romantic attachments in the chapters that follow. The lesson of Fujitsubo's perfection is developed in the Kiritsubo narrative beginning in "Wakamurasaki" (chapter 5), which focuses on Murasaki, the girl who replaces the now inaccessible Fujitsubo in Genji's affections. The other lesson, about the erotic appeal of lower-ranking women or women who have fallen in rank, is developed in the Broom Tree narrative through the stories of four women: Utsusemi in the "Broom Tree" and "Utsusemi" (chapters 2 and 3); Yūgao in chapter 4; Suetsumuhana in chapter 6; and Gen no Naishi in "Momiji no Ga" (chapter 7).

Genji's relationships with the four women of the Broom Tree narrative are developed primarily through his sexual competition with Tō no Chūjō. Repeatedly in the Broom Tree narrative, Genji desires women who have—or who once had—an erotic connection to Tō no Chūjō. If we think of the Broom Tree narrative as a narrative of male friendship, the Broom Tree women serve as mediators in that friendship, not in a way that subordinates them but rather in a way that makes them central figures in the tale. In addition to their intrinsic erotic appeal for Genji, he pursues these women because of the ways they bind him to Tō no Chūjō and allow him to compete with his friend. Genji shares two of the Broom Tree heroines, Yūgao and Gen no Naishi, as lovers with Tō no Chūjō, and both men court Suetsumuhana, whom Genji wins in a bittersweet victory. In each of these cases, Tō no Chūjō's presence as a rival is what stimulates Genji's desire for the women, and in each case their friendship is contested in a new way. Only in the story of Utsusemi, first of the Broom Tree women, is Genji's rivalry with Tō no Chūjō irrelevant. Instead, the woman's younger brother, Kogimi, serves an intermediary role that prefigures Tō no Chūjō's role as Genji's rival for the other women.

Anegimi / Utsusemi

Near the end of the "Broom Tree" and immediately after the rainy-night critique of ranks, Genji pays a visit to his wife, Aoi, at her father's Sanjō mansion. She and the entire household await him in a state of expectant readiness, but the narrator tells her readers that Genji feels uncomfortable in the woman's presence because of her demanding nature. A directional taboo spares Genji from having to spend the night with Aoi and provides him with the opportunity for an erotic adventure with a woman of the middle ranks. She will be his first actual experience of a type of woman that he learned about abstractly during the recent rainy-night critique of ranks. Genji achieves an initial sexual encounter with her, but he subsequently meets with two major deflections. In the first case, she rebuffs Genji so vehemently that, in his anger and frustration, he ends up sharing his bed with her younger brother, Kogimi, at the end of chapter 2. The woman is referred to as Anegimi (elder sister) in the text, in relation to Kogimi, her brother. In relation to Genji, however, she soon develops an alternate persona as Utsusemi ("locust shell") because of the way she sheds her robe like a locust shedding its shell, in order to flee Genji's unwelcome visit in the next chapter.

This second deflection occurs early in "Utsusemi" (chapter 3), after Genji has spied on Anegimi and her stepdaughter through a door that was left slightly ajar. It is a classic scene of *kaimami* ("peeping through a gap in a fence"), which constitutes a voyeuristic prelude to lovemaking in Heian narratives. Just as Genji was forced to substitute Kogimi for the boy's elder sister in the preceding chapter, here he must substitute the stepdaughter for the wily Anegimi, who manages to elude him. The initial encounter with Genji has aroused powerful and conflicting feelings of attraction and revulsion in Anegimi. She is married to the Provincial Governor of Iyo, a much older man and not the best match for her. Had she succeeded in securing service at court in her youth, she might have freely pursued a love affair with the youthful Genji, but she understands that acquiescing to Genji's desires for her now would only bring disaster and heartache. She distrusts the extravagant hopes Genji raises in her through his passionate avowals of love and tells herself that it is too late for her to develop a lasting relationship with a man of Genji's status. In her resistance to Genji, it is her realistic sense of self that is the source of her strength, which Genji likens to the strength of stalks of bamboo—pliant but nearly impossible to break. Genji is deeply angered and frustrated at first, as observed in the scene where he brings her brother, Kogimi, to his bed as her substitute, but with time he develops a respect for her resistance to him and an appreciation of the emotional toll his attentions have exacted from her. Many years later, after the death of her husband, Genji is finally able to bring Anegimi/Utsusemi, now a nun, into his circle of women.

Tokonatsu/Yūgao

During the rainy-night critique of ranks, Tō no Chūjō tells the story of a former lover whom he refers to in a poem as Tokonatsu ("wild carnation"). He describes her as a naive young woman of perhaps sixteen who quietly accepted his infrequent visits without any show of resentment. Then one day she disappeared without a trace, taking with her the infant daughter she had borne him. Tō no Chūjō calls the lost infant "Nadeshiko," another name for "wild carnation." Genji learns later in the narrative that the woman was so frightened by threats of violence from Tō no Chūjō's in-laws (the Minister of the Right and Kokiden) that she vanished without telling Tō no Chūjō where she had gone, but Tō no Chūjō is never privy to this information. In the rainy-night discussion, Genji senses a resonance between the woman's fate and that of his mother, who many years before had suffered threats, issued by the same people, that led to her sudden decline and premature death.

At the beginning of "Yūgao" (chapter 4), Genji has a fateful encounter with Tō no Chūjō's lost love. This comes about when he pays a visit to the house of his former wet nurse, who is ill. The wet nurse is the mother of Koremitsu, one of Genji's closest attendants and his "breast brother." Genji is at this point in the tale about seventeen years old. While he waits for Koremitsu to open the gate to the house, Genji notices a vine covered with white blossoms on a fence at the house next door. After inquiring about the name, a male attendant tells him that they are blossoms of the *yūgao,* or "evening face," a kind of gourd. Genji asks the attendant to pluck a blossom for him and is surprised when a little girl emerges from the house with a fan. The attendant passes the fan to him, and Genji discovers a poem written in a delicate hand. The poem implies that the woman who sent it has recognized Genji and seeks to make contact with him. Genji is intrigued and orders Koremitsu to make inquiries to discover her identity. Unlike the *kaimami* in the Anegimi/Utsusemi story, where Genji himself spies directly on Utsusemi and her stepdaughter through a gap in a door, he this time assigns Koremitsu to do the spying in a surrogate *kaimami.*

As Genji ponders the possibility of another and perhaps more satisfying affair with a woman of the lower ranks, the narration makes it clear that he is aware that his excitement is inspired by the rainy-night critique of ranks. He is also acutely uneasy about the possibility of another embarrassing defeat such as the one he suffered at the hands of Anegimi/Utsusemi. The earlier disastrous affair thus haunts his thoughts at the very beginning of his relationship with the woman we come to know as Yūgao. The narrative diverts briefly from the Yūgao story to tell us, in quick succession, that Genji has an official audience with the Provincial Governor of Iyo, Anegimi/Utsusemi's husband, and learns that the Governor is about to leave the capital with his wife and daughter; that Genji immediately contacts the woman's brother, Kogimi, to arrange another meeting with her, but she once again rebuffs him; that Genji is neglecting his proud wife, Aoi, and this has produced resentment among his in-laws at Sanjō; and that his feelings for the highborn Rokujō no Miyasudokoro have cooled due to her extreme possessiveness. In the context of cooled desire, only Yūgao continues to excite Genji. Why is this?

When the text returns to the Yūgao story, it is to give an account of Koremitsu's surrogate *kaimami,* done on Genji's behalf in hopes of identifying the author of the fan-poem about the gourd flower. Koremitsu has been able to learn only that the woman has some connection to Tō no Chūjō, for he has observed that the women in the household showed great excitement when Tō no Chūjō drove past their house in his carriage. Genji immediately senses that she is the same Tokonatsu, or "wild carnation," that Tō no Chūjō had spoken of on that rainy night. The knowledge inflames Genji's desire for her. From the very start, part of Genji's desire for Tokonatsu/Yūgao involves the half-repressed knowledge that the woman once belonged to Tō no Chūjō. Genji is not engaged in a typical rivalry or competition for the woman, for Tō no Chūjō has no idea of her whereabouts. Rather, Genji unilaterally and secretively pursues the woman. That she was his friend's former lover becomes an element in Genji's own desire and compounds it. We learn later from the woman's attendant, Ukon, that Yūgao had long ago guessed Genji's identity, but Genji sublimates his own knowledge of her connection to Tō no Chūjō until after her untimely death.

The problem of secrecy and its relation to heightened desire acquires further resonance when we learn in the next chapter of Genji's love affair with his father's consort, Fujitsubo. The relationship is fraught with guilt on several levels: Genji cuckolds his father, Fujitsubo betrays the Emperor, and the lovers are involved in symbolic incest—in the sense that Fujitsubo had initially served as a kind of surrogate mother to Genji. This forces us to consider the possibility that Genji's repression of the knowledge of the origins of his feelings for Tokonatsu/Yūgao in the Broom Tree narrative is related at an even deeper level to repression of his betrayal of his father in the Kiritsubo narrative. Fujitsubo is a replacement for Genji's dead mother in the minds of both the Emperor and Genji, and Genji comes to link Tokonatsu/Yūgao to his mother in terms of her persecution by the political forces aligned with the Minister of the Right. By juxtaposing the Tokonatsu/Yūgao story in the secondary narrative with the Fujitsubo story in the primary narrative, the author of the *Genji* seems to be suggesting that Genji's repression of his knowledge of Tokonatsu/Yūgao's connection to Tō no Chūjō in "Yūgao" (chapter 4) is capable of illuminating some of the unspeakable aspects of his transgressive affair with his stepmother, Fujitsubo, in "Wakamurasaki" (chapter 5). In the logic of the guilt borne by Fujitsubo and Genji for their betrayal of the Emperor, Yūgao's sudden death has aspects of ritual sacrifice. It is as if the tale makes Yūgao die in Fujitsubo's stead and, through her sacrificial death, punishes Genji for their sin. Seen in this light, the Broom Tree narrative seems to exist to address and resolve one of the most vexing psychic dilemmas created in the Kiritsubo narrative. Tō no Chūjō's uncharacteristic failure to discover Genji's affair with Tokonatsu/Yūgao parallels the Emperor's willful ignorance of Genji's affair with Fujitsubo. This is the tenuous link a reader might establish in retrospect between the twin Kiritsubo and Broom Tree narratives.

Returning to the Tokonatsu/Yūgao story, the text states that Genji made his first excursion to meet the woman as soon as he received Koremitsu's report. He is in disguise and accompanied by a small retinue consisting of Koremitsu, a bodyguard, and an attendant. The text suggests just how far Genji was willing to go to remain innocent of the knowledge of the woman's connection to Tō no Chūjō: "[Genji] did not ask the woman [Yūgao] if she was that person [i.e. the one Tō no Chūjō could not forget], nor did he identify himself [to her]."[27] In other words, Genji does not want to consciously acknowledge Yūgao's identity as Tō no Chūjō's "wild carnation," for to do so would mean that he could not pursue her without guilt. At the same time, the repressed knowledge of her connection to Tō no Chūjō is part of his fascination with her.

The woman herself seems to find Genji's secrecy strangely incomprehensible *(ito ayashiku kokoroenu kokochi nomi shite)*[28] and is in fact eager to know who he is, to the extent that she has his messengers tailed to see what route he takes home when he leaves her at dawn. Genji's repeated visits lead him to ponder the mysterious source of the woman's appeal. Although of good birth, she is, after all, of relatively low rank, and her childlike demeanor hides obvious knowledge of men. Even so, he finds himself irresistibly drawn to her and cannot fully explain the power of her appeal for him. The text states that Genji's deepest fear is that the woman will "slip away and hide,"[29] suggesting the insecurity he feels ever since the Anegimi/Utsusemi affair. Retrospectively, in the light of events in the following chapter, "Wakamurasaki," readers might relate his sense of insecurity to his fear of losing Fujitsubo, which stems in turn from the earlier loss of his mother. The fear makes particular sense if we remember that "slipping away and hiding" was the exact manner in which Tokonatsu/Yūgao escaped the threats of the Minister of the Right and extricated herself from the relationship with Tō no Chūjō. To allay his own mounting fears, Genji contemplates the extraordinary action of moving Tokonatsu/Yūgao in secret to his Nijō mansion and making her his wife.

Tokonatsu/Yūgao would seem to be functioning as an Anegimi/Utsusemi substitute in the Broom Tree narrative when Genji contemplates the move, and in retrospect she can also be understood as a Fujitsubo surrogate in relation to the Kiritsubo narrative. While she might succeed in helping him erase the memory of his failure with Anegimi/Utsusemi, she is ultimately unsuitable as a surrogate for his mother and Fujitsubo, due to her low rank, her lack of a blood link to Fujitsubo (what the text calls the "link to the color purple," *murasaki no yukari*), and her sexual past, symbolized by the child Nadeshiko. Tokonatsu/Yūgao's mysterious death makes sense fictionally if we think of her as preparing the way for a more suitable heroine, the young Murasaki, who enters the Kiritsubo narrative as a child without a sexual past, a blank slate to be written upon as Genji saw fit, who also had the requisite blood link to Genji's mother-surrogate, Fujitsubo. Genji's hopes of finding a replacement for Fujitsubo and Anegimi/Utsusemi come to fruition later in "Suetsumuhana" (chapter 6) when he succeeds in bringing Murasaki to live with him at his Nijō mansion. There Genji raises her to become his ideal companion and wife. Tokonatsu/Yūgao is the most important forerunner of the woman who so fully satisfies Genji's need for love. Here, again, the relationship between the Kiritsubo and Broom Tree narratives is intricate and profound; the Broom Tree narrative explores aspects of Genji's character that prepare the reader for further, related developments in the Kiritsubo narrative.

To return once more to the Yūgao story, Genji finds himself one evening forced by the woman's gentle and obedient nature to recall the way Tō no Chūjō had similarly described his lost Tokonatsu on the occasion of the rainy-night critique. He is perilously close to achieving conscious understanding of the role Tō no Chūjō plays in his affection for her. The issue of

Genji's refusal to identify himself to Tokonatsu/Yūgao surfaces shortly thereafter when Genji takes her to a deserted mansion to escape the distractions of her lowly residence and his constricted life at court. Here, seeking a new level of intimacy with the woman, he for the first time reveals his own face to her and asks her to tell him her name. She refuses, calling herself only a "fisherman's, or diver's, daughter" *(ama no ko)* who has no fixed abode. Genji understands the rebuff to be her way of blaming him for maintaining his anonymity for so long. There is a humorous pun in his reply, "I brought it on myself, then" *(yoshi, kore mo ware kara nari),*[30] for *ware kara* is a type of seaweed or sea creature. Shortly after this very intimate scene, Yūgao dies at this very mansion in mysterious circumstances involving spirit possession.

The next morning, a distraught Genji returns alone to his mansion at Nijō. Tō no Chūjō calls on him to ask why he was absent from a concert at the palace the night before. Genji receives Tō no Chūjō at a distance, keeping him standing *(tachinagara)* during the conversation and speaking to him from behind blinds *(misu no uchi nagara).* Both aspects of Genji's reception were consistent with court protocol when visitors were received by someone who had suffered a defilement. Genji explains that the defilement resulted from the sudden death of a servant at the home of his wet nurse, Koremitsu's mother, while he paid her a visit. Tō no Chūjō knows Genji too well to accept this explanation at face value, but Genji refuses to reveal the truth. Genji has ascertained the girl's identity, although he continues to pretend ignorance, and he clearly feels guilty for having kept her whereabouts a secret from Tō no Chūjō while she was alive.

A few pages later the lady's serving woman, Ukon, reveals the truth to Genji of Tō no Chūjō's connection to the woman. She left him not because of his neglect, which is how Tō no Chūjō described the reason for her disappearance in the rainy-night critique of ranks, but because of a threat from the Minister of the Right. Genji recalls the existence of a child the lady bore Tō no Chūjō and begs Ukon to bring the little girl to him as a memento *(katami)* of the lost woman. He admits to himself, "I should tell my friend Tō no Chūjō, I suppose, but why invite criticism?"[31] His feelings of guilt are reiterated a few pages later at the end of the chapter: "His [Genji's] heart raced each time he saw Tō no Chūjō. He longed to tell his friend that 'the wild carnation' [*nadeshiko*] was alive and well; but there was no point in calling forth reproaches."[32] This last line is more literally rendered "but he did not bring the matter up because he feared [Tō no Chūjō's] accusations" *(kagoto ni ōjite uchi ide tamawazu).*[33] The chapter ends with the departure of

Anegimi/Utsusemi and her husband, the Provincial Governor of Iyo, for his post in the province. Genji's final poem bids farewell to two women, the one who gave herself to him and died (Tokonatsu/Yūgao) and the one who refused him and now goes away (Anegimi/Utsusemi).

The simple, innocent friendship of Tō no Chūjō and Genji that was first sketched out at the beginning of the "Broom Tree" (chapter 2) has become characterized by complex feelings of secrecy and guilt due to Genji's encounter with Tokonatsu/Yūgao. Genji explains the lady's death to himself as punishment "for a guilty love."[34] According to Abe Akio, the punishment for a guilty love *(ōkenaku arumajiki kokoro no mukui)* is to be taken to refer to Genji's love of Fujitsubo, his father's consort.[35] Thus Genji's betrayal of his father in the Kiritsubo narrative, which is introduced to the reader only later, comes to be superimposed retrospectively upon his betrayal of Tō no Chūjō in the Broom Tree narrative. In terms of the order of chapters in the tale, events in the Broom Tree narrative once again prepare the reader for events that will shortly unfold in the Kiritsubo narrative.

Many aspects of Genji's friendship with Tō no Chūjō that are central to Genji's brief relationship with Tokonatsu/Yūgao in "Yūgao" (chapter 4) are explored obliquely through the figure of Koremitsu, Genji's so-called breast brother. Koremitsu's comparatively low status makes it impossible for him to be Genji's friend in the same way that Tō no Chūjō is, but an undeniable bond between the two men develops in the course of the chapter in ways that mimic the developments in Genji and Tō no Chūjō's friendship. Just as Tokonatsu/Yūgao links Genji and Tō no Chūjō erotically and emotionally, she similarly functions to link Genji and Koremitsu. This is clear from the moment that Genji assigns Koremitsu to spy out the lady's identity. The surrogate *kaimami* threatens to unravel because, unbeknownst to Genji, Koremitsu becomes interested in her for himself, even as he continues to act as Genji's go-between. On the night when Genji takes the woman to the abandoned mansion where she later dies, Koremitsu makes it clear that he covets her, expressing what the narrator calls an extraordinary thought *(mezamashiu omoioru),*[36] that "he could have had her himself, had he not been so generous."[37] The competition for the same woman overtly expressed in the mind of Koremitsu in the text is an oblique reflection of what is going on in Genji's mind vis-à-vis Tō no Chūjō. Genji knows that he should tell Tō no Chūjō of her existence if she is indeed his friend's "wild carnation," but he escapes this obligation through his carefully maintained charade of ignorance. As it is, her sudden death forces him to face her true identity and leaves him with a bitter knowledge of his betrayal of his friend. Koremitsu's overt desire for Genji's Yūgao is frustrated until after her death, whereas Genji's covert desire for Tō no Chūjō's Tokonatsu is given free rein until her death.

Koremitsu's desire for Genji's woman—the one who could have been his had he not been so generous—takes an extraordinary turn when Genji relinquishes her dead body to him, allowing Koremitsu to hold it, lift it into a carriage, and accompany it to a temple for burial. Koremitsu's reaction to the body is not revulsion, as one would expect in response to a corpse, but attraction more appropriate to a living body. From the moment Tokonatsu/Yūgao passes from Genji's hands into Koremitsu's, he revels in his access to her. Just as the lady passed from Tō no Chūjō to Genji by means of a disappearance as abrupt as death, she now passes from Genji into the hands of Koremitsu through death. Her death breaks Genji's pathway of access to Tō no Chūjō, but for Koremitsu it opens up new means of access to Genji. Koremitsu's attraction to Yūgao's corpse is a product of her identity as Genji's former lover, just as Genji's attraction to her derived to a great extent from her identity as Tō no Chūjō's former lover. The pathways of male connection crisscross Tokonatsu/Yūgao as much in death as in life.

Back in his rooms at Nijō, Genji regrets not accompanying Koremitsu in the carriage with the lady's body. He is anguished by the thought that she may revive and think herself abandoned by him. In the evening, after Tō no Chūjō has come and questioned Genji about his absence at court the night before, Koremitsu returns from the temple where he has taken the body. He informs Genji that she is indeed dead and that the body will be cremated the next day. Genji insists on "seeing her again," and Koremitsu reluctantly agrees to lead Genji to her for a last visit. Once there, both men note that her face is unchanged by death and that she remains strangely beautiful. This characteristic of being beautiful even in death links Tokonatsu/Yūgao most notably to Murasaki herself, who is described similarly in "Minori" (chapter 40).

Genji's love affair with Tokonatsu/Yūgao ends abruptly with her death, but the lingering implications of the affair become fully apparent later in the tale beginning with "Tamakazura" (chapter 22) when Genji receives Nadeshiko/Tamakazura (the daughter of Tō no Chūjō and Tokonatsu/Yūgao) as his long-lost daughter and uses her to compete against Tō no Chūjō and his sons for prestige at court. Both Tokonatsu/Yūgao and her daughter, Nadeshiko/Tamakazura, are fated to carry the competition between Genji and Tō no Chūjō across their bodies, thereby linking the two men in a friendship characterized by sexual rivalry.

The Hitachi Princess/Suetsumuhana

"Suetsumuhana" (chapter 6) begins with an account of Genji's longing for the dead Yūgao and of his desire to discover another pretty and charming woman like her. Chapter 6 also narrates Genji's continued bitterness over his failure with the lady of the locust shell, Utsusemi, who resisted his advances so assiduously in chapters 2 and 3. The dual figures of Yūgao and Utsusemi thus provide the pretext for Genji's interest in a royal Princess, daughter of the late Prince Hitachi and born in his old age, who is living an impoverished existence at her father's estate not far from the palace. Might she be the pretty and charming replacement for Yūgao that he seeks? Might he have success with her to drive away the bitterness of his failure with Utsusemi? These two thoughts motivate him to pursue what turns out to be a hilariously misguided affair.

The bringer of tidings about Prince Hitachi's daughter is Tayū no Myōbu, a female version of Koremitsu who plays much the same intermediary role that Koremitsu played in the Yūgao affair. Like Koremitsu, Tayū no Myōbu is the child of one of Genji's former nurses. She is in court service attending to the needs of Genji's father, the Emperor, but instead of residing at the palace she travels there each day from Prince Hitachi's former estate, where she now lives. Tayū no Myōbu professes little knowledge of the Princess' character or looks, but she claims to share with her a love of music. It is this report that initially excites Genji's interest in her. Genji is apparently familiar with the musical skills of her late father, Prince Hitachi, and speculates that the Princess is endowed with similar skills on the koto. Desiring to hear the Princess play, Genji and Tayū no Myōbu pick a quiet spring evening for Genji to pay his first visit. Secretly ensconced in Tayū no Myōbu's room in the mansion, he hears just enough of the Princess' playing to be fascinated. He considers making his presence known to her, but being aware of her high rank, he fears being thought childishly impulsive *(uchitsuke)* by her, so he desists. Genji is eighteen years old at the time.

When Tayū no Myōbu returns to the room where Genji has been listening in secret, he begs her to take him to the Princess, but she refuses out of fear for the effect such an encounter might have on the naive and sexually inexperienced lady. Genji agrees to postpone his visit, but for quite a different reason. It seems that Genji is intimidated by the woman's rank. Her brief concert makes her desirable to him at the same time that her rank cools his ardor and ultimately makes it impossible for him to invade her chamber as he would like to. The possibility is beginning to form in Genji's mind that the Hitachi Princess, far from being a winsome and approachable Yūgao, may be as unapproachable as all the other highborn ladies he finds so trying, among them his proud wife, Aoi, and the imperious Rokujō no Miyasudokoro. Claiming another commitment, Genji excuses himself to Tayū no Myōbu and prepares to take his leave of the Hitachi mansion.

At this point, three or four pages into the story of the Hitachi Princess, it is not clear what direction the love affair will take. For Genji to follow through and make love to the Princess, it seems that a *kaimami* must take place. In other words, Genji must spy on the Princess and be inspired by her beauty to invade her room and possess her. We learn later, of course, that the Hitachi Princess is no beauty except for her long and luxurious tresses, but for now that fact must be kept from Genji. Here the author devises an inspired solution to the problem of keeping secret the Princess' plainness while still providing Genji with a motive to pursue the woman. The solution is a deflected *kaimami* in which Genji, seeking a glimpse of the Princess, spies a rival suitor instead. The man is none other than Tō no Chūjō. Through another instance of the sort of sexual rivalry first observed with Tō no Chūjō in the story of Yūgao, Genji blunders into a most unlikely relationship.

The scene develops after Genji leaves Tayū no Myōbu. He does not head straight home to his mansion but instead makes his way to the Shinden, the central hall of the Princess' living quarters, where her interview with Tayū no Myōbu has just ended. Genji is no doubt on the prowl, desiring a glimpse of the Princess herself, and to that end he quietly takes a position behind a decrepit bamboo fence. From there, he spies a man who seems to have been standing there for some time. Genji dismisses him as a young gallant *(sukimono)* and pulls back into the shadows. It later becomes clear that the man is Tō no Chūjō and that he was equally impressed by the same brief concert on the koto that Genji heard, but Genji fails to recognize him and quietly prepares to leave in order to avoid discovery. Genji's initial failure to recognize his friend is reminiscent of his earlier refusal to recognize Tō no Chūjō's identity as the former lover of Tokonatsu/Yūgao. At this point in the text, Tō no Chūjō intervenes. He identifies himself to Genji with a poem and accuses him once more of betrayal. The narrative backtracks to explain that the two friends had left the palace together that evening and that Tō no Chūjō had trailed Genji in secret to this desolate place. Genji is amused but also a bit irritated at being discovered on such an expedition, which contradicts his reputation as a man of probity *(mamebito)*. The effect of Genji's deflected *kaimami* that leads to the encounter with Tō no Chūjō is to increase the urgency of his desire for the Princess. When Genji's eyes fall on the adventurous *sukimono* instead of on their intended female target, Genji's ardor is inflamed as surely as a glimpse of the Princess, were she beautiful, would have inflamed him. Genji does not desire Tō no Chūjō, but he desires what Tō no Chūjō desires.

Genji is annoyed to be discovered on one of his amorous escapades, but at the same time he gloats that he has been able to keep the Yūgao affair secret from Tō no Chūjō, calling it a "difficult trick" *(omoki kō)* to have done so.[38] The sexual rivalry that occurs with the Hitachi Princess is fundamentally different from the rivalry in the Yūgao incident, although Tō no Chūjō's presence is crucial to both. In the case of Yūgao, Tō no Chūjō's former presence in her life is necessary to excite Genji's continued desire for her, yet the presence is so uncomfortable for Genji that it must remain unacknowledged until after her death. The sexual rivalry that emerges between the friends in the deflected *kaimami* scene in the Hitachi Princess' central hall relies on an entirely different dynamic. Here Genji does not replace Tō no Chūjō, as he did in the case of Tokonatsu/Yūgao, but must preempt him. The two forms of sexual rivalry are fundamentally different and banal enough that they require techniques of the writer's trade to resolve them interestingly. The rivalry is made interesting and even exciting, in the first case, by Yūgao's death and, in the second case, by the Hitachi Princess' plainness.

After Genji and Tō no Chūjō discover each other spying on the Princess, they ride to Sanjō in a single carriage *(hitotsu kuruma ni norite).*[39] As they ride, they play on their flutes in the evocative moonlight of a misty night. It is an image of extraordinary intimacy between the men. They act as co-conspirators as they quietly pull into a secluded gallery, change unnoticed into court dress, and, flutes still in hand, proceed to the main hall as if they had just arrived directly from night duty at court. A concert ensues, and dawn comes with the memory of the Hitachi Princess' koto echoing in their minds. Tō no Chūjō imagines her as a charming woman living sadly in her grand and dilapidated house. Genji's thoughts, on the other hand, are clearly affected by his failure with Utsusemi and his knowledge of Tō no Chūjō's rivalry, and they focus on his fears of another humiliating failure.

Subsequently, both men write to the Hitachi Princess, but she does not deign to answer either of them, a situation that Tō no Chūjō finds particularly outrageous: "What a man wanted was a woman who though impoverished had a keen and ready sensibility and let him guess her feelings by little notes and poems as the clouds passed and the grasses and blossoms came and went. The Princess had been reared in seclusion, to be sure, but such extreme reticence was simply in bad taste."[40] Tō no Chūjō's ardor begins to wane as a result. He asks Genji if he has received any response from the Princess, and Genji's ambiguous reply succeeds in making him feel that he may have lost the battle for the woman's affections. Despite the smug impression Genji gives Tō no Chūjō, the text tells us that in fact Genji is also annoyed with the Princess' silence. The only thing that encourages Genji in his pursuit is Tō no Chūjō's earlier desire for her, observed by Genji in the deflected *kaimami:* "Genji was not in fact very interested in her, though he too found her silence annoying. He persisted in his efforts all the same. Tō no Chūjō was an eloquent and persuasive young man, and Genji would not want to be rejected when he himself had made the first advances."[41]

Genji's reluctance to admit defeat in the rivalry with Tō no Chūjō, motivated by his sense of Tō no Chūjō's desire for the Princess, leads him to discuss with Tayū no Myōbu the possibility of arranging a tryst, but she dissuades him from what she considers an ill-considered match. Genji's judgment is clouded, however, by memories of Yūgao: "'From what you say, she would not appear to be a lady with a very grand manner or very grand accomplishments. But the quiet, naive ones have a charm of their own.' He was thinking of 'the evening face.'"[42] Spring and summer pass uneventfully, we are told, while Genji suffers from bouts of malaria. This brings the story in line chronologically with the earlier events of the previous chapter, "Wakamurasaki," which begins with Genji's retreat to the hills for treatment for malaria in the care of a monk. There he stumbles on the child, Murasaki, who is to change his life.

It is not until autumn, the season of Yūgao's death the previous year, that Genji is assailed with lonely thoughts of the dead lady, and he revives his pursuit of the Hitachi Princess. Still receiving no answer to his frequent notes, Genji suddenly becomes desperate to make contact with her: "In his annoyance he almost felt that his honor was at stake. He was not to be outdone."[43] Tayū no Myōbu is astonished by Genji's insistent requests to meet the Princess, and she has trouble comprehending the source of his powerful feelings. She is of course unaware of the impact of Tō no Chūjō's rivalry on Genji's heightened desire for a meeting, or of his longing for the dead Yūgao. Tayū no Myōbu's perplexity is mixed with her own feelings of guilt for instigating the affair. It was she, after all, who first told Genji the tantalizing story of a highborn Princess who had fallen on hard times. What was she to do?

Tayū no Myōbu finally hits upon a plan: "She would find a suitable occasion to bring Genji to the Princess's curtains, and if he did not care for her, that would be that. If by chance they were to strike up a brief friendship, no one could possibly reprove Tayū herself."[44] With Genji's assurances that he would not act rashly, Tayū arranges an audience between Genji and the Princess. Genji is taken aback by the lady's inept conversation, but contrary to Tayū no Myōbu's expectations Genji's interest remains strong:

> He [Genji] talked on, now joking and now earnestly entreating, but there was no further response. It was all very strange—her mind did not seem to work as others did. Finally losing patience, he slid the door open. Tayū was aghast—he had assured her that he would behave himself. Though concerned for the poor Princess, she slipped off to her own room as if nothing had happened.[45]

From the description of the Princess' response, we can surmise that it was her first sexual encounter. The lady "was in a state of shock, so swiftly had it happened," and "was incapable of anything but dazed silence."[46] Genji is perplexed by the incongruities of the Princess, unlike anything he has experienced before. She is of the highest birth, but impossibly reticent; well-bred, but incapable of the simplest poetic exchange. Once back in his rooms at Nijō, he remains in bed until late in the morning, overwhelmed with feelings of deep remorse, not for the Princess' sake but for his own. Clearly, this woman is not the replacement for Yūgao he had hoped for. In fact, she is not even close to his ideal, but because of her high status he feels that he cannot simply discard her the way he might a lower-ranking woman. At exactly this juncture, Tō no Chūjō appears and immediately notices Genji's melancholy. Genji keeps the affair to himself, even though questioned by Tō no Chūjō to explain his reasons for sleeping so late. Tō no Chūjō knows that Genji is, as usual, withholding information from him, but the possibility that it might involve the Hitachi Princess never seems to cross his mind. He has lost interest in the strange Princess who never responds to his letters, and he does not appreciate the extent to which his earlier courtship of her has inspired Genji to rivalry. The two friends again share a carriage to the palace to make preparations for a royal outing by Genji's father, the Emperor, which takes place in the next chapter, "Momiji no Ga." The event requires Genji's attendance at the palace all day, and it is evening before he finally dispatches the requisite morning-after poem to the Hitachi Princess. The text reveals how humiliating the delay must have been: "Tayū felt very sorry for the Princess as the conventional hour for a note came and went. Though embarrassed, the Princess was not one to complain."[47] Genji's poem seems to suggest that he has no plans to visit again, sending the

Princess' household into the deepest gloom. Unbeknownst to the Princess' attendants, however, the text tells us that Genji has decided to assume full responsibility for the Princess: "He must look after her to the end."[48]

Nevertheless, he makes no further attempt to contact the Hitachi Princess through the entire autumn. One day, during final rehearsals for the royal excursion to view autumn leaves, Tayū no Myōbu pays him a visit and tells him just how cruelly his neglect has affected the Princess. Genji's excuse is that Murasaki has kept him fully occupied, to the extent that he has been neglectful of that far more demanding lover, Rokujō no Miyasudokoro. It would seem that the Hitachi Princess is simply not very high on his list of priorities. Nevertheless, he manages to retain some curiosity about her, though its source is mostly in his ever-hopeful imagination: "Her excessive shyness made him suspect that she would not delight the eye in any great measure. Yet he might be pleasantly surprised. It had been a dark night, and perhaps it was the darkness that had made her seem so odd. He must have a look at her face—and at the same time he rather dreaded trimming the lamp."[49]

Genji finally rouses himself one snowy night to pay the Princess a visit. The visit begins with another unsuccessful attempt at *kaimami* at her door. This time Genji manages only to glimpse five old serving women sharing what appears to be an unappetizing and scanty meal. As they eat, they complain of the bitter cold. Genji closes the door and taps on a shutter to announce himself as if he had just arrived. As the Princess prepares to receive him, something about the scene brings back memories of Yūgao one year ago: "Snow was piling in drifts, the skies were dark, and the wind raged. When the lamp went out there was no one to relight it. He thought of his last night with the lady of 'the evening faces.' This house was no less ruinous, but there was some comfort in the fact that it was smaller and not so lonely. It was a far from cozy place all the same, and he did not sleep well. Yet it was interesting in its way. The lady, however, was not. Again he found her altogether too remote and withdrawn."[50] In this pathetic scene, Genji's desire for the dead Yūgao makes him feel all the more poignantly the inadequacies of the Hitachi Princess. It is the second time in the text that Genji and the Hitachi Princess are sexually intimate.

On the morning of this second visit, by the light reflected from freshly fallen snow, Genji for the first time has a chance to observe the Princess' features; the narrator describes a bulging forehead, an emaciated body, bony shoulder blades, a long face, and a pendulous red nose. The lady's one redeeming feature was her long and luxuriant hair, the typical mark of a heroine in a romance. As Genji leaves the Princess' residence by carriage, his friend Tō no Chūjō comes to mind: "He thought of a very cold lady with a very warmly colored nose, and he smiled. Were he to show that nose to Tō no Chūjō, what would his friend liken it to? And a troubling thought came to him: since Tō no Chūjō was always spying on him, he would probably learn of the visit."[51] If his friend were to find out about the visit, Genji's humiliation would be complete. This thought leads to musings about the view he had of Utsusemi in the successful *kaimami* in "Utsusemi" (chapter 3). She had not been beautiful, but she had possessed certain charms that made her unforgettable, and he had lost her. The Hitachi Princess' plainness becomes linked in Genji's mind with two other losses: the death of Yūgao and the departure of Utsusemi for the provinces; one had been taken away by fate, and the other by her own fierce resistance of Genji.

As the year draws to a close, the Hitachi Princess sends Genji a year-end gift, a gesture expected of a nobleman's wife. It is a bright red robe that Genji finds to be unfashionable and ill-fitting. Amused by the utter inadequacy of the Hitachi Princess' taste, he writes a poem that Tayū no Myōbu, reluctant deliverer of the robe, reads over his shoulder: "Red is not, I fear, my favorite color. Then why did I let the safflower stain my sleeve?"[52] The safflower *(suetsumuhana)* produces a highly prized red dye, and in court poetry it was normally a symbol of outspoken passion, but Tayū no Myōbu immediately recognizes that in Genji's poem the safflower is a reference to the Princess' red nose, and she feels deeply embarrassed for her. From this moment in the tale the Hitachi Princess will be known as Suetsumuhana, the "Safflower Princess." It is a comic appellation, but it places her in the company of the other Broom Tree women, Anegimi/Utsusemi and Tokonatsu/Yūgao (and still later Nadeshiko/Tamakazura), who have dual appellations and dual identities that are associated with Genji's friendship with Tō no Chūjō (or, in the case of Anegimi/Utsusemi, with Tō no Chūjō's precursor, Kogimi). In the New Year, Genji pays the Hitachi Princess/Suetsumuhana another intimate visit and notes some improvements in both the Princess and her household. Yet later, back at his own quarters in Nijō, he shares an amusing moment with Murasaki when, to Murasaki's delight, he draws a figure of a woman with a red nose and then dabs red color on his own nose. The "Suetsumuhana" chapter ends with a question: What will happen hereafter to these people?

The question is answered, of Suetsumuhana at least, in "Yomogiu" (chapter 15), where quite surprisingly she enjoys the distinction of becoming one of the women Genji brings to live in his Nijō residence. She makes brief appearances in "Tamakazura" (chapter 22), "Hatsune" (chapter 23), "Miyuki" (chapter 29), and finally "Wakana I" (chapter 34), where we learn that she is in poor health. Otherwise, "Yomogiu" is the last time she figures in any significant way in the tale. In the chapter, Genji has returned from his years of self-imposed exile in Suma and Akashi and become master of the realm under the reign of Genji's reputed brother (and actual son), the Reizei Emperor. Genji is now twenty-eight or twenty-nine years of age, and a decade has passed since the time of his first visits to the Hitachi Princess recounted in "Suetsumuhana" (chapter 6). "Yomogiu" describes how the Princess, abandoned by Genji both during and after his exile, was reduced to utter poverty. Her attendants have all moved into more favorable positions elsewhere, except for the faithful Jijū, who is like a sister to her.

The Princess has an aunt who invites her to join her in Tsukushi Province in Kyushu, where her husband has assumed the provincial governorship. Prince Hitachi had looked down on this aunt, his sister, for marrying a man of the provincial governor class, which he considered a humiliation for a woman of royal birth. Now that the Prince is dead and his daughter is reduced to poverty, the aunt gloats on her good fortune and heaps scorn on the Princess for clinging so stubbornly to her royal past, which she sees as no more than an obstinate pretension. The Hitachi Princess is true to her father's spirit, however, and refuses the invitation outright. In exasperation, the aunt abandons the Hitachi Princess to her fate and sets out to her husband's post in Tsukushi. To the Princess's shock, Jijū, who is practical enough to realize that the aunt is her only hope of survival, goes with them.

At this sad juncture, the tale takes an unexpected turn. Genji, more by chance than design, stumbles one evening upon Prince Hitachi's former estate, now reduced to little more than a "wormwood patch" (*yomogiu,* thus the title of the chapter). Koremitsu is with him, and together they make their way through the undergrowth to reach the dilapidated gate of the mansion. Genji is so moved to discover that his Safflower Princess is still there, having waited faithfully for him all these years, that he decides on the spot to take responsibility for her care and support. Genji appeared at the gate of the Hitachi Princess/Suetsumuhana at a strangely opportune moment: "Though he [Genji] did not know it, he had chosen a moment of heightened feeling. She had been napping and she had dreamed of her father. Afterwards, as if on his order, she set someone to mopping the rainwater that had leaked into a penthouse, and someone else to rearranging cushions, and in general it seemed as if she had resumed housekeeping."[53] A poem highlights her emotional focus on her father: *My sleeves still wet from tears for him who died / Are wetter yet from rain through ruined eaves.*[54] Genji is impressed with her faithfulness, which he misinterprets as being directed at himself, but he is touched also by her loyalty to the household and to the estate of her dead father: "Her stoicism in the face of poverty gave her a certain dignity. It made her worth remembering. He hated to think of his own selfishness through the years."[55] Though he cannot bring himself to spend the night with her, Genji is filled with a new sense of her strange preciousness to him and subsequently sees to the repair of her mansion. Two years later, with her former serving women once more assembled around her, Genji moves her to the newly built east lodge at his Nijō estate. Her story concludes with the thought, "It could no longer be said that he treated her badly."[56]

There is something mysterious, the text recognizes, about Genji's liaison with the Hitachi Princess/Suetsumuhana: "People had always said that Genji chose superior women to spend even a single night with. It was very odd: everything suggested that the Hitachi Princess in no respect rose to mediocrity. What could explain it? A bond tied in a former life, no doubt."[57] The text articulates the mystery this way, but the author has given us another explanation for the unlikely liaison, locating it in Genji's sexual rivalry with his friend, Tō no Chūjō. In "Suetsumuhana," Genji is looking for a woman to substitute in various ways for the elusive Utsusemi and the dead Yūgao. His rivalry with Tō no Chūjō gives him the necessary motive to approach the Hitachi Princess, despite his misgivings about her suitability for him. He finds a woman who seems to betray his every yearning for Utsusemi and Yūgao, but in time he comes to admire her faithfulness to the memory of her father. Her intrinsic quality of single-minded devotion, in the end, endears her to him. Through the events of "Yomogiu," Genji becomes a mature man who at least takes responsibility for his actions, even if he cannot explain them, and is himself reconfigured into a faithful lover by his appreciation of the Princess' faithfulness.

Gen no Naishi

In "Momiji no Ga" (chapter 7), the element of sexual rivalry in the friendship of Genji and Tō no Chūjō becomes mutually self-conscious through their simultaneous affairs with Gen no Naishi, a lady-in-waiting to the Emperor, Genji's father. The woman's age is given in the text as "fifty-seven or fifty-eight,"[58] a ripe old age by Heian standards, and part of what attracts the two young men to her is the outlandishness of her sexual coquetry toward them. Compared with the repressed consciousness of Genji's rivalry with Tō no Chūjō in the affair with Tokonatsu/Yūgao and the secrecy of Genji's competition with Tō no Chūjō for the Hitachi Princess/Suetsumuhana, the affair with Gen no Naishi reveals deep affection and humor between the men. At no other time in the *Genji* do the two friends share such physical intimacy as in the climactic mock sword fight between them in Gen no Naishi's chambers. The scene cannot match the emotional intimacy of the "Suma" friendship sequence, but it is equally vivid and memorable.

"Momiji no Ga" begins at the imperial palace with a dress rehearsal of the Chinese and Korean dances and music to be performed on a royal excursion later in the Tenth Month. The Emperor greatly regrets that Fujitsubo, who is with child, will not be able to accompany him on the excursion, and for her sake he brings the preliminary rehearsal to the palace. The highlight of the performance is Genji and Tō no Chūjō's dance of "Waves of the Blue Ocean." After dwelling on Genji's extraordinary beauty as he intones the lyrics of the song, the text contrasts it with Tō no Chūjō's more commonplace good looks: "Tō no Chūjō was a handsome youth who carried himself well, but beside Genji he was like a nondescript mountain shrub beside a blossoming cherry."[59] That night the Emperor praises the performance of Genji and Tō no Chūjō in a conversation with Fujitsubo. The reader is aware that Fujitsubo's enjoyment of the dance is marred by certain unspeakable occurrences (a reference to her affair with Genji), and this knowledge makes the Emperor's innocent question about what she thought of the dance seem all the more poignant. After the actual performance during the royal excursion, Genji and Tō no Chūjō are rewarded with promotions in court rank.

"Momiji no Ga" relates the birth of Fujitsubo's son by Genji, and for that reason the chapter clearly belongs to the Kiritsubo narrative. The episode with Gen no Naishi, however, links "Momiji no Ga" to the Broom Tree narrative in one very important way: Gen no Naishi is not a typical partner in rank or age for Genji. She thus represents one facet of the lesson that Genji learned from the rainy-night critique of ranks in the "Broom Tree," that even a woman who might not be what is conventionally thought of as a good match for a nobleman of Genji's status may nonetheless make an interesting sexual partner for him. In fact, Abe Akio identifies the Gen no Naishi episode as the origin and inspiration for the entire Broom Tree narrative, which as we have seen explores Genji's relations with women of the lower and middle ranks in the context of his friendship and sexual rivalry with Tō no Chūjō.[60]

Scholars have situated Gen no Naishi in relation to various of Genji's women who are prominent in the chapters that constitute the Kiritsubo narrative. According to Haruo Shirane, "Mitani Kuniaki has argued [that] the Gen no Naishi incident may be taken as a parody of Genji's secret liaisons with the Fujitsubo lady in the first half of 'Momiji no ga' and with Oborozukiyo in [the next chapter] 'Hana no en.'"[61] Shirane concludes that in contrast to the Oborozukiyo case, which has serious political reverberations and leads to Genji's exile to Suma and Akashi, the Gen no Naishi incident is trivial, little more than a "private joke between two male friends."[62] Norma Field follows Mitani in seeing the incident with Gen no Naishi as "yet another parodic version of Genji's secret violation of Fujitsubo."[63] Later, in "Aoi" (chapter 9), when Gen no Naishi offers to give up her place in the viewing stands to make room for Genji and Murasaki's carriage at the Kamo Festival, Field suggests that Genji links Gen no Naishi in his mind to Rokujō no Miyasudokoro: "Naishi, who in the interest of decency should have forsaken flirtation long ago, becomes a caricaturized Rokujō Lady. Although the latter is never ludicrous, the implied comparison is hardly flattering."[64] Field further argues that this insult was another reason for Aoi's possession by a malign spirit (presumably Rokujō's) and her subsequent death in the same chapter.

When considered in terms of the role she plays in Genji and Tō no Chūjō's friendship, Gen no Naishi is perhaps better understood as being linked to the other women of the Broom Tree narrative, particularly Tokonatsu/Yūgao and the Hitachi Princess/Suetsumuhana. Gen no Naishi is introduced as one of the women who attends the Emperor, Genji's father. What sets her apart is that, despite her advanced years, age has not dulled her erotic appetite. She makes it clear that she is interested in Genji, who is approximately eighteen years old at the time, and he responds to her largely out of curiosity. Genji soon decides to end the affair, fearful lest "the world see him as the boy lover of an aged lady."[65] The reaction of the Emperor to the affair is amusement, but Tō no Chūjō is intrigued: "He had thought his own affairs varied, but the possibility of a liaison with an old woman had not occurred to him. An inexhaustibly amorous old woman might be rather fun."[66] Not to be outdone, he secretly arranges his own rendezvous with Gen no Naishi. Tō no Chūjō's desire for Gen no Naishi is presented as a product of his sexual rivalry with Genji, and without Genji's prior contact with the woman it is hard to imagine that he would have approached her on his own. It is a reversal of the pattern of Tokonatsu/Yūgao and the Hitachi Princess/Suetsumuhana, where Genji's desire for the women arose in large part due to Tō no Chūjō's connection with them. In the affairs with Tokonatsu/Yūgao and the Hitachi Princess/Suetsumuhana, Genji keeps secret that he has gotten the better of Tō no Chūjō in the rivalry. With Gen no Naishi, however, it is Tō no Chūjō who has the upper hand and keeps his visits a secret. Genji fails at first to realize that he has been replaced.

That Tō no Chūjō maintains secret knowledge over Genji in the Gen no Naishi affair helps explain why Gen no Naishi is the only woman of the Broom Tree narrative who possesses a single identity. The other dual identities—Anegimi/Utsusemi, Tokonatsu/Yūgao, and the Hitachi Princess/Suetsumuhana—are all a product of the author's exploration of sexual rivalry emerging from Genji's friendship with Tō no Chūjō (and Tō no Chūjō's precursor, Kogimi). Genji's desire for Utsusemi is enabled by the woman's identity as Anegimi, the elder sister of Kogimi; his desire for Yūgao is enabled by the woman's identity as Tō no Chūjō's Tokonatsu; his desire for Suetsumuhana is enabled by her desirability as the Hitachi Princess to Tō no Chūjō. The men's sexual rivalry "doubles" the woman because of the duplicity of Genji's consciousness: Genji has knowledge of Tō no Chūjō's presence in the women's lives, but Tō no Chūjō is in ignorance of Genji's secret access to them. The asymmetry of knowledge achieves symmetry in the Gen no Naishi episode, and this in part explains the extraordinary intimacy of the culminating scene.

The affair with Gen no Naishi introduces into Genji's and Tō no Chūjō's friendship a new level of physical and psychological intimacy, surpassing even the earlier deflected *kaimami* of the Hitachi Princess when they shared a single carriage home. The culminating scene begins one evening when Genji chances to hear Gen no Naishi playing most evocatively on her lute: "She was a unique mistress of the instrument, invited sometimes to join men in concerts before the emperor. Unrequited love gave her playing tonight an especial poignancy."[67] Drawn by the sound, he approaches her rooms and adventurously accepts her invitation to spend the night. Meanwhile, Tō no Chūjō has been looking for an opportunity to chasten Genji for his affairs: "Tō no Chūjō had long resented Genji's self-righteous way of chiding him for his own adventures. The proper face Genji showed the world seemed to hide rather a lot. Tō no Chūjō had been on the watch for an opportunity to give his friend a little of what he deserved. Now it had come. The sanctimonious one would now be taught a lesson."[68]

Tō no Chūjō slips into Gen no Naishi's chambers as Genji dozes. In the darkness, Genji hears an unknown man enter and, hoping to escape discovery, seeks shelter behind a screen. Genji suspects it is the superintendent of palace repairs come to visit Gen no Naishi, and he does not want to be caught in her company. Much like the scenes of nonrecognition in his affairs with Tokonatsu/Yūgao and the Hitachi Princess/Suetsumuhana, Genji is unable to discern Tō no Chūjō's identity. The unknown man brandishes a sword as if ready to attack Genji, and Gen no Naishi intervenes, pleading with them not to fight. When Genji realizes the identity of his assailant, Tō no Chūjō bursts into laughter. Tō no Chūjō refuses to return Genji's clothes, which he found beside the bed Genji has just shared with Gen no Naishi. In the face of this humiliation, Genji suggests, "Well then, let's be undressed together,"[69] and proceeds to remove his friend's sash and strip him of his robes. The masculine physicality of this raucous scene is unprecedented in the tale. Having abandoned all discretion, standing there disrobed and in disarray, the two young men are finally able to see the humor of the situation and reconcile with each other. When they gather their things and go out of Gen no Naishi's rooms together, arm in arm, they leave "the best of friends."[70] Gen no Naishi is outraged at being left high and dry by her "boy lovers" in this manner, and the next morning she sends Genji a poem expressing her unhappiness: *No complaint of mine could relieve my misery, now the double wave that dashed itself on my shore has again slipped out to sea.*[71]

Gen no Naishi makes two brief appearances after this in the tale, but neither involves Tō no Chūjō. The first is in "Aoi," where she relinquishes her place to Genji in the viewing stands for the Kamo Festival. Murasaki is with him in his carriage, and for that reason he finds the erotic adventurousness of Gen no Naishi's poetic banter especially out of place. The scene is interwoven with the troubled feelings of Rokujō no Miyasudokoro, who was humiliated at the earlier installation service of the Kamo Priestess when Aoi's carriage clashed with her own. The juxtaposition suggests the unflattering link, noted earlier by Norma Field, between Gen no Naishi and Rokujō. The final appearance of Gen no Naishi is in "Asagao" (chapter 20). The chapter covers the period of mourning for Empress Fujitsubo, whose death occurs in the previous chapter, "Usugumo." Genji distracts himself with visits to the estate of Princess Asagao, who implacably resists his advances, and there he discovers that Gen no Naishi, by now in her seventies, is still among the living. He cannot help but contrast the longevity of that woman with the brevity of Fujitsubo's far more precious life. Beyond that, the tale informs us of nothing further regarding Gen no Naishi's fate.

Gen no Naishi appears to be a pivotal character among the women of the Broom Tree narrative. In her original appearance in "Momiji no Ga," she brings intimacy into the friendship of Genji and Tō no Chūjō consistent with the role of other female characters such as Tokonatsu/Yūgao and the Hitachi Princess/Suetsumuhana. In her later appearances in "Aoi" and "Asagao," however, she serves to illuminate aspects of women from the Kiritsubo narrative, most notably Fujitsubo and Rokujō no Miyasudokoro. Gen no Naishi's appearance in "Momiji no Ga" is structurally significant, for it creates a direct link between the women of the Kiritsubo and Broom Tree narratives. By contrast, the depictions of the other women of the Broom Tree narrative are far more oblique in their exploration of the difficult questions raised by the Kiritsubo narrative: Genji's relationship with Fujitsubo was explored, as we have seen, through Genji's betrayal of Tō no Chūjō with Tokonatsu/Yūgao; and Genji's substitution of Murasaki for Fujitsubo was explored through his failed attempt to replace the Hitachi Princess/Suetsumuhana for his lost loves, Yūgao and Utsusemi.

Anegimi / Utsusemi

As noted earlier, one of the defining characteristics of the Broom Tree narrative is Tō no Chūjō's dramatic prominence. Although he is not a factor in Genji's attraction to Anegimi/Utsusemi, it is worth reconsidering her story in relation to Genji and Tō no Chūjō's friendship. It was stated earlier that Anegimi/Utsusemi's brother, Kogimi, serves as an immature precursor of the intermediary role played later by Tō no Chūjō. Kogimi enters the narrative toward the end of the "Broom Tree" and immediately after the rainy-night critique of ranks. As we have seen, Genji returns from the palace to the house of his wife, Aoi, at Sanjō, and when he is unable to stay at Sanjō due to a directional taboo, he gratefully accepts the invitation of the Governor of Kii, a man not much older than Genji, to stay at the Governor's house. Also at the Governor's house that night, due to a ritual purification, are all of the women from the house of the Governor of Iyo, who is the father of the Governor of Kii. Among the Governor of Kii's attendants is a boy of twelve or thirteen who catches Genji's eye because of his unusual beauty *(ito kehai ateyaka nite)*.[72] Inquiring into his background, Genji learns that he is Kogimi, the orphaned brother of the Governor of Iyo's young wife, Anegimi. Genji immediately develops an interest in the woman, but from the start Genji's interest in Anegimi's brother is implicated in his desire for her.

That night, Genji is placed in an area of the house adjacent to the woman's room. He overhears her speaking with Kogimi. Thinking how unpleasant it is to spend the night alone *(itazurabushi)*,[73] Genji follows the boy's voice to where Anegimi is sleeping, tries the door, and finds it unlocked. This carelessness seals the woman's fate. Genji enters, picks the woman up in his arms, and carries her back to his room. When Anegimi's attendant, Chūjō, tries to stop him, he coolly replies, "Come for her in the morning."[74]

Anegimi puts up a valiant psychological resistance and makes it clear to Genji that, as much as she might have wished to respond to him sexually and emotionally, she is a married woman and cannot allow herself to love him.[75] The married woman's recognition of Genji's emotional and sexual appeal anticipates the complexity of Fujitsubo's response to Genji, developed beginning in "Wakamurasaki" (chapter 5). Genji, for his part, reflects on the woman's appeal to him in terms of the rainy-night critique of ranks that took place just the night before: "She was no beauty, but she seemed pretty and cultivated. Of the middling rank, he said to himself. The guards officer who had seen them all knew what he was talking about."[76]

Having made love to her, Genji's next concern is how to reestablish contact with the woman, and he strikes upon a scheme to use Kogimi as his intermediary. Although Kogimi functions as a go-between in the relationship, in other ways it is the sister, Anegimi, who serves to link Genji and Kogimi in a bond of unusual intimacy. Anegimi's mediation between her brother and Genji anticipates the role of the other women of the Broom Tree narrative in mediating Genji and Tō no Chūjō's friendship. There is an element of adolescent clumsiness (recall that Genji is about age seventeen or eighteen) in Genji's pursuit of Anegimi. She appears in Genji's life before his competition with Tō no Chūjō achieves its central focus, as it will in the cases of Tokonatsu/Yūgao and the Hitachi Princess/Suetsumuhana. The role of Kogimi prefigures the role to be played later by Tō no Chūjō with one crucial difference: Kogimi easily becomes a substitute object of desire when Genji's true object, Anegimi, eludes him.

Toward the end of the "Broom Tree," Genji summons the Governor of Kii and tells him of his wish to offer Kogimi a position in his household. The boy is brought to Genji several days later, and Kogimi is thrilled and pleased *(ito medetaku ureshi to omou)*[77] to receive Genji's attentions. Kogimi is startled when Genji hints to him what has taken place with Anegimi. The boy's first assignment is to convey a love letter to her. Being a married woman, she is embarrassed when her brother delivers such a letter to her and disclaims any knowledge of it. When Kogimi reveals his certainty that the letter is intended for her, she experiences feelings of utter humiliation. The text tells us at this juncture that the Governor of Kii has taken an interest in his stepmother and is also cultivating his friendship with Kogimi for purposes similar to Genji's. Kogimi is doubly desirable to Genji when he realizes he must compete for the boy's loyalty against the Governor of Kii. To fully gain Kogimi's trust, Genji tells him, "You shall be my son" *(ako wa waga ko nite o are yo)*.[78] Genji also tells the boy that his adoptive father, the Governor of Iyo, will not live long enough to provide him with the backing he needs to succeed at court, and he should therefore place his hopes in Genji instead. The text tells us that Genji treated Kogimi like a true son *(makoto ni oyamekite atsukai-tamau)*,[79] taking him to court with him and dressing him in clothes from his personal wardrobe. In this way Genji grooms Kogimi to act as go-between with the sister Genji desires, while at the same time enjoying his physical and psychological proximity to Kogimi. Kogimi in some ways seems to foreshadow Genji's other roles as surrogate father, with Murasaki (who goes from being Genji's surrogate daughter to his wife), with Akikonomu (who goes from being Genji's surrogate daughter to his daughter-in-law), and with Tamakazura (who goes from being acknowledged as Genji's surrogate daughter to being recognized as Tō no Chūjō's daughter). In each case, Genji's assumed identity as father barely hides sexual intentions, and if Akikonomu and Tamakazura escape it, it is as much a result of his political calculation as it is their resistance. If Genji's desire for his "daughters" characterizes his adult sexuality, his desire for Kogimi as a son appears here to be a characteristic of his youth.

Genji's next opportunity to visit Anegimi comes when a directional taboo forces him once more toward the Governor of Kii's mansion. There Genji asks Kogimi to search out his sister so that he can rendezvous with her. This time, however, she anticipates Genji's move and has taken refuge in her attendant Chūjō's quarters in a secluded gallery. When Kogimi finally tracks her down, she scolds him bitterly for agreeing to bring Genji to her, but Kogimi is less concerned with the feelings of his sister than he is that Genji might be displeased with him. Barely suppressing his tears, Kogimi cries, "But he will think me completely useless."[80] Kogimi returns to Genji and reports that he has failed in his mission, whereupon Genji pulls Kogimi into bed with him. The "Broom Tree" ends with these suggestive lines: "The boy was delighted, such were Genji's youthful charms. Genji, for his part, or so one is informed, found the boy more attractive than his chilly sister."[81]

The "Broom Tree" comes to an end with these words, and the opening lines of the next chapter, "Utsusemi," are a continuation of the same scene. This device has long puzzled scholars of the *Genji,* for there is no other chapter break like it in the tale. If there is any literary logic to starting a new chapter in the middle of the scene (and we do not know if the break is the result of the author's decision or—more likely—a later accretion), it could be that the break draws attention to the concluding lines of the "Broom Tree," emphasizing that Kogimi's mediation between Genji and his sister has gone awry and that Kogimi himself has become the recipient of Genji's attentions. A similar but more oblique displacement will occur later with Tō no Chūjō in the scene of Genji's *kaimami* at the house of the Hitachi Princess, when Genji's gaze takes in Tō no Chūjō instead of the intended Princess. The way the two men afterward ride to Sanjō in a single carriage is the emotional equivalent of Genji's pillowing Kogimi, the difference being that Genji's adolescent feelings for a boy who is like a son to him can be expressed intimately and unguardedly, but courtly propriety demanded that Genji observe certain boundaries with a friend and sexual rival such as Tō no Chūjō.[82]

"Utsusemi" begins with Genji's berating Kogimi for his failure to take him to the sister. Kogimi is eager to regain Genji's trust and willingly serves once more as go-between. It is a warm summer evening when the Governor of Kii is absent from the house, serving at his provincial post. Due to the heat, curtains are raised that would normally block the women of the house from being observed. Genji's view is unobstructed. Like the carelessly unlocked door at Genji's first visit, inattentiveness to the details of female security seems about to seal Anegimi's fate once more. Genji scrutinizes the woman and her companion, a daughter of the Governor of Iyo (and thus Anegimi's stepdaughter). Genji observes them at his leisure until Kogimi returns to him. Kogimi suggests that Genji wait until Anegimi has gone to bed, and then he will signal Genji to enter for his rendezvous with her. What they fail to realize is that the stepdaughter has decided to share the sister's sleeping quarters that night.

When the two women have settled in for the night, Genji makes his way in the darkness toward their sleeping place. Anegimi immediately senses danger and, slipping out of her robe, flees from the room as Genji approaches. Unaware of her flight, Genji reaches the bed and, finding a woman there, proceeds to make love to her. Too late, he realizes the mix-up. Before Genji takes his leave from the stepdaughter's bed in the morning, Genji picks up Anegimi's robe and takes it with him as a replacement for the elusive woman. Back in his rooms at Nijō, Genji spreads the robe, which is imbued with the woman's fragrance, and lies on it with Kogimi at his side. Genji is faced with two surrogates for the woman, her brother and her discarded robe, and he must choose between them: "It's not that you aren't a nice enough boy, and it's not that I'm not fond of you. But because of your family I must have doubts about the durability of our relationship," Genji tells Kogimi. The comment "plunged the boy into the darkest melancholy."[83] Genji's ability to transfer his desire for Anegimi onto a fetish object such as her robe instead of onto her brother is preparing him for his competition with Tō no Chūjō for the other women of the Broom Tree narrative.

The story of Anegimi/Utsusemi and Kogimi achieves resolution in "Sekiya" (chapter 16). We learn there that Utsusemi's husband, the Governor of Iyo, had subsequently been assigned a post as Governor of Hitachi and that Kogimi was living with his sister and her husband there, having abandoned Genji during his period of banishment in Suma and Akashi. The Governor and his entourage are now returning to the capital upon the completion of his term of duty. It is about a year since Genji's return from exile, and Genji is on a pilgrimage of thanksgiving to Ishiyama to celebrate the birth of his daughter, the Akashi Princess. The two parties meet, fittingly enough, at the Ōsaka Barrier, a location that serves as a poetic placename for a meeting between lovers. Its poetic associations figure in a subsequent exchange of poems between Genji and Utsusemi. Genji here receives a chastened Kogimi with open arms and reveals that even though his feelings could not be what they were in the past, he "still numbers Kogimi among the closest members of his household" *(nao shitashiki iebito no naka ni wa kazoe-tamaikeri).*[84] Kogimi is touched and, as a favor to his former guardian, once more conveys a letter from Genji to his sister.

Shortly after this reunion at the Ōsaka Barrier, Utsusemi's husband dies, leaving her at the mercy of her stepson, the former Governor of Kii, who is now the Governor of Kawachi. To escape his advances, she is left with no recourse but to take the tonsure and become a nun. In "Hatsune" (chapter 23), we learn that she is living as a nun in Genji's mansion at Nijō, where she remains—along with the Hitachi Princess/Suetsumuhana—after Genji moves his other ladies to the newly built Rokujō estate. It seems to be the fate of the two surviving women of the Broom Tree narrative (Yūgao is dead and the ancient Gen no Naishi all but so) to share their final years in the empty Nijō mansion on the periphery of the tale, while the women of the Kiritsubo narrative flourish in the center at the Rokujō estate. The only Broom Tree woman to make the transition to Rokujō, however temporarily, is Nadeshiko/Tamakazura. She embodies the joining together of the Kiritsubo and Broom Tree narratives that begins in "Tamakazura" and continues through "Makibashira," a sequence that covers from chapters 22 through 31. Ultimately, her marriage to Higekuro relegates her, too, to the periphery of the tale, along with the other Broom Tree women.

Male Friendship in Political Rivalry

If the sexual rivalry between Genji and Tō no Chūjō unifies the Broom Tree narrative, there is a perceptible shift to political rivalry after Genji's return from exile and the beginning of the Reizei Emperor's reign. The stories of the women of the Broom Tree narrative are resolved in "Yomogiu" (chapter 15), "Sekiya" (chapter 16), and "Hatsune" (chapter 23), and it is now political rivalry that occupies the men. Beginning with "Miotsukushi" (chapter 14), as Genji and Tō no Chūjō enter their political ascendancy, their friendship is inexorably politicized by their need to situate their sons and daughters favorably at court. The two men are often at odds as a result, and Tō no

Chūjō suffers repeated political betrayals at the hands of Genji. This political rivalry is mediated by their children. At the end of "Akashi" (chapter 13), Genji is summoned from exile by his half brother, Emperor Suzaku, who suffered severely from an eye ailment during Genji's absence from the capital. The ailment healed immediately upon Genji's return, indicating that the proper political order had been restored. Genji's triumphant return is followed in "Miotsukushi" with the Suzaku Emperor's abdication and the installation of the Emperor Reizei, the secret son of Fujitsubo and Genji. The new reign brings with it generous promotions for Genji and Tō no Chūjō. In addition, the retired Minister of the Left, Tō no Chūjō's father, is persuaded to come out of retirement and accept the position of Chancellor. The text tells us that "Tō no Chūjō had a troop of sons by his various ladies which quite filled Genji with envy."[85] Genji could boast only Yūgiri, his son by Tō no Chūjō's sister, Aoi. The Reizei Emperor could not, of course, be publicly acknowledged as his son. In "Miotsukushi" the Akashi Lady gives birth to a baby girl, Genji's daughter. These three—Yūgiri, Reizei, and the Akashi Princess—are Genji's only children.

When Genji is in his ascendancy as Minister in service to Emperor Reizei, he shows political favoritism to Tō no Chūjō by making his daughter by the Fourth Princess, Kokiden's sister, a consort to the Reizei Emperor, while rejecting the candidacy of Prince Hyōbu's second daughter. This arrangement suits Genji's plans to frustrate the political ambitions of Prince Hyōbu. Although Hyōbu was the brother of Fujitsubo and the father of Murasaki, the two women Genji loved most deeply, Genji wishes to punish him for his support of the Kokiden faction during his years of exile. Genji's support of Tō no Chūjō wanes, however, when Rokujō no Miyasudokoro dies in "Miotsukushi" and leaves her daughter, Akikonomu, in Genji's care. Genji carries deep feelings of guilt about his neglect of Rokujō, and he is determined to make amends through his conscientious treatment of her daughter. It was Rokujō's destiny never to become Empress, because of the death of her husband, the Crown Prince. Her fondest wish was that her daughter should succeed where she had failed. Genji is determined that Akikonomu realize her mother's ambitions. The desire to make amends is so great that Genji is willing to betray both his half brother, the retired Emperor Suzaku, and his friend Tō no Chūjō in order to bring his plans to fruition.

After consultation with Fujitsubo, Genji makes Akikonomu a Consort to the Reizei Emperor (their son), even though Genji knows of the retired Suzaku Emperor's wish to have Akikonomu for himself. Tō no Chūjō and the former Minister of the Left are the powerful male backers of Tō no

Chūjō's daughter as Consort to the Reizei Emperor, and they are now positioned as Genji's rivals because he is the sole powerful male backer of the arrangement. The threat posed by Akikonomu to the fortunes of Tō no Chūjō's daughter as the Emperor's Consort produces the famous picture contest in "Eawase" (chapter 17). Genji knows how much the Reizei Emperor loves painting and encourages him to spend more time in the Plum Pavilion with Akikonomu, who is an accomplished painter. Aware of this threatening development, Tō no Chūjō assembles a large number of artworks for the Emperor to enjoy on a quiet day in the Third Month. The purpose is to get Reizei to spend more time in Tō no Chūjō's daughter's rooms in the Kokiden Pavilion. On the advice of Fujitsubo, who is herself an avid appreciator of art despite her current status as a nun, the Plum Pavilion of Akikonomu and the Kokiden Pavilion of Tō no Chūjō's daughter are divided into two sides for competing in a picture contest, to be judged by three serving women on each side. Genji hears of the contest between the two women's salons and suggests that the final judgments be made in the Emperor's presence. The retired Suzaku Emperor takes advantage of the event to send paintings from his own collection to the Kokiden faction through his mother, clearly an act of vengeance for Genji's betrayal of his desire to have Akikonomu for himself. Nevertheless, Genji clinches victory for the Akikonomu faction with his own very moving paintings of his years in exile in Suma and Akashi. Akikonomu's side is on the left, Tō no Chūjō's daughter on the right. Symbolically, Genji's friend Tō no Chūjō now occupies enemy territory in the court structure by being associated with the side traditionally antagonistic to Genji.

It is at this time that Genji begins to seriously contemplate retirement from court, but he is prevented from following through on his wish by concern for his children's future. Most pressing is the care of his young daughter, born in Akashi. He resolves to bring her to the capital and place her in the care of Murasaki for training and education. When Tō no Chūjō's father, the Chancellor, dies in "Usugumo" (chapter 19), the burden on Genji increases to provide advice on governmental matters to the Reizei Emperor. Likewise, the death of Fujitsubo later in the same chapter deals a devastating blow to both Genji and the Emperor, her son. Disquieted by the chain of unhappy events, the Emperor learns from a bishop in his service the shocking fact that Genji is his real father. The revelation leads Reizei to consider restoring Genji to royal status and turning the throne over to him, but Genji is adamant that his own father's decision to remove him from the imperial succession be honored. At this time, Genji thinks again of his trusted friend: "Tō no Chūjō was a general and councilor. When he had advanced a step or two Genji might safely turn everything over to him and, for better or worse, withdraw from public life."[86]

In "Otome" (chapter 21), three major developments occur in Genji's and Tō no Chūjō's friendship, all related to their children. The first is the coming-of-age of Yūgiri, Genji's son by Aoi. Tō no Chūjō has taken considerable responsibility for his nephew's training in Chinese because the boy has grown up at Sanjō in the care of Ōmiya, the boy's grandmother, ever since Aoi's death in childbirth in "Aoi" (chapter 9). The second development is the naming of Akikonomu as Empress to the Reizei Emperor, a move that spells defeat for the other Imperial Consorts, the daughters of Tō no Chūjō and now of Prince Hyōbu. Genji feels that he has successfully atoned for his shabby treatment of Akikonomu's mother, Rokujō no Miyasudokoro, by raising the daughter to the exalted position she had coveted. We are told that this issue was acknowledged at court: "There were many remarks upon the contrast between her fortunes and those of her late mother."[87] The third development involves Genji's son, Yūgiri, and another daughter of Tō no Chūjō's, Kumoinokari. Both children had been raised in the Sanjō house with their grandmother Ōmiya, but they had been separated when they were ten years old because it was considered inappropriate for girls to have male playmates beyond that age.

The issue of Yūgiri and Kumoinokari's relationship revitalizes the fictional role of Tō no Chūjō and transforms him into an active, even central, character for the first time in the tale. In a scene between Tō no Chūjō and his mother, Ōmiya, during one of Kumoinokari's music lessons, Tō no Chūjō expresses his resentment at Akikonomu's success at court and acknowledges the threat that the Akashi Princess poses to Kumoinokari's chances of marrying the next crown prince. Ōmiya voices her anger at Genji's betrayal of her late husband, the former Minister of the Left, and his high hopes for the girl: "Your father was all wrapped up in his plans to send your little girl to court, and he thought it extremely unlikely that an empress would be named from any house but ours. It is an injustice which would not have been permitted if he had lived."[88] Yūgiri enters at this point in the scene, and Tō no Chūjō tells him how much pleasure his fine flute playing gives him. Later, however, when Tō no Chūjō discovers that Yūgiri is spending time with his daughter, he is very upset. He opposes a marriage between them partly because the defeat of his first daughter for the position of empress still rankles him. His first daughter may have failed to achieve the pinnacle for a woman at court, but he still hopes that Kumoinokari will be able to succeed as consort to the next emperor. Two days later, Tō no Chūjō angrily confronts his mother, Ōmiya, and accuses her of encouraging the romance, a charge she vehemently denies. In the end, Tō no Chūjō brings both Kumoinokari and Reizei's Consort home so that he can keep a close eye on them. Tō no Chūjō thinks of Yūgiri as being beneath consideration as a marriage partner for Kumoinokari due to the boy's long university training, which has delayed his advancement in rank. Here Tō no Chūjō is in disagreement with his mother, Ōmiya, who favors Yūgiri as a partner for Kumoinokari on the basis of his studious nature and the very sobriety inculcated in him by his university education.

Eventually, in "Fuji no Uraba" (chapter 33), Tō no Chūjō reconciles himself to the marriage of Yūgiri and Kumoinokari. This represents another humiliating defeat for him, since he had hoped to present Kumoinokari in the service of the Crown Prince, a position now filled by Genji's daughter, the Akashi Princess. The politically astute and manipulative Genji issues this warning to Yūgiri about Tō no Chūjō's character: "You may think him a calm, unruffled sort of man, but he has a strain of deviousness that does not always seem entirely manly and does not make him the easiest person in the world to get along with."[89] At the end of "Otome" (chapter 21), Genji establishes his Rokujō estate in the eastern part of the city and assembles his women there: Murasaki in the southeastern quadrant, in a garden emphasizing spring-blooming varieties of flowers and trees; Akikonomu in the southwest quadrant, as a home away from the palace when she is not serving as Reizei's Empress, in a garden planted for fall colors; the Lady of the Orange Blossoms in the northeast quadrant, a place planted with bamboo and trees that offer cool summer shade; and the Akashi Lady in the northwest quarter, a place surrounded with pines and designed to look their best covered in snow. Murasaki and the docile Lady of the Orange Blossoms move into their new quarters on the same day, followed by Akikonomu several days later, and the Akashi Lady in the following month. The arrangement of Genji's women in this place consolidates for Genji all of the women populating the earlier chapters of the Kiritsubo narrative and brings structure to Genji's past. Time slows in the tale as the activities centered at Rokujō become the focus of the story. The stage is now set for the development of Nadeshiko/Tamakazura's story beginning in "Tamakazura" (chapter 22).

By the end of "Otome" (chapter 21), we are able to discern the entire outline of Genji and Tō no Chūjō's friendship and rivalry as mediated by their children in their middle years. On Genji's side are Tamakazura (Tō no Chūjō's daughter temporarily in Genji's care); Akikonomu (in Genji's care since the death of Rokujō no Miyasudokoro); his only daughter, the Akashi Princess; and his two sons, the Reizei Emperor and Yūgiri. Arrayed against them on Tō no Chūjō's side are three daughters—the Ōmi Lady, the Kokiden Consort to Emperor Reizei, and Kumoinokari—and a son, Kashiwagi. Through the intricate play of power among these characters in the second generation of the tale, the author enacts new dimensions of Genji and Tō no Chūjō's friendship and rivalry. No longer are women's bodies being contested in a sexual rivalry, as in the Broom Tree narrative. Instead, the bodies of sons and daughters are contested by their fathers in a competition for political dominance at court.

Nadeshiko/Tamakazura provides an interesting example of political rivalry in the friendship between Genji and Tō no Chūjō because it is colored by their earlier sexual rivalry. The girl is Tō no Chūjō's daughter, of course, but Genji covets her as a memento of Yūgao, her mother. The girl links the men in more complicated ways than their mother did and represents an extension in new directions of the connections initiated between the two men through her mother. The beginning of "Tamakazura" summarizes events from "Yūgao" (chapter 4), in which Tokonatsu/Yūgao died, and brings the story of her child up to the narrative present of the tale. We are told that Ukon, Yūgao's lady-in-waiting, is still living in Genji's care as one of Murasaki's attendants. The nurse was never informed of the mother's fate, and she was afraid to approach Tō no Chūjō about the child lest he take her away from them. The child eventually was taken to Kyushu when the husband of the child's nurse was appointed to a post there. For that reason, she ended up being raised in the provinces, the worst possible fate for a highborn girl. The text mentions that "sometimes, rarely, one of them would dream of the dead mother. She would have with her a woman who might have been her twin, and afterwards the dreamer would fall ill. They had to conclude that she was no longer living."[90] The "twin" image is consistent with her dual identity in the tale. For Genji, she is Yūgao, the lady of "the evening faces." For Tō no Chūjō, however, she will always be Tokonatsu, the "wild carnation." The dead woman is doubled in another sense through her daughter's existence, who herself bears as an infant the appellation of "wild carnation" *(nadeshiko).* She, like her mother, changes appellations in the tale and comes to be known as Tamakazura, the "jeweled chaplet," from this chapter forward. We learn that Nadeshiko/Tamakazura's guardian, the former Deputy Viceroy of Kyushu, took ill and died suddenly when she was ten. She was left in the care of his sons and their mother, her nurse, but when she was twenty, they were forced to flee their adopted home in Hizen Province to escape the advances of a boorish provincial official from Higo who had demanded to have her in marriage.

Once back in the capital, the girl and her guardians undertake a pilgrimage to Hatsuse, a shrine outside the capital, to pray for their future well-being. Fate brings the girl's entourage to the same lodging where Ukon is housed, and shortly thereafter the girl is almost magically integrated into Genji's life. Genji keeps silent to her father, Tō no Chūjō, about her reappearance and presents her at court as a long-lost daughter of his own. Jealous that Genji has discovered such a fine young woman, Tō no Chūjō searches for a long-lost daughter of his own to perhaps compensate for the less than satisfying accomplishments of his other two daughters, Reizei's Kokiden Consort and Kumoinokari. In one of the *Genji*'s most humorous scenes, Tō no Chūjō suffers utter humiliation when the daughter he finds, the countrified Ōmi Lady, turns out to be an unmitigated disaster. Meanwhile, Genji considers making Nadeshiko/Tamakazura his wife, but he ultimately decides against such a move, partly out of deference to Murasaki's feelings and partly to avoid putting himself into the awkward position of being Tō no Chūjō's son-in-law. When Genji finally tells Tō no Chūjō the truth about her, Tō no Chūjō welcomes the girl into his household. She soon becomes the wife of Higekuro, not as fine a match as Genji could have finessed for her, Genji notes with some satisfaction.

Stages of Friendship

"Wakana I" (chapter 33) depicts Tō no Chūjō celebrating Genji's fortieth birthday with music and nostalgic conversation. The tearful scene signals that the period of political rivalry between the two men that began with the Emperor Reizei's ascension is finally over. In "Wakana II" (chapter 34), Reizei abdicates the throne, and both Genji and Tō no Chūjō relinquish their government positions, taking a less active role thereafter in affairs of state. This move brings the two men back to the sort of equilibrium they enjoyed in the years of the Emperor Suzaku's reign before and during Genji's banishment, when the hostile Minister of the Right held sway at court and Genji and Tō no Chūjō shared life in the shadows. The period of competition ushered in by the Emperor Reizei's rule represented their political prime, and competition between them came close to overwhelming the friendship at the same time that it confirmed the existence of a powerful bond between them. In the two "Wakana" chapters a mature friendship is revealed. Having passed political power to the next generation, they can forgive the many bitter experiences of earlier years and luxuriate in the sort of friendship that is based on a shared past.

The friendship of Genji and Tō no Chūjō thus goes through three distinct stages in the course of the tale, based on changes in the political status of the men. During the reign of Genji's father in the first nine chapters, Genji and Tō no Chūjō's youthful friendship is developed around their competition for the women of the Broom Tree narrative: Anegimi/Utsusemi in chapters 2 and 3; Tokonatsu/Yūgao in chapter 4; the Hitachi Princess /Suetsumuhana in chapter 6; and Gen no Naishi in chapter 7. Genji and Tō no Chūjō are not yet politically mature men in these chapters. Genji is estimated to be about seventeen and eighteen, and Tō no Chūjō is only slightly older. As we have seen, their sexual rivalry changes after the abdication of Genji's father in "Sakaki" (chapter 10), when Suzaku becomes emperor and ushers in a period when the Minister of the Right and Kokiden dominate the court. Genji's subsequent self-banishment in "Suma" and "Akashi" (chapters 12 and 13), signals the end of their youthful sexual rivalry and leads to a brief period in which their friendship serves primarily to comfort them in a period of political setback. It is at this point in the narrative that the *Genji*'s author draws most upon Chinese elements in her depiction of male friendship. Afterward, beginning in "Miotsukushi" (chapter 14), the men move into a period of political ascendancy that follows Genji's return from exile and is ushered in by the reign of the Reizei Emperor. This reign signals Genji's and Tō no Chūjō's political maturity, at which point their friendship ceases to be a sexual rivalry and turns into a competition for courtly status through the careers of their children (chapters 14, 17–31). This period continues into the final years of their lives, albeit less intensely, as the two men relinquish power to their children and are observed fondly sharing memories of the past (chapters 34–41). The three stages of their friendship are demarcated by the three reigns that govern the tale as long as Genji and Tō no Chūjō live, and in each reign their friendship is characterized differently: as a sexual rivalry, as providing comfort in defeat, and finally as a political rivalry.

There is, however, one more bitter experience for the two men to share that results from the actions of Tō no Chūjō's son, Kashiwagi, who had hopes of marrying the Suzaku Emperor's daughter, the Third Princess. When she goes to Genji instead, the heartbroken Kashiwagi marries her sister Ochiba. He is never able to forget the Third Princess, however, and he finally succeeds in making love to her. The result of their liaison is that she bears him a son, known as Kaoru. When Genji discovers that Kaoru is not his own, the revelation has tremendous ramifications for the tale. The Third Princess, to make amends for her betrayal of Genji, takes the tonsure and becomes a nun, and a remorseful Kashiwagi starves himself to death. After Kashiwagi's death, his best friend, Yūgiri, marries Ochiba. This precipitates Kumoinokari's decision to divorce Yūgiri. When Kumoinokari returns to her home in "Yūgiri" (chapter 39), her father, Tō no Chūjō, sends Ochiba a harsh poem accusing her of destroying his daughter's marriage.

The Third Princess' affair with Kashiwagi seems to destroy Genji's spirit. In particular, he regrets his marriage to the Third Princess because it was a betrayal of Murasaki and precipitated her decline. Nevertheless, Genji refuses to allow Murasaki to devote herself to her prayers and become a nun as she wishes, for he cannot bear the thought of life without her. When she finally dies in "Minori" (chapter 40), Tō no Chūjō is alone among Genji's friends to comfort him in his sorrow. This final act of friendship ends the story of the two men, who both pass from the tale without elaboration as to the manner or time of their deaths. The *Genji* continues for thirteen more chapters with a new hero at its core: Tō no Chūjō's grandson Kaoru.

Chapter 5

The Uji Chapters

"Maidens of the Bridge"

The *Genji* starts in "Kiritsubo" with what might be called a foundational relationship between Genji's parents, the Emperor and the Kiritsubo Consort, from which radiates the central dynamic of multiple substitutions in the tale. Both the Emperor and Genji try to solve the problem of the Kiritsubo Consort's death by replacing her with a new consort, Fujitsubo, who bears a physical resemblance to the other. This strategy amounts to a denial of the loss they have suffered. When Genji loses access to Fujitsubo as mother substitute and lover, he replaces her in turn with Murasaki. As we have seen, substitution is also a major factor in the Broom Tree narrative, wherein Genji thinks of Yūgao as bringing him comfort after the loss of Utsusemi and thinks of Suetsumuhana as possibly filling the void left by both women after Yūgao's death.

With the passing of Genji and Tō no Chūjō from the tale after "Maboroshi" (chapter 41), the author establishes a new hero and a new foundational relationship for the tale beginning in "Hashihime" (chapter 45). The new hero is Kaoru, and the foundational relationship is between Kaoru and the Eighth Prince, Genji's half brother. The Prince lives in seclusion in the village of Uji, outside the capital, and it is to Uji that Kaoru is repeatedly drawn by his longing for the Prince. The tale's new locus in Uji is the reason that the final chapters (45–54) are commonly referred to as "the ten Uji chapters" *(uji jūjō)*. When the Eighth Prince dies in "Shiigamoto" (chapter 46), his death reverberates throughout the remainder of the tale in the form of another pattern of multiple substitutions, similar to the one created by the death of Genji's mother in "Kiritsubo." In contrast to Genji's quest for the memory of his lost mother—and then his lost mother figure and lover, Fujitsubo—which occupies the early chapters of the *Genji,* the final chapters of the tale center upon Kaoru's quest for the memory of his male friend, the Eighth Prince, coupled with the quest for knowledge of his real father,

Kashiwagi. Substitution in the Uji chapters takes a very different form from substitution in the first part of the *Genji* because the Uji narrative explores Kaoru's need to replace a father/friend, not a mother/lover as was the case with Genji. Moreover, Genji's strategy for substitution is to replace one woman with another, but when Kaoru loses the Prince, he does not replace the Prince with another man he can call friend; instead, he first seeks access to the lost Prince in the Prince's eldest daughter and spiritual heir, Ōigimi. She accepts his friendship but rejects his love and chooses to die rather than become his wife. Bereft of his primary link to the Prince, Kaoru shifts his longings onto Ōigimi's sister Nakanokimi and finally onto a half sister, Ukifune. At their core, the Uji chapters depict Kaoru's attempts to keep alive the memory of his friendship with the Eighth Prince by pursuing a displaced intimacy with the Prince's three daughters.

Kaoru and Niou are the heirs in the Uji chapters of the youthful sexual rivalry between Genji and Tō no Chūjō. Their relationship dates from early childhood, when both are being raised at Genji's Rokujō estate, and their story is introduced in three intermediate chapters, "Niou Miya" (chapter 42), "Kōbai" (chapter 43), and "Takekawa" (chapter 44), before the action of the tale shifts from the capital to the village of Uji, beginning in "Hashihime" (chapter 45). In contrast to Genji and Tō no Chūjō, Kaoru and Niou suffer no political setbacks that might have inspired a profound display of friendship on the order of the "Suma" friendship scene, and their story never reaches a period when they might have competed with each other to place their children advantageously at court as Genji and Tō no Chūjō did. Instead, the friendship of the two men begins and ends in the realm of sexual rivalry. What distinguishes it from the sexual rivalry of Genji and Tō no Chūjō hinges primarily on the depiction of the Eighth Prince's daughters, for whom they compete. Unlike the women of the Broom Tree narrative, the daughters of the Eighth Prince are keenly aware of the rivalry between Kaoru and Niou and are shown to be astute observers of the friendship that inspires it.

Niou is the third son of the reigning emperor and Genji's daughter, the Akashi Princess. Of all Genji's grandchildren, he was Murasaki's favorite. While she lived, Murasaki took complete responsibility for raising him as she had his mother, the Akashi Princess. Niou's connection to Murasaki places him in a maternal constellation of relationships of special importance to Genji, including Fujitsubo and going back to Genji's own mother. After Murasaki's death, Niou inherits her Nijō house as his private residence, though he is free to visit the palace whenever he wishes to be with his parents, the Emperor and Empress.

Kaoru is thought by everyone at court to be Genji's son by the Third Princess, but he is always aware of Genji's estrangement from him and suspects otherwise. At the end of Genji's life, Genji entrusts him to the care of the retired Emperor Reizei, and the text tells us that Reizei lavished Kaoru with unprecedented attention. Reizei and Akikonomu (Rokujō no Miyasudokoro's daughter) have no children of their own, and Kaoru serves as an adopted son for them. Reizei places Kaoru on an equal footing with the Reizei Princess, his only child, by a daughter of Tō no Chūjō's. Kaoru's mother, the Third Princess, has lived in seclusion as a nun since Kaoru's birth, and he takes his role as his mother's protector so seriously that people at court come to associate his attentiveness for her welfare with his relative lack of interest in erotic adventures with women. Kaoru is lavished with attention at court, yet he gravitates toward isolation and introspection.

The innate spirituality of Kaoru from his earliest years is often contrasted with Genji's eager competition in the erotic and political arenas in his youth. Genji comes to spiritual understanding only gradually, in his old age, and only after having experienced life's pleasures and sorrows to their fullest. Genji is shown putting aside erotic and political entanglements in his later years as a cumulative result of his experience of the emotional cost of competing in the public world of the court. Kaoru follows the opposite trajectory: he gradually forgets his youthful insights into the spiritual cost of involvement in human affairs and becomes increasingly entangled in courtly competition, both political and erotic. As Haruo Shirane has noted, "Kaoru appears to be a spiritual reincarnation of the mature Genji, taking up where his predecessor left off. But instead of fulfilling these expectations, Kaoru follows a path almost the reverse of that trod by Genji."[1]

Kaoru's failure to achieve the expectations of spiritual attainment he evoked in his youth is usually explained by scholars as being the result of his erotic entanglements with the daughters of the Eighth Prince, his spiritual tutor. According to that account, Kaoru first develops a passion for Ōigimi and, after her death, enacts and reenacts the mechanism of substitution first with her sister Nakanokimi and then with their half sister, Ukifune. The interpretation I propose here of Kaoru's entanglement in the world of Uji hinges on his experience of male friendship. In this account, Kaoru's spiritual reversal is directly related to the nature of his friendship with the Eighth Prince. Generally, the Eighth Prince's significance has been underestimated by *Genji* scholars, who see it mainly in terms of shifting the locus of activity of the tale from the capital to Uji and of drawing the Prince's three daughters into the scope of Kaoru's and Niou's vision. Norma Field states, for example, "The Eighth Prince, after all, cannot generate a tale."[2] I wish to argue that, on the contrary, the Eighth Prince can indeed generate the tale told in the Uji chapters, and the author does this by deploying a mechanism of displacement to try to restore the friendship between Kaoru and the Eighth Prince that was broken with the Prince's death. The first of the Uji chapters, "Hashihime," thus marks a fundamental shift in the dynamic of the tale, from Genji's need to recover a mother/lover figure to Kaoru's need to recover a father/friend figure. As proof of this shift, the multidimensional friendship embodied by Genji and Tō no Chūjō in the first part of the *Genji* is split in two and distributed between two pairs of men: Kaoru and the Eighth Prince inherit the narrative of comfort in political defeat that reached its culmination in the "Suma" friendship scene, and Kaoru and Niou inherit the narrative of youthful sexual rivalry.

Genji's experience of friendship with Tō no Chūjō was profound, but in one sense it was incomplete, for Genji was never required to experience the death of his friend in the course of the story. If we think of the lesson of friendship's rupture through death that concludes the poems on friendship in *Poems to Sing*, and of the final episodes of the *Ise* that depict the hero at the end of his life, friendless and alone, it is clear that Genji was spared this form of grief. Perhaps he was spared because his character is shaped and defined almost exclusively in terms of the experience of female loss (mother, surrogate mother, lover, surrogate lover, and so on). It is left to Kaoru to confront in the Uji chapters friendship's deepest and most unacceptable truth, that even friends are subject to mortality and leave us bereft when they die. In contrast to Genji, Kaoru is a character who is defined by his experience of male loss, including his paternal identity, estrangement from his supposed father, Genji, and ultimately the death of his Intimate Friend and Imperial Prince, the Eighth Prince.

Just as death of the mother/lover was unacceptable to Genji and required substitution to make it bearable, the death of Kaoru's Prince was made bearable only through a strategy of displacement. We might say that Genji succeeded for a time in regaining his bearings through the figure of Murasaki, who seemed to answer so fully his longings for Fujitsubo, but Genji's decision to take the higher-ranked Third Princess, Kaoru's mother, as his wife destroys both his fragile equilibrium and Murasaki herself, the woman he loves most. This error is Genji's fundamental tragedy. In contrast, Kaoru never truly regains his bearings after the death of the Eighth Prince. When Kaoru seeks access to the memory of the Prince through the Prince's daughters, he is destined instead to reap only sorrow due to his insincere sexual rivalry with Niou. Kaoru's tragedy lies in the terrible toll he exacts from the women who are the ambivalent object of his pursuit.

Kaoru and the Eighth Prince

Kaoru first hears of the Eighth Prince at the beginning of "Hashihime" during an audience between his adoptive father, Reizei, and an Abbot from Uji. He learns that the Eighth Prince retired to Uji years ago after suffering defeat in a succession dispute and has since engaged himself in solitary spiritual pursuits. The Prince's present isolation and loneliness are emphasized in the description. The dispute leading to the Prince's retirement directly involved Genji and Reizei. In the years after Genji's return from exile and prior to the abdication of the Emperor Suzaku, the Eighth Prince had been put forward with the support of the Minister of the Right as a candidate for crown prince in competition with Reizei (the Tenth Prince). The Eighth Prince had lost this competition. It was primarily Genji's support of Reizei—Genji's secret son by Fujitsubo—that led to the Eighth Prince's political defeat, and with Genji's backing, Reizei eventually ascended to the throne.

As the audience between Reizei, Kaoru, and the Abbot continues in "Hashihime," the Abbot speaks of the Eighth Prince's spiritual devotion to the Buddhist teachings and of his two motherless daughters and informs the men that it is the Prince's concern for his daughters that prevents him from severing completely his ties with the world. Reizei recalls having heard others call the Prince a "worldly saint" *(zoku hijiri),*[3] and he immediately reflects on the fate of the two daughters, even fantasizing that after the Prince's death he might become their guardian (husband), following the example of Genji's marriage to Suzaku's youngest daughter, the Third Princess (Kaoru's mother). This romantic fantasy, characteristic of Genji's thinking earlier in the tale and of Niou's later in the Uji chapters, highlights the very different characters of Kaoru and Reizei. Perhaps to accentuate the contrast, Edward Seidensticker's translation interpolates a sentence at this point in the text: "Kaoru was less interested in the daughters than in the father."[4] A more literal rendering of the text would be "Kaoru's deepest longing was to see the Prince face to face engaged in his devotions."[5] The crucial point conveyed by these words is that Kaoru's imagination is immediately drawn to the Eighth Prince, whereas Reizei's imagination is drawn to the Eighth Prince's daughters. From the perspective of the Princely paradigm of friendship in the *Ise,* Kaoru is ready to play the hero who brings comfort to a defeated Prince, just as Narihira did to Prince Koretaka. The narrative then proceeds to show us Kaoru's pursuit of the heroic passion he conceives at that moment for the Eighth Prince.

The Eighth Prince's political defeat at the hands of the Genji-Reizei imperial line places him in an antagonistic relationship to it that parallels Kaoru's own. While Kaoru is the reputed son of Genji and has been adopted by Reizei and the Empress Akikonomu, who are childless, Kaoru's genealogy as the actual grandson of Tō no Chūjō aligns him with Genji's rivals and gives him natural affinities with the faction of the Minister of the Right at court, who supported the Eighth Prince. These affinities make Kaoru particularly susceptible to the Prince. From the moment Kaoru hears the Eighth Prince referred to as a worldly saint, he experiences uncanny feelings of longing and self-recognition that go far beyond the ordinary and bring him to a virtual crisis of identity, which centers on the question of his paternity. Not only will Kaoru comfort the Prince with his friendship, but he also will find in him the surrogate father he longs for on account of his personal history.

When the Abbot returns to Uji and tells the Eighth Prince of Kaoru's desire to meet him, the Prince appears to be deeply moved and expresses his admiration for Kaoru's youthful spiritual discernment, as reported by the Abbot. Like Genji, the Prince came to understand spiritual truths only after experiencing devastating political setback at court. The Prince tells the Abbot that he is not equal to the task of being a spiritual mentor to the young man, but he suggests an alternative model for their relationship: rather than being a pupil, let him be "a friend in the teachings [of the Buddha]" *(nori no tomo).* The most important aspect of the Prince's suggestion is that it reveals his desire to engage himself with Kaoru as a friend *(tomo).*

> WALEY: "Tell him that if he comes it must be not as a pupil, but as *a friend and equal in the Law.*"[6]
>
> SEIDENSTICKER: "No, I am afraid I would be a scandalously bad teacher. Let him think of me as *a fellow seeker after truth,* a very humble one."[7]
>
> TYLER: "Still, I doubt that I have much time left now, and considering how approximate my mode of life really is and how little likely I am ever to fully understand the past or future, he will be *a friend in the Teaching* before whom *I* should properly feel deficient."[8]

The Eighth Prince's extraordinary suggestion that Kaoru should be his spiritual friend begins a relationship that, ironically, draws Kaoru into the opposite trajectory, away from the spiritual and toward a profane attachment with the Prince as his friend and father figure. Kaoru's devoted attentions to the Eighth Prince also reconcile the Prince with his reputed half brother, Reizei, and reintegrate him into court circles in a way the Prince has not known for years. Suddenly, the Uji house has visitors again, bringing with them gifts from the capital. What begins as a spiritual quest ends by entangling both noblemen further in the very mechanisms of political competition they had sought to avoid. In the hands of the *Genji*'s author, male friendship is as dangerous an attachment as the Prince's love of his daughters in frustrating the men's higher spiritual aspirations.

Time accelerates in the narrative at this point, as if the author is intent to move the tale quickly to the next significant moment in the plot. Within the space of a page, the bishop arranges for a meeting between Kaoru and the Eighth Prince; they form a devoted friendship; and "three years go by" *(sannen bakari ni narinu).*[9] The three uneventful years of intimacy between the two friends are never explicated in the narrative, but it is in those unheralded years that the tale's new foundational relationship is formed and from which the rest of the Uji narrative emanates. From their first meeting, Kaoru's concern for the Prince is described as "attentive" *(nemugoro ni).* Kaoru acknowledges the Prince's two daughters, who live in the same house, but he fails to show any overt erotic interest in them. The daughters and the Prince both note this fact approvingly. In short, we are given the impression that the Prince provides exactly the sort of male companionship that both men have desired for so long. The terms used to describe the friendship between Kaoru and the Prince are in fact remarkably intimate: "After repeated visits Kaoru came to feel he wanted to be always at the Prince's side, and he would be overtaken by intense longing when official duties kept him away for a time."[10] Kaoru's feelings of longing *(koishiku oboetamau)* especially resemble those expressed in the Chinese verses from *Poems to Sing* and in the paradigm of the Intimate Friend in the *Ise.* The emptiness Kaoru feels when away from the Prince is intensified by his past experience of masculine loss, including the death of his reputed father, Genji, and his persistent doubts about his true paternity. The fact that absence from the Prince generates such longing suggests that the Prince satisfies Kaoru's need for male friendship in a way that his adoptive father, Reizei, cannot.

What are we to make of the three years that elapse during which nothing "happens" in the tale?[11] One way to interpret the gap is to say that it was not the author's intention to write an extended tale about the happy relationship of two male friends or that perhaps such a tale simply could not yet be written. To do so would mean dramatically reconceptualizing male friendship outside of its relationship to erotic adventure. The narrative elides three years of contentment in the lives of these characters in order to bring the story quickly to a point where we can measure Kaoru against the conventional literary hero as a "lover of women and a friend of men." In that sense, the span of three years functions as a magical number that represents the period that must elapse before the time is ripe for certain events to occur. The idea that important events can occur only when the time is ripe is common in myth and fairytale narratives with oral roots and derives from a way of narrating time that is generally thought of as inconsistent with the chronologically unfolding narrative mode of a tale such as the *Genji.* In the *Genji,* temporality is sometimes manipulated within chapters, whether stretched or slowed down, and earlier events are frequently recounted in subsequent chapters through flashbacks or embellishment. Between chapters, it is not uncommon to see temporal leaps, either backward or forward in the narrative chronology. But only in this instance in its description of the friendship between Kaoru and the Eighth Prince does the text revert to a magical number in order to accelerate the tale to a point, three years ahead, when the time is ripe for events to occur. The technique gives special significance to what follows: the Prince is absent one rainy night in late autumn, and Kaoru's attention is drawn for the first time to the Prince's daughters. Kaoru's response to the Prince's absence establishes a pattern that will be repeated when the Prince dies in the next chapter. In that sense, the scene is Kaoru's foretaste of the Prince's death.

When Kaoru arrives for his usual visit, he learns that the Prince has gone on a week-long retreat to the Abbot's monastery nearby. The text tells us that the Prince's retreat is motivated as much by a desire to escape the noise of fishermen on the river (a profane motive) as to complete the autumn observances of scripture reading (a spiritual motive). The Prince's reputation as a *zoku hijiri* (worldly saint) is confirmed by his dual motives for making the fateful journey to the Abbot's monastery. The very Abbot who earlier brought the two men together here serves to separate them. The Prince's absence accentuates the sense that Kaoru's spiritual desire to learn the Buddhist truths is in conflict with his profane desire for the Prince's companionship. After three years of uninterrupted friendship between them, the Prince's absence also represents a shocking rupture to Kaoru. He is in danger of losing the sole companion whose presence has brought him emotional equilibrium.

The next few pages of the text describe with great psychological insight Kaoru's complex response to the unexpected absence of the Prince. The Prince's absence resonates with the numerous absences of the father figures in Kaoru's life: Genji, who at some level rejected him and whom he rejected; the Reizei Emperor, who treasured him like a son but whose companionship Kaoru abandoned for the Eighth Prince's; and ultimately, the father he never knew, Kashiwagi. The narrative devotes great detail to describing the difficulty of Kaoru's journey to Uji that night, on horseback and without his usual retinue of men, as if to emphasize Kaoru's isolation and vulnerability. The treacherous path to Uji accentuates the loneliness of the fatherless man. As Kaoru approaches the Prince's house that night, he hears the plucking of a stringed instrument and assumes that it must be the Prince who is playing. When he is met outside by a guard and learns that the Prince is away, he realizes that one of the Prince's daughters is playing the instrument. The guard offers to send word immediately to the Eighth Prince of Kaoru's arrival—the monastery is not so distant that the tolling of its bell cannot be heard from the house—but Kaoru declines to interrupt the Prince's retreat and prepares to return to the capital, his clothes drenched with rain.

Kaoru pauses, however, to listen in secret to the music being played so compellingly by the daughter. This represents the first time Kaoru turns to the daughters to fill the void created in him by their father's absence. Kaoru is uncharacteristically forceful in expressing to the guard his wish to hear the daughter's playing. After some hesitation, the guard reluctantly allows Kaoru to eavesdrop on the sisters. As if to mimic Genji's deflected *kaimami* earlier in the tale, when on just such a night he encountered Tō no Chūjō outside the chambers of Suetsumuhana, the Safflower Princess, Kaoru's eavesdropping brings him to an encounter with an old and garrulous serving lady, Bennokimi. She represents an uncanny figure in the narrative who addresses the disturbance in Kaoru's psyche caused by the Prince's absence, for she begins to reveal to him information about the circumstances of his birth and, more importantly, the true identity of his father. Both are hesitant to go too deeply into the revelation, surrounded as they are by other serving women, and when they part, it is with the understanding that they will meet again to continue the conversation on another occasion. Kaoru is deeply affected by the oblique revelation of his paternity. Bennokimi is the first person to provide direct and firsthand knowledge of his father to him. She is therefore a most precious link to him and plays an increasingly important role as mediator in the mechanics of Kaoru's quest for his dead father.

On that night thick with mist, Kaoru composes the poem that commences his first poetic exchange with the sisters. It is a poem about losing "one's way home" *(ieji)* in the fog and expresses poetically the threat that the knowledge of his paternity poses to the fragile equilibrium of his friendship with his beloved Prince. Kaoru's poem is thus occasioned by both the absence of the Prince and the appearance of the shadowy figure of his real father, the dead Kashiwagi, that night.

asaborake ieji mo miezu tazunekoshi maki no oyama wa kiri kometekeri
Day now is breaking, but the path I must take home is invisible, and the wooded hills I crossed lie thickly shrouded in mist.[12]

In her reply, the Prince's eldest daughter, Ōigimi, chooses to describe the path to their door as a *kakeji,* a precarious bridgelike path built into the side of a steep mountain.

kumo no iru mine no kakeji o akigiri no itodo hedatsuru koro ni mo aru kana
Yes, this is the time when clouds sit upon the peaks and the autumn mists shroud all the paths up to the heights, to remove them from our world.[13]

The poem states that she and her sister always feel as isolated and alone, as Kaoru now feels. The autumn mist affects them even more keenly now that their father, who has contrived to keep their existence a virtual secret, has abandoned them for a week-long monastic retreat. A deep, mutual sympathy communicates itself between Kaoru and Ōigimi in the poetic exchange, hinging on their common sense of precariousness in the absence of their shared father and friend, the Eighth Prince, which stirs their fears of abandonment and reminds them of past losses. In a sense, the shared situation of Kaoru and Ōigimi (and, by extension, her sister Nakanokimi) makes of them pseudosiblings, similarly orphaned by their absent father.

The effect of Ōigimi's poem on Kaoru is profound, for he suddenly sees in her a kindred spirit: the "evidence of loneliness made him reluctant to leave."[14] Previously, the Prince's friendship had been all that Kaoru needed or desired, but now he finds himself drawn to the man's daughter by feelings of sympathy for her plight or perhaps by a sense that they share a common plight of being abandoned and fatherless. Kaoru finds himself on the verge of an erotic adventure, but with a new and remarkable difference. He desires to bring comfort to Ōigimi, in a way more appropriate to a nobleman comforting a male friend. Kaoru seems to pose to himself a question: what sort of relationship is possible with this woman? She is not exactly a figure of erotic attraction to him, but a figure of friendship, the result of displacement from its primary object, her father. He expresses his feelings poetically to her as he watches boatmen ferrying goods across the Uji River outside the house.

hashihime no kokoro o kumite takase sasu sao no shizuku ni sode zo nurenuru

What drops wet these sleeves, when the river boatman's oar, skimming the shallows, sounds out the most secret heart of the Maiden of the Bridge![15]

To Kaoru, Ōigimi is the *hashihime,* or Maiden of the Bridge, who can join him to his Prince. The relationship he desires with her is as much sympathetic as it is erotic: he knows her longing for the Prince because he feels it too. Together they will serve as each other's comfort, linked by their longing for the absent Prince. Her reply assures Kaoru that she shares his sentiment:

sashikaeru uji no kawaosa asayu no shizuku ya sode o kutashi hatsuran
These drops day and night while the Uji ferryman plies the running river soak these ever-moistened sleeves till they may soon rot away.[16]

Her loneliness and sorrow are suggested by the image of the ferryman's water-soaked sleeves, which for her result from constant weeping. By equating herself to the ferryman, who carries travelers from one side of the river to the other, Ōigimi seems to acknowledge her new role of linking Kaoru to her father.

Kaoru returns to the capital after this pivotal night at Uji, and the following day his mind is filled with thoughts of Bennokimi's remarks and of the Prince's daughters. He senses that a turning point has occurred in his friendship with the Prince and that he is now linked to him no longer by friendship alone but through the sympathy he has developed for the daughters. He also has the bleak realization that because of these newly established links to the Prince, it will now be even more difficult to fulfill his spiritual desire to renounce the world. Back at Uji, meanwhile, the Prince assures Ōigimi that Kaoru is incapable of posing a sexual threat to her: "He possesses a manner that is unlike that of the typical young man" *(rei no wakōdo ni ninu onkokorobae nameru o).*[17] The Prince even takes credit for Kaoru's newfound interest in the daughters: "I have no doubt that his thoughts have turned to you because I once chanced to hint at a hope that he would watch over you after my death."[18] The Prince would have Kaoru replace himself in his daughter's lives as their provider and confidant, but Kaoru's own motives seem to be far more complex.

When Kaoru makes his first visit to Uji after the Prince's retreat, the Prince entertains him throughout the night, along with the Abbot and others invited from the nearby monastery. The Prince obliges Kaoru's request for a musical performance by playing a brief tune on the koto, which Kaoru accompanies on the lute. The scene is on the surface exactly like the intimate scenes Kaoru enjoyed with the Prince for three years, but in fact a radical transformation has occurred. Due to the Prince's absence on Kaoru's previous visit, Kaoru has established a sympathetic link to the Prince's daughters; moreover, the truth of Kaoru's paternity is about to be revealed. At dawn the Prince retires for his morning devotions, and Kaoru is at last able to meet with Bennokimi, who completes the story begun at his last visit. During a tearful meeting, Bennokimi hands Kaoru a sealed pouch entrusted to her by the dying Kashiwagi. Later that day, back in the capital, Kaoru discovers that the pouch contains several love letters from his mother, the Third Princess, to Kashiwagi, along with Kashiwagi's last testament to her. He immediately goes to pay his mother a visit, but he cannot bring himself to reveal this newfound knowledge to her. He hides the secret, rather than disrupt her devotions. With this act of kindly deception, the pivotal "Hashihime" chapter comes to a close.

"Shiigamoto" (chapter 46) explores in detail the consequences of Kaoru's discovery of his father's identity. It also gives us a direct view for the first time into the heart of the Prince, unfiltered by Kaoru's perceptions. The Prince's deepest concern is the future of his daughters, now ages twenty-five and twenty-three, who are in the full bloom of beauty. With the help of Kaoru, Niou has struck up a correspondence with them that their father encourages, lest they be despised as untutored in the courtly art of poetry, but he is always careful of the sexual threat Niou poses: "'You must answer him,' the young ladies' father explained, 'although you should avoid any hint of courtship. That would just incite him more.'"[19] At the same time, the Eighth Prince senses that Niou's determination to have the daughters is so powerful that it might be his destiny to marry one of the them. Sensing, too, that death is approaching, the Eighth Prince reiterates his hope that Kaoru will see fit to look after his daughters. In what proves to be their last meeting, the Prince talks movingly to Kaoru about the past, especially the musical performances he grew up listening to at the palace, and about the future of his daughters. The two concerns come together in a scene where the Prince coaxes them to play for Kaoru, after which the Prince retires, weeping, to return to his devotions. Their final, poignant exchange of poems suggests Kaoru's commitment to the Prince's hopes for his precious daughters.

ware nakute kusa no iori wa arenu to mo kono hitokoto wa kareji to zo omou

After I am gone, this grass hermitage of mine may well fall to ruin, yet I know that you will be true as ever to your word.[20]

ikanaramu yo ni kakare semu nagaki yo no chigiri musuberu kusa no
iori wa
*In what age to come will that solemn promise fail, when I gave my word for all
time not to forsake this, the hermitage you made?*[21]

The depiction of Kaoru's strategy of dealing with the Prince's absence after the Prince retires that night is reminiscent of the earlier scene in "Hashihime," when the Prince had gone to perform devotions at the Abbot's monastery. Kaoru first summons Bennokimi to learn further details about his father, Kashiwagi, and later converses with the sisters in a manner that shows his complete sympathy and poses no sexual threat to them. Even as they talk quietly together, Kaoru realizes how unlike other men he is. He has become emotionally attached to the daughters, and yet he struggles to describe to himself the nature of that attachment. Compared with Niou, who is eager for erotic adventure, and despite the Eighth Prince's open encouragement of Kaoru, he is in no rush to make love to them. He enjoys instead, as the seasons pass, the simple pleasure of conversing with them about the spring blossoms and the autumn leaves, communicating their deepest feelings to each other *(orifushi no hana momiji ni tsukete aware o mo nasake o mo kayowasu ni).*[22] In short, what they fulfill in him is his need for non-erotic companionship or friendship, a role normally filled by a man.

When the Eighth Prince dies later in the chapter, Kaoru is plunged into grief, wishing "if only they might have another quiet evening together."[23] His thoughts turn often to that final meeting, which he had refused to imagine might indeed be their last. In keeping with his promise to the Prince, he soon turns his attention from his own grief to the grief of the daughters, who feel even more acutely the precariousness of their existence. In a touching scene when Kaoru first visits the sisters after the period of initial mourning, Ōigimi receives Kaoru freely, for she senses his deeply felt sympathy and is comforted by the memory he brings of her father. At the same time, Kaoru takes comfort in the access Ōigimi provides him to the Prince's memory. They appear to be developing a friendship unlike any other in the literature, in that it is between a nobleman and a Princess, rather than a Prince.

Overcome with emotion, Ōigimi withdraws from Kaoru's presence, and the scene shifts to Kaoru's conversation with Bennokimi, whom he thinks of as an "improbable replacement" *(koyonaki on-kawari).* It is an interesting phrase, interpreted in various ways, but perhaps the most convincing is that he thinks of the old serving woman as a replacement for that constellation of absent father figures (Genji, Reizei, and his true father, Kashiwagi) that now includes the Eighth Prince and, by association, Ōigimi. Through a sort of wizardry of nostalgia, Bennokimi is able to conjure the father for Kaoru as well as in Kaoru, when she sees the image of Kashiwagi in him: "She felt as if she were looking at Kashiwagi himself."[24] The conflation of Kaoru with his father takes a further twist when, later in the chapter, Kaoru composes a poem in which he equates the deceased Eighth Prince with an oak tree, a symbol of his father, Kashiwagi. The poem is preceded by a scene depicting Kaoru's acute feelings of longing for the Prince as he observes the Prince's old chambers being swept clean of dust that has accumulated since his death: "Long ago, the prince had promised that they would be companions in prayer if Kaoru were to renounce the world."[25]

> tachiyoramu kage to tanomishi shii ga moto munashiki toko ni narinikeru kana
> *The oak tree I sought to give me happy refuge under spreading shade is no more, and where he lived emptiness and silence reign.*[26]

Kaoru's feelings of longing for the dead Prince focus on the chamber's empty bed *(munashiki toko)* and are so intense that all who observe the scene are moved to tears.

The author of the *Genji* creates in Kaoru a very different sort of hero from that of Genji, primarily through her depiction of Kaoru's lingering attachment to the memory of the Eighth Prince. This becomes apparent in the next chapter, aptly titled "Agemaki," or "Trefoil Knots" (chapter 47), in which the threads that bind Kaoru, Ōigimi, and the Prince will finally unravel due to Kaoru's increasingly sexual rivalry with Niou. The chapter opens with a poem by Kaoru, addressed to Ōigimi, and written during the first anniversary memorial services held at Uji for the Prince.

> agemaki ni nagaki chigiri o musubikome onaji tokoro ni yori mo awanamu
> *In these trefoil knots may you secure forever our eternal bond, that our threads may always merge in that one place where they meet.*[27]

The image of the trefoil (three-looped) knot in Kaoru's poem is usually taken to indicate his erotic desire to join in marriage with Ōigimi. In the context of the Prince's memorial service on the anniversary of his death, however, the ones with whom Kaoru wishes to always remain entwined must be construed as the Prince and his daughter; thus the "trefoil knot." Ōigimi prefers that her relationship to Kaoru remain a friendship of a sisterly kind, as if they shared the same father, and this coincides with Kaoru's own needs and wishes, but he is goaded on by Niou's competition to push for more from her, with disastrous consequences. Through a series of increasingly tragic episodes, Kaoru succeeds in bringing Niou together with Nakanokimi, the Prince's second daughter, so that he can have Ōigimi to himself, but the marriage between Niou and Nakanokimi only pushes Ōigimi into making a desperate decision. Contrary to Kaoru's expectations, she arrives at the grim conclusion that her only means of escaping marriage to Kaoru is to die. She stops eating, the same method Kaoru's father, Kashiwagi, used earlier to end his life after his disastrous affair with the Third Princess. After Ōigimi's death, Kaoru is left utterly bereft, without his most precious link to the Prince.

Kaoru and Niou

When Kaoru comes of age before "Hashihime," he finds himself in a friendship with Niou that is characterized by rivalry in various forms. The rivalry first takes the form of a "competition to be pleasantly scented,"[28] and from this derive the appellations by which they are known, "Niou" being "perfume" and "Kaoru" being "fragrance." "Niou" connotes pale light or the faint smell of perfume. The name immediately conjures associations with Genji, who was given the appellation of the Shining Prince *(hikaru kimi)* in the opening chapter of the tale. In contrast, Kaoru gets his appellation from the extraordinary fragrance he exudes naturally. His exclusive association with scent represents in some ways a repudiation of the metaphor of light indicated by the names of the shining Genji and his dimmer grandson Niou. From the start of the friendship between Kaoru and Niou, it is the Imperial Prince Niou who envies what Kaoru possesses, not the other way around.

The first female figure to serve as an object of sexual rivalry in the friendship between Kaoru and Niou is Kaoru's adoptive sister, the Reizei Princess. As Tō no Chūjō's granddaughter and daughter of an Emperor, she is deemed of sufficiently high birth to be a fitting match for Niou, an Imperial Prince. Kaoru himself has forsworn erotic interest in the Reizei Princess and is well aware of how carefully his adoptive father, Reizei, has protected her from scandal. Nevertheless, Kaoru takes advantage of the fact that he shares the Reizei house with the Princess to excite Niou with his knowledge of her while himself remaining aloof. Kaoru derives a peculiar pleasure from this tantalizing game, as if his erotic indifference to the Reizei Princess is designed merely to torment Niou for Kaoru's enjoyment. The element of sexual cruelty, established in this initial scene with the Reizei Princess, remains a feature of Kaoru's friendship with Niou throughout the Uji chapters.

Sexual rivalry comes into full play in Niou and Kaoru's friendship in "Hashihime," following the scene when the Prince is absent and Kaoru first takes notice of the two sisters. Kaoru does his best to goad Niou to jealousy by telling him of the beautiful daughters of the Prince. Judging from the apparent depth of Kaoru's feelings for them, Niou imagines that they must be remarkable beauties, since he has observed that "Kaoru was not one to be drawn to any ordinary woman."[29] Kaoru uses his discovery of the sisters to make Niou envious of him, even though Kaoru has little genuine erotic interest in them. Furthermore, it seems clear that he excites Niou's interest while knowing full well that Niou has little hope of immediate satisfaction. The thrill of Kaoru's sexual rivalry with Niou in "Hashihime" is in some way related to his deeper feelings of anxiety regarding Bennokimi's revelation of his father's identity. Though he does not allow Bennokimi to reveal all that she knows, he hears enough to realize for the first time that, as he has long suspected, his father is Kashiwagi. His heart is in a pitiable state of turmoil as a result. Then comes a pivotal sentence in which his own paternal anxieties drown out his feelings for the Uji sisters: "At heart the Captain [Kaoru] was ever more deeply absorbed by what the old woman's talk had suggested, and he cared relatively little that a young woman should be seen as delightful or called a pleasure to look at."[30] Having engaged Niou in a competition for the sisters, Kaoru realizes that the actual act of competing for them does not interest him that much.

As we have seen, "Shiigamoto" (chapter 46) provides Niou with an opportunity to learn more about the Eighth Prince's daughters. The chapter begins in the Second Month with Niou and Kaoru paying a visit at Yūgiri's Uji mansion, located across the river from the Eighth Prince's residence, when they are on their way to a pilgrimage at Hatsuse. Niou is struggling to arrange a glimpse of the Prince's daughters, while Kaoru's thoughts turn to the Prince himself. The contrast is reminiscent of the former Emperor Reizei's reaction and Kaoru's opposite reaction when they first heard of the Prince and his daughters in a conversation with the Abbot at the beginning of the previous chapter. When a poem arrives from the Prince, Niou welcomes the chance to respond with a poem of his own, and Kaoru takes it upon himself to deliver it. During the Eighth Prince's lifetime, a state of affairs continues in which Kaoru is given more and more responsibility for the two women while he blocks Niou's access to them. Immersed in his own friendship with the Prince, Kaoru engages with Niou in a period of extended foreplay before he allows actual contact to occur.

Only after the Prince's death does Kaoru openly act to bring the women together with Niou, as if he were his friend's procurer: "I have made myself his 'guide to your seashore,'" he admits to them.[31] After hearing Kaoru's defense of Niou as being a serious sort of fellow, Ōigimi is persuaded to reply to Niou's letters (a reply that makes it clear that heretofore Nakanokimi had been his correspondent), and that is when Niou begins to approach the sisters more boldly, in a betrayal of Kaoru's report of his sober character. Ōigimi's reaction to Niou's blatantly sexual overtures is to recoil from him so as to obey the spirit of her dead father *(naki on-tama),* who wished more than anything that they should avoid humiliation and scandal. Ōigimi has the acute sense that even to consider an erotic attachment would be an act of sacrilege to her father's wishes. Kaoru's letters, by contrast, she answers freely, for they seem less sexually charged and give evidence of a gentle sympathy that reinforces rather than threatens the memory of her father. Only later, when Kaoru argues Niou's case, does Ōigimi begin to feel that he is unworthy of the trust her father placed in him and that perhaps she can no longer rely on him for sympathy and support. She seems to be aware that Kaoru's increasingly sexual demeanor toward her is a result of his competition with Niou. Her sense of Kaoru's betrayal empowers her to take charge of being the one to protect her sister and herself from humiliation: "Ōigimi wondered whether it might now be her duty to take the place of her father."[32] The obligation to care for them, which the Prince had passed to Kaoru, Ōigimi now takes upon herself.

At first Kaoru is not completely sure how to distinguish the sisters: they seem to be "two ladies with but a single heart."[33] Ōigimi's determination to protect herself and her sister takes a selfish turn when she flees her bed one night to avoid Kaoru's advances, leaving her sister to fend for herself. After this experience, Kaoru no longer has any difficulty distinguishing them. Almost perversely, from Ōigimi's perspective at least, Kaoru now becomes determined to show his commitment to her by refusing to establish an erotic attachment with Nakanokimi. On a day when Kaoru and Niou are staying at Genji's Rokujō estate, Kaoru comes to the conclusion that he can best reserve Ōigimi for himself as a link to the Prince and impress her with his faithfulness to the Prince's wishes by encouraging the marriage of Niou and Nakanokimi: "Though it might seem cruel to go against Ōigimi's wishes, his own affections did not seem prepared to jump lightly to her sister. He must see that Nakanokimi went to his friend."[34] The plan succeeds almost too well, and Nakanokimi and Niou are soon wed after the customary three consecutive nights of lovemaking. Kaoru's idea that he can thereby maneuver Ōigimi into marriage turns out to be a miscalculation, and Ōigimi only becomes more determined to adhere to her perception of her father's wishes for her to remain chaste.

Ōigimi wills herself to die by refusing to eat. Her distrust of men has been confirmed by Kaoru's betrayal of his promise not to force himself on her and by Niou's apparent neglect of Nakanokimi after their marriage. Death is her escape from the intolerable options before her. She would not give herself to Kaoru as a lover, for to do so would compromise her sense of self, which at some level seems to be male-identified. As long as Kaoru responds to her as a friend, as a link to her father, they could be of comfort to each other. But as soon as Kaoru begins to treat her as an object of sexual competition with Niou, she would rather die than submit. Ōigimi's rejection of Kaoru can be looked at from the perspective of male friendship in the tale as a demand to be treated "as a man." In addition, her death seems to imply that if there must be an erotic dimension to their relationship, then it must be posthumous, and Kaoru must make his approach to her memory through an intermediary, just as he approached the memory of her father. In interesting ways, the author of the *Genji* places Ōigimi in the realm of male friendship and imagines for her a bond of friendship with Kaoru.

Norma Field's analysis perceives the true nature of Ōigimi's remarkable attempt to link herself to Kaoru in a marriage of the minds.

> When Bennokimi comes to plead Kaoru's cause . . . , Ōigimi discloses her intent to commend Nakanokimi to his care in her stead. She puts her case this way: "If he is truly faithful to the past [i.e., to the Prince's wishes], let him think of us as one. Sharing the same flesh *(mi),* I will have yielded to her everything in my heart *(kokoro),* and thus I will surely be disposed to see him." An extraordinary vision this: shrouded and thus invisible in her sister's body, Ōigimi will be able to see (possess) Kaoru's and conclude a marriage of true minds."[35]

In a sense, Ōigimi is searching for a mechanism that would allow her the same sort of friendship that Kaoru enjoyed with her father as his "friend in the Buddhist teachings." Her desire is to possess the male prerogative of a friendship with Kaoru by forcing the typically female erotic role on her sister and reserving her father's de-eroticized role for herself. Field captures the mechanism of male friendship motivating Ōigimi's dilemma when she states, "Ōigimi attempts to conceal her flesh in her sister's and achieve a disembodied union with Kaoru. She insists upon denying her own material being, and when all efforts to persuade Kaoru to cooperate fail, she has no choice but to die."[36] Simply put, Ōigimi wanted to be Kaoru's (male) friend in a non-erotic "disembodied union," not his (female) lover.

Ōigimi's death leaves Kaoru exactly where she wanted him to be, forced to access her memory and the memory of her beloved father through Nakanokimi. When Nakanokimi moves to Niou's house in the capital as his wife, she finds solace in Kaoru's frequent visits. Niou detects Kaoru's distinctive fragrance on Nakanokimi's robes one night and is furiously jealous. His feelings of sexual rivalry with Kaoru intensify. For Kaoru, however, the visits to Nakanokimi are less erotic than friendly, and Nakanokimi increasingly takes on a dimension of surrogacy for her sister. What Kaoru desires most in Nakanokimi is not a lover but someone to replace Ōigimi's function as a link to the Eighth Prince. The words for substitution introduced by Kaoru in the Uji chapters in reference to Ōigimi—describing her variously as a *hitogata* (doll), *nademono* (fetish object), and *katashiro* (substitute figure)—all indicate functional replacements, not emotive or affective substitutes as in the chapters of the tale that centered on Genji. Genji sought physical contact and erotic love in his female substitutes, while what Kaoru seeks in his replacements is not a new male friend but access to his memory of the Prince's friendship. Field recognizes the complex nature of Kaoru's displacements when she asks: "Does this make Kaoru the master of substitution? Perhaps. . . . By finding names for the dominant form of action in that world [of the *Genji*], he manages to substitute for substitution itself."[37] Another way of saying this might be that the mechanism of substitution in the Uji chapters is altered by the fact that the foundational relationship of the Uji narrative is between two men (Kaoru and the Eighth Prince) rather than between a man and a woman (the Emperor and his Consort, duplicated in Genji and his mother substitutes), as in the first part of the tale.

Nakanokimi senses the danger posed to her marriage to Niou by Kaoru's continued visits, and in "Yadorigi" (chapter 49), she responds by committing a further act of displacement in the saga of Kaoru's friendship with her father and her sister, Ōigimi. She reveals to Kaoru the existence of a half sister. This woman comes to be known in the tale as Ukifune (drifting boat). The effect on Kaoru is immediate, and he has no difficulty thinking of her as a suitable replacement for Ōigimi. Through a remarkable exchange of poems, Kaoru and Nakanokimi negotiate Ukifune's fate. As Field notes, "The cumulative effect of their conspiratorial word play is simultaneously to make Ukifune into the expendable (and therefore) cleansing object of Kaoru's lust and the (presumably) enduring object of his devotions."[38] The bifurcation Field sees here between Ukifune as a dual object of love and worship can be understood as a product of Ōigimi's dual role: she linked Kaoru to her father, his true object of devotion, as a friend; and she became the object of his erotic desires in response to Niou's sexual rivalry. The same dual role that drove Ōigimi to her death will lead to Ukifune's eventual near-destruction.

Due to a series of misadventures, Ukifune's mother, who is married to the Governor of Hitachi, asks Nakanokimi to take Ukifune into her residence for protection. Niou discovers her there and begins courting her, still unaware of her identity, but Nakanokimi commends her to Kaoru's care and Kaoru soon manages to move Ukifune and her attendants into the Uji house where her half sisters had once lived with their father. He is disappointed with her countrified ways at first, but she is a quick student and increasingly pleases him. Field interprets Kaoru's motives as going no further than the desire for a substitute for Ōigimi: "Ukifune provides the living tissue for the statue of Ōigimi that Kaoru intends to erect in the villa-turned-temple."[39] But Kaoru is determined to make Ukifune a link to her father as well. In a scene back at the capital when a contest in Chinese poetry composition is interrupted by a storm, Niou, Kaoru, and the others seek shelter in Niou's rooms, where they are served a meal. Afterward, Kaoru is called out to receive a message from Uji. Niou is greatly disturbed at the sign of Ukifune's possible interest in Kaoru and of Kaoru's clear infatuation with her: "Clearly his friend's feelings for Ukifune passed the ordinary. He had hoped that the lady at the bridge [*hashihime*] had spread her cloak for him alone, and it was sad and annoying that Kaoru should have similar hopes."[40] With this reference to Ukifune as a Maiden of the Bridge, the circuit from Ōigimi to Nakanokimi to Ukifune is complete. All three sisters have been dubbed Maidens of the Bridge, signifying their central importance in linking Kaoru to the memory of their father and to Niou as a sexual rival in the Uji narrative. The intimate friendship of Kaoru and the Eighth Prince and the friendship of sexual rivalry between Kaoru and Niou seeks a kind of unification in the three sisters, but in each case the wholeness of friendship—of "two cranes flying wing to wing," such as Genji experienced with Tō no Chūjō—eludes Kaoru. The reasons for this are clarified through the figure of Ukifune in particular.

Nakanokimi first reveals Ukifune's existence to Kaoru in "Yadorigi," at about the same time he is preparing to marry an Imperial Princess, a half sister of Niou's, called the Second Princess. The marriage, his first, is one aspect of Kaoru's spiritual reversal in the sense that it binds him more firmly than ever to the profane world of courtly power, and he goes through with it only reluctantly at the urging of the Emperor, her father. Secretly, he would prefer her sister, the First Princess, who is a daughter of the Akashi Empress, Niou's mother. Kaoru's relative indifference to his new wife, the Second Princess, is in contrast to his profound fascination with Ukifune. He has rebuilt the Uji villa that belonged to her father, whom she never knew, and turned it into a temple suitable for him to perform his devotions, but he now begins the process of building a new house near it where she will live. Occupied with matters at court, he cannot visit her as often as he wishes, but each visit increases his appreciation of her resemblance to Ōigimi and Nakanokimi.

The chaste nature of Kaoru's fascination with Ukifune becomes apparent when Niou impersonates him one night and makes love to her at the Uji villa in "Ukifune" (chapter 51). Niou suffers a certain amount of guilt for deceiving Kaoru ("What a thing to do to the man who had then always taken him there in a spirit of extraordinarily close friendship!"),[41] but he is also angry that Kaoru and Nakanokimi have conspired to keep her existence a secret from him, and his erotic adventure with her is thus a form of vengeance that brings him some satisfaction in the rivalry with Kaoru. Ukifune herself is aghast but powerless to do much about the deception, and she finds herself increasingly drawn to Niou for the very passionate avowals of love that at first horrified her.

The complex repercussions of Niou's visits to Ukifune are a product of the layers of friendship and surrogacy involving Kaoru's feelings for the Eighth Prince. For one, Niou returns to the capital in such a state of agitation after leaving Ukifune that he masks it as jealousy rather than lovesickness. He confronts Nakanokimi with his suspicions that she and Kaoru are having an affair, forcing Nakanokimi to reflect on the cause of his accusations in these terms: "This is what has earned me his [Niou's] contempt: the mistake I made when I relied too greatly on someone [Kaoru] whom nothing obliged to assist me, and when I began to feel grateful for everything he had done."[42] In other words, there was no sexual affair but rather a sympathetic bond of something like friendship between Nakanokimi and Kaoru that Niou was incapable of imagining because of his relentlessly erotic feelings toward the women. Ukifune, for her part, cannot help but compare the two men and their very different natures. Kaoru's sympathy and loyalty are very precious to her, and she cannot imagine life without him; yet, at the same time, she must admit to herself that it is Niou who thrills her erotically: "How wrong it is of me, and how giddy, to prefer instead the one who insists on pursuing me with such mad abandon!"[43] Kaoru notices a brooding quality in Ukifune in a subsequent visit and takes it as a sign of her boredom with life in Uji. The evidence of suffering also endears her to him and spurs him to promise to move her to a new house in the capital in the near future. When Niou catches wind of the plan, he decides that he must make the first move. He informs Ukifune that he has found a place for her in the capital and will come to Uji to take her there.

Kaoru shortly discovers the affair. He is mortified and angry with Niou for the betrayal and reflects on his own considerable restraint in his dealings with Niou's wife, Nakanokimi, even though his feelings for her are far more profound than Niou's for Ukifune. Kaoru contemplates yielding Ukifune to him, but in the end he cannot bear the thought of breaking off with her. The loneliness he would feel reverberates far beyond his feelings for Ukifune and encompasses all the other losses associated with Uji, including the Eighth Prince, Ōigimi, Nakanokimi, and even his father, Kashiwagi. For that reason, he cannot harbor a grudge against Ukifune for long and continues with construction of a new house where he plans to situate her in the capital. Kaoru sends Ukifune a poem indicating that he knows of the affair, but she deftly avoids admitting her guilt by returning it with a note suggesting that the poem must have been delivered to her by mistake. Nevertheless, she agonizes over what Kaoru must be thinking of her betrayal. At the same time, she continues to receive long, passionate letters from Niou, far longer, she notes, than the letters that come from Kaoru, and she cannot reconcile the conflicting emotions they inspire in her. She realizes grimly that her only recourse is to die if she wishes to avoid completely disgracing her name.

Determined to die, she burns her papers and letters in preparation for throwing herself into the Uji River. She longs to write letters of farewell explaining herself to Kaoru and Niou, so that they might know her true feelings for them, but she is constrained by one thought: "That if she did so, these two fast friends might in time compare what she had sent to each. No, she thought, I shall just leave both wondering what happened to me."[44] Her—and her sisters'—awareness of the inseparable bond *(hanarenu onnaka)* between the men shows a level of observation of male friendship far surpassing that of the women of the Broom Tree narrative toward Genji and Tō no Chūjō.

"Kagerō" (chapter 52) opens with the discovery by Ukifune's attendants that their mistress is gone, an apparent suicide by drowning. Niou is the first to learn of her disappearance, and Kaoru is informed shortly thereafter. There is a hasty cremation of her bedding by the serving women, who are eager to hide what they believe to be the disgraceful truth of her suicide. Anxious to know more about the details of her final days, Kaoru goes to Uji to speak with Ukifune's attendants. For Kaoru, her loss triggers reflections about the whole trajectory of his life since that first visit to Uji seven years previous: "All the way there he pondered the past and wondered what bond from lives gone by had first led him to seek out His Late Highness [the Eighth Prince]. And ever since then, he reflected, I have looked after his daughters, even to the strange end of this last and least expected of them, and suffered constantly over them! He was such a saintly man, and our tie was always our hope for the life to come, under the Buddha's guidance, but for me it led only to error and sin—which I suppose must have been the Buddha's way of bringing me to the truth after all."[45] These thoughts reflect Kaoru's awareness of the way in which his friendship with the Prince has betrayed his spiritual aspirations and led to "error and sin." His profound error, which he is unable to articulate, is his lingering attachment to the Prince's daughters as links to the man. With the loss of this last daughter, the way is finally clear for Kaoru to embrace the Buddhist truths. He develops a previously unthinkable distaste for Uji and the former villa of the Eighth Prince: "for many years, affection had drawn him here, back and forth over those rough mountain roads, but he hated the place now; he did not want even to hear the sound of its name."[46]

In the next chapter, "Tenarai" (chapter 53), we learn that Ukifune is discovered mentally shattered and alone at a neighboring estate on the banks of the Uji River by a group of people associated with the Bishop of Yokawa, a high-ranking Buddhist prelate revered for the efficacy of his prayers. The Bishop's sister has recently lost a daughter of about the same age and takes on an immediate protective and nurturing role in caring for the mysterious young woman. She is soon taken to a temple in Ono, a day's journey from Uji, where a group of Buddhist nuns care for her, but her recuperation is slow, and an exorcism conducted by the Yokawa Bishop is deemed necessary. The exorcism is a difficult one, but it finally produces a confession from a male spirit, which, as Field notes, "is the first male possessing spirit to be granted speech" in the tale.[47] The identity of this spirit is unclear, and we know only that it belongs to a former monk with a grudge that had taken up residence in the Uji house many years before.[48] The words spoken by the exorcist's medium implicate the spirit in the death of Ōigimi, and it is only through the Bishop's intervention that Ukifune is spared. Scholars of the *Genji* usually explain Ukifune's breakdown as a result of her being torn between the love of two men, but when looked at in terms of the depiction of male friendship in the Uji chapters, we might conclude instead that the nature of her desire for each man was fundamentally different, that she was sexually drawn to Niou but emotionally drawn to Kaoru as a friend. From this perspective, the breakdown was a product of the impossibility of integrating the conflicting claims of erotic desire and a desire for friendship that divided her own heart. As Ukifune's mind mends in the care of the nuns at Ono, she makes this observation: "What a fool I was then—for now I see my ghastly mistake—to entertain the slightest feeling of love for that Prince [Niou]! He is the one who ruined my life! Why did I listen so gladly to those promises he made me by the green trees on the islet? She was heartily sick of him, and it was that gentleman [Kaoru], never really passionate yet always patient, whom she now remembered sometimes with very great pleasure."[49]

Ultimately, it would seem that one important purpose of the Uji chapters is to explore the impossibility of friendship between a man and a woman from two different angles: the perspective of the Eighth Prince's daughters, who each in her own way desires a non-erotic connection to Kaoru; and the perspective of Kaoru, who desires a connection with them that is motivated by nostalgia for their dead father. Kaoru comes to desire Ōigimi's friendship as a surrogate for her father through a mechanism of displacement, and Ōigimi similarly longs for a kindred spirit to fill the loss of her father. The depiction of her being drawn to Kaoru, not as a lover but as a friend, challenges the expectation that noblemen and noblewomen should engage with each other only in erotic terms in the tale. In the hands of the *Genji*'s author, Kaoru suggests a new kind of hero that cannot divide the love of women and the friendship of men in the same way as his literary predecessors. Kaoru felt no urgency to make Ōigimi his lover, but preferred instead a heartfelt exchange of feelings with her about the blossoms and the autumn leaves. Likewise, Kaoru's sympathy and loyalty to Nakanokimi are appreciated and reciprocated by her in a nonsexual way, something that her husband, Niou, was incapable of imagining. Ukifune, too, senses that the difference between the two men lies in the way one approaches her from a desire for comfort as a treasured memory of friendship, while the other comes to her filled with erotic desire. Had Kaoru not sought to restore the Eighth Prince through the Prince's daughters, and had he been able to disengage himself from a halfhearted sexual competition for them with Niou, he might have spared the Maidens of the Bridge much suffering. But the story of female suffering is, in a sense, exactly the tale that the *Genji*'s author chooses to tell. In the process, the Uji chapters further convey a truth about male friendship, consistent with the accounts in *Poems to Sing* and the *Ise,* that was left incomplete in the lengthy depiction of Genji and Tō no Chūjō: friends may bring comfort in defeat and competition in love, but they are still subject, tragically and unacceptably, to loss through death. How Kaoru's heart confronts the death of his friend is the story that reverberates throughout the Uji chapters.

Afterword

In *Politiques de l'amitié* (Politics of friendship), Jacques Derrida notes the existence of a double exclusion in Western philosophical treatises on friendship: "on the one hand, the exclusion of friendship between women; on the other, the exclusion of friendship between a man and a woman."[1] As we have seen, the same double exclusion does not hold in Heian depictions of friendship. *Poems to Sing* and the *Ise* certainly depict friendship between men to the exclusion of other forms of friendship, and in doing so they reflect a Chinese discourse of friendship that is also exclusively masculine. The other texts in this study have shown, however, that friendships are addressed in a variety of ways that are inclusive of the feminine. In the *Heichū,* for example, friendships between women are depicted primarily in terms of the opportunities for love that they present to the tale's hero, and the subject is still the male hero rather than the women themselves. In the *Kagerō,* the female narrator's friendships are depicted in terms of the comfort she brings to others around her, and they to her; and female friends are definitely in the subject position. Finally, in the *Genji,* the issue of the impossibility of friendship between a man and a woman is addressed through the figure of Kaoru and the daughters of the Eighth Prince. Drawn exclusively to the Prince, Kaoru is driven to seek him out in the sisters in a process of displacement that is initiated by the Prince's absence in "Hashihime" and then by his death in "Shiigamoto." Kaoru's failure to establish the memorializing bond he seeks with the sisters in the Uji chapters is a product of his inability to escape the pull of sexual rivalry with Niou, a dimension of male friendship that had been integrated much less problematically into Genji and Tō no Chūjō's earlier friendship.

The future of these multifaceted Heian depictions of courtly male friendship was played out in a post-Heian world where the court's literary legacies became dispersed among other emerging elites outside the capital. Literary arts in the medieval world were dominated no longer by noblemen but by military leaders and poet-priests who cultivated through them the refinement they associated with nobility. In time, the *Ise* became, along with the *Kokinshū*, one of the most important texts transmitting what it meant to be cultured to a class of people that admired the courtly attainments. The focus on the *Ise* represented a constriction of Heian discourses of friendship into an exclusively masculine mode in which Derrida's double exclusion prevailed. Proof of the abiding influence of the *Ise*'s depiction of male friendship can be found in a medieval sequence of one hundred linked verses known as "Sōgi dokugin nanihito hyakuin" (1499, "Sōgi's solo sequence of one hundred verses related to person"), composed by the master poet Sōgi (1421–1502) three years before his death. Sōgi seems to have intended it as a final word of instruction to his students in the art of linked-verse *(renga)* composition. Perhaps for this reason the sequence has been widely admired as Sōgi's masterpiece, imbued as it is with a lifetime of feeling and artistry.[2]

Verses 13 and 14 of the "Solo Sequence" contain a reference to episode 9 of the *Ise*. In the episode, the tale's hero journeys from the capital to the eastern provinces with one or two male friends and eventually reaches the banks of the River Sumida, in the area of modern-day Tokyo. Sōgi's reference to the episode is the only allusion *(honsetsu)* to a classical prose text in the "Solo Sequence," and as such it must have possessed special significance for Sōgi.

13. itsukite ka sumidagawara ni mata mo nen
When shall I come to the banks of the Sumida to sleep once more?

14. hanareba tsurashi tomo to suru hito
It is painful to be apart from the man who is my friend.

15. chigiriki ya aranu noyama no hana no kage
We exchanged vows on nameless hills and fields beneath the blossoms.

16. yo o nogarete mo haru wa mutsumaji
Though I abandoned the world, yet I still love the springtime.

17. mi wo kakusu io wa kasumi o tayori nite
I can only rely on the [spring] haze to hide me in my hermitage,

18. kien keburi no yukue so matsu
And there await my fate: to vanish in the smoke.[3]

The allusion to the *Ise* episode begins a conceptually discrete sub-sequence within the larger "Solo Sequence" in which the male poetic subject expresses first the longing he feels for his friend (verses 13–14), then a sense of frustration because of his persistent feelings of attachment to the friend and to the blossoms beneath which they spent the night together (verses 15–16). In relation to verse 14, the vows the men exchanged *(chigiriki)* beneath the blossoms in verse 15 refer to vows of love between the subject and his friend, consistent with the practice of *nanshoku* (male love) in Sōgi's day.[4] But when read in relation to verse 16, the vow in verse 15 changes to one addressed by the poetic subject to the cherry blossoms, in which he confesses his love for spring. Verse 17 expresses the subject's ironic reliance on spring haze to hide him from the sensual appeal of the world, and the final verse announces his sense of calm resignation as he waits for the extinction of death. In the six-verse sub-sequence from 13 to 18, Sōgi explores human suffering in terms of a man's yearning for his absent friend, thereby creating a poignant meditation by an aging master on the timeless Buddhist problem of the appeal of the sensual *(iro),* here represented by a friend and the blossoms in springtime. In the *waka* tradition based on the courtly aesthetic of the *Kokinshū,* such a meditation might have addressed the problem of the appeal of the sensual in terms of the feelings aroused by blossoms and women; but in linked verse, where the bond of friendship between men was an appropriate theme, Sōgi was able to manipulate the image of the male friend from episode 9 of the *Ise* to great poetic effect.

The *Ise*'s influence in the fifteenth century on a poet like Sōgi was made possible by generations of court literati who accorded the text special status as an expression of courtly taste. The most important of these was probably Fujiwara no Teika, who compiled the standard Tempuku-bon version from many competing versions in circulation at the late Heian court. Another was Nijō Yoshimoto (1320–1388), whose high regard for the *Ise* was especially crucial to the text's ultimate canonization. Like Teika before him, Yoshimoto was a nobleman who possessed extraordinary talents in the composition of *waka* and *renga,* and his tastes dramatically reshaped and revived the courtly literary culture of his day. Although in the fifteenth century Shinkei (1406–1475) was to call Yoshimoto and his fellow fourteenth-century *renga* masters "amorous men par excellence" *(kashikoki irogonomi)* for their stylish practice of erotic adventure and poetry,[5] Yoshimoto and his followers seem to have been sensitive to the way male friendship coexisted alongside erotic adventure in the *Ise,* for place-names and images reflecting both dimensions of the hero as friend and lover were incorporated from the *Ise*'s prose episodes into *renga*'s diction at about this time.

Yoshimoto's most famous poetic compilation was arguably the *Tsukuba shū* (1357, Tsukuba collection), containing more than 2,100 stanzas of linked verse, 87 of them composed by Yoshimoto himself. That it was organized into twenty volumes, along the lines of the prestigious imperial anthologies, showed just how highly Yoshimoto regarded *renga.* By incorporating words and moods from the prose episodes of the *Ise* into *renga,* Yoshimoto and his fellow *renga* masters elevated linked verse to the level of traditional *waka* while giving it a distinctive poetic language all its own.

After Yoshimoto's passing in 1388, Shōtetsu (1381–1459) was one of the first *renga* masters whose instruction of the *Ise* to his students can be historically verified. Sōgi extended this tradition among *renga* masters, lecturing widely on the *Ise* both to provincial students of linked-verse composition and to the highest court nobles. Records from 1487 show Sōgi discussing the *Ise* before the future Emperor Go-Kashiwabara (1464–1526, r. 1500–1526), and in 1488, when Sōgi was named Shogunal Administrator of the Bureau of Renga Contests at the Kitano Shrine, he lectured on the *Ise* to the Shogun himself and to other provincial magistrates.[6] Sōgi's influential commentary on the poems of the *Ise,* the *Yamaguchi ki* (ca. 1489, also known as the *Yamaguchi shō*), was composed of lectures he gave to the Lord of Suō Province (modern Yamaguchi), Ōuchi Masahiro. Furthermore, two commentaries survive that consist of verbatim notes of earlier lectures given by Sōgi: *Ise monogatari shōmon shū* (1477, also known as *Ise monogatari kikigaki*), compiled by Sōgi's pupil Botanka Shōhaku (1443–1527); and *Ise monogatari shō,* by the monk Sōkan, a contemporary of Shōhaku's.[7] The impact of the *Ise* on practitioners of linked verse is nowhere more evident than in the one-hundred-verse sequence called "*Ise monogatari* kotoba hyakuin" (1521, One hundred verses using words from the *Tale of Ise*). Each of the hundred verses contains an allusion to the *Ise,* and the phrase *tomo to suru hito,* "the man who is my friend" (used earlier in Sōgi's "Solo Sequence") appears in the fifth verse of the sequence.[8]

In sum, the *renga* poets of the fourteenth to sixteenth centuries who transmitted the *Ise* to their numerous students in the capital and throughout the provinces played an extraordinarily important role in popularizing the narrative and shaping its reception, particularly with regard to the perception of the tale's hero as a devoted friend of men, not simply a passionate lover of women. The references to the male friend in Sōgi's "Solo Sequence" of 1499 and in "One Hundred Verses Using Words from the *Tale of Ise*" of 1521 owe a great deal to Yoshimoto's practice from a century earlier of drawing from the *Ise* in order to introduce into *renga*'s poetic repertoire a new diction and imagery of erotic adventure and friendship not found in the standard *waka* tradition.

Sōgi and other fourteenth- and fifteenth-century *renga* poets were drawn to the *Ise*'s formulation of male friendship because of its relevance to their own world of masculine relations. As the commentaries attributed to Sōgi attest, he and his fellow *renga* masters made sense of the *Ise*'s depiction of male friendship largely in terms of their own social experience. Their interpretation of that depiction shaped the medieval canon and held sway until early modern times, but the choice of the *Ise* had in some ways already been made for them by their literary forbearers, Fujiwara no Teika and Nijō Yoshimoto. Teika and Yoshimoto elevated the *Ise,* with its exclusive focus on friendship as a male experience, and downplayed other texts that explored female friendships and friendships between men and women, and in doing so, they created a more constricted legacy for the depiction of friendship than was actually the case in Heian literature.

Notes

Introduction

1. I. Morris, *The World of the Shining Prince,* 93.

2. See, for example, W. McCullough, "Japanese Marriage Institutions in the Heian Period," and Nickerson, "The Meaning of Matrilocality."

3. Major studies of Heian literature informed by feminist perspectives include the following: Bargen, *A Woman's Weapon;* Field, *The Splendor of Longing;* Okada, *Figures of Resistance;* Sarra, *Fictions of Femininity;* and Shirane, *The Bridge of Dreams.*

4. For a critique of the modern tendency to equate the Heian period with the feminine, see Mostow, "Modern Constructions."

5. A copy of the *Lie-zi* [J: *Resshi*] is recorded in the *Nihonkoku genzaisho mokuroku* (A catalog of [Chinese] books presently existing in the land of Japan), proof that the text was available to Heian courtiers from at least ca. 891, when the catalog was compiled by Fujiwara no Sukeyo (847–897).

6. Mann, "Women's History, Men's Studies," 86.

7. Ury, "Chinese Learning," 342.

8. LaMarre, *Uncovering Heian Japan,* 3.

9. For examples of Heian women's knowledge of Chinese, see Mostow, "Mother Tongue and Father Script," 121–127.

1. *Poems to Sing* and the Hope for Transcendence

1. Rimer and Chaves, *Poems to Sing,* 219–221. The study and complete English translation by Rimer and Chaves is based on Ōsone and Horiuchi, *Wakan rōei shū.* In English, see also Harich-Schneider, *Rōei: The Medieval Court Songs of Japan.*

2. Rimer and Chaves, *Poems to Sing,* 13.

3. Keene, *Seeds in the Heart,* 134.

4. Ōsone and Horiuchi, *Wakan rōei shū,* contains 803 poems, whereas Kawaguchi, *Wakan rōei shū,* contains 804. Little is known about the actual musical per-

formance of the poems; see Stephen Addiss, "Singing the *Wakan rōei shū*," in Rimer and Chaves, *Poems to Sing*, 244–259.

5. For translations into English, see Rodd and Henkenius, *Kokinshū*, and H. McCullough, *Kokin Wakashū*.

6. Rimer and Chaves, *Poems to Sing*, 9.

7. *Nihon koten bungaku daijiten*, 2:679.

8. Kimbara Tadashi, *Heianchō kanshibun no kenkyū*, 353.

9. Rimer and Chaves, *Poems to Sing*, 303.

10. Kawaguchi, *Wakan rōei shū*, 239.

11. Rimer and Chaves, *Poems to Sing*, 303.

12. Watson, *The Complete Works of Chuang Tzu*, 215.

13. Ibid.

14. Kaneko Motoomi and Emi, *Wakan rōei shū shinshaku*, 471.

15. For a detailed study of this important figure and his times, see Borgen, *Sugawara no Michizane*.

16. Kaneko Motoomi and Emi, *Wakan rōei shū shinshaku*, 474, give the date 929 for the reunion.

17. Throughout the book, I use modern orthography in my transcriptions of Japanese. Transcriptions of Japanese poems appear in roman type, and English translations in italics. When quoting translations of *waka*, I have indicated the translator's breaks between verses with a slash, but my own translations present *waka* as a single line.

18. *Shin senzai shū* identifies the poem as being by an unknown poet on an unknown topic, but Ōsone and Horiuchi, *Wakan rōei shū*, 276, cite fragmentary documents from an undated poetry contest as evidence that the poem was composed on the assigned topic of "Frustrated Love."

19. Kaneko Motoomi and Emi, *Wakan rōei shū shinshaku*, 475.

20. Keene, *Seeds in the Heart*, 343.

21. Ōsone and Horiuchi, *Wakan rōei shū*, 277.

22. Kawaguchi, *Wakan rōei shū*, 241.

23. Rodd and Henkenius, *Kokinshū*, 156.

24. Ibid., 159.

25. Ibid., 162.

26. *Gosen shū*, vol. 7, Autumn (2), poem 380.

27. *Gyokuyō shū, ihonka*, poem 2807. The same poem appears in the imperial anthology *Fūga shū* (1349, Collection of elegant *waka*), vol. 13, Love (4), poem 1232, but without attribution to Ono no Komachi.

28. H. McCullough, *Tales of Ise*, 230.

29. Rodd and Henkenius, *Kokinshū*, 234. I have slightly modified their punctuation.

30. Kaneko Motoomi and Emi, *Wakan rōei shū shinshaku*, 385.

31. Rimer and Chaves, *Poems to Sing*, 145–146.

32. Ibid., 172.

33. Ibid., 226–227.
34. Ibid., 227.

2. Paradigms of Friendship in the *Tale of Ise*

1. For a discussion of the erotic adventurer as a literary trope, see Yokota-Murakami, *Don Juan East/West.* For a good summary of Origuchi Shinobu's influential approach to *irogonomi,* see Takahashi, *Irogonomi no bungaku to ōken.* See also Nishijima, *Nihon bungaku no dansei zō,* especially the chapter by Hirose, "Irogonomi no kikōshi," 45–65.

2. Bowring, "The *Ise monogatari,*" 419.

3. Shirane, *The Bridge of Dreams,* 47. In the same study, Shirane describes the *Ise* as "neutral in gender" (236 n. 18), presumably in the sense that it is unmarked as a male text written in *kanbun* (Chinese) or as a female text written in *kana* from a female perspective. I would argue, however, that the *Ise,* like the *Tosa nikki* (Tosa diary), is an early example of a male *kana* text that carves out a distinctly male subject position within the vernacular language. For a different perspective on the *Tosa Diary,* as a blend of male and female discourses, see Miyake, "*The Tosa Diary:* In the Interstices of Gender and Criticism."

4. Field, *The Splendor of Longing,* 35. Jin'ichi Konishi would probably disagree with Field's assessment, noting, "Some scholars of Japanese literature with ethnological interests [i.e., Origuchi Shinobu] have seen the man's journey to the East Country as a crude example of the motif of the nobleman wandering through strange lands, but this approach immoderately magnifies the role of setsuwa motifs [in the *Tale of Ise*]" (*A History of Japanese Literature,* 2:359).

5. The following studies of the *Ise* in English are all extremely useful, but none articulates a role for friendship: Vos, *A Study of the Ise-Monogatari;* H. McCullough, *Tales of Ise;* Marra, "A Lesson to the Leaders: *Ise Monogatari* and the Code of *Miyabi,*" chap. 2 in *The Aesthetics of Discontent;* Okada, "Sexual/Textual Politics and *The Tale of Ise,*" chap. 5 in *Figures of Resistance;* and Bowring, "The *Ise monogatari:* A Short Cultural History."

6. For the three-stage theory, see Katagiri Yōichi et al., *Taketori monogatari, Ise monogatari, Yamato monogatari, Heichū monogatari.* See also Marra, *The Aesthetics of Discontent,* 36–37, 48–49.

7. Okada, *Figures of Resistance,* 152.

8. Konishi, *A History of Japanese Literature,* 2:356.

9. Okada, *Figures of Resistance,* 145–146.

10. Konishi, *A History of Japanese Literature,* 2:359.

11. Marra, *The Aesthetics of Discontent,* 35.

12. I follow Konishi's assertion that the *Ise* hero's failure and disappointment are a literary invention and inconsistent with the facts of Narihira's life. See Konishi, *A History of Japanese Literature,* 2:359. For a contradictory assessment, see H. McCullough, *Tales of Ise,* 42.

13. Marra, *The Aesthetics of Discontent,* 53.

14. Tsukahara, *Ise monogatari no shōdan kōsei,* 178.

15. Unless otherwise noted, all translations of the *Ise* are from Vos, *A Study of the Ise-Monogatari,* vol. 1. Vos' literalness, and his policy of bracketing words not in the original, makes his translations most useful for a study of this sort.

16. Ellipsis points are in the original.

17. Tsukahara, *Ise monogatari no shōdan kōsei,* 153.

18. Ibid., 153–155.

19. Vos, *A Study of the Ise-Monogatari,* 1:167.

20. The shift in the hero's position from subject to object is a product of his move from capital to province. As a nobleman, the proper object of his amorous pursuits is a woman at court, but in the provinces the hero's status as courtier makes him desirable to provincial women or their parents for the potential access he provides them into the court. In the capital, women of the highest rank could solidify and even elevate the status of the noblemen they married, but the reverse was true in the provinces, where it was the nobleman who elevated the status of a provincial woman he might marry.

21. Tsukahara, *Ise monogatari no shōdan kōsei,* 158.

22. Ibid., 160.

23. Yura, *Ise monogatari kōsetsu,* 1:107.

24. Ibid., 106. Yura describes this clumsiness in terms of the repetition of certain phrases (*yuku o, ima wa,* and *yo no tsune* each appear twice) and a syntax filled with oppositions.

25. Ibid., 108.

26. Episode 38 is related in interesting ways to episode 48, in which the *Ise* hero is kept waiting in vain by an unnamed man for whom he has prepared a farewell dinner. In this case, however, the act of waiting becomes an occasion not for male-male intimacy but for a renewal of male erotic adventure directed at women. The hero, realizing how unpleasant it is to wait for someone who does not show, vows to be more attentive in the future to the women who lie awake at night, longing for him.

27. Takeoka, *Ise monogatari zen hyōshaku,* 645.

28. Yura discusses, and rejects, the "morning-after" thesis. Yura, *Ise monogatari kōsetsu,* 1:264.

29. Katagiri et al., *Taketori monogatari, Ise monogatari, Yamato monogatari, Heichū monogatari,* 166 n. 13.

30. For Chinese examples, see Takeoka, *Ise monogatari zen hyōshaku,* 648–649.

31. Rodd and Henkenius, *Kokinshū,* 162. Compare Helen McCullough's translation, which erases the suggestion of intimacy in the poem: "Mitsune. Composed when he said good-bye after having chatted with Prince Kanemi for the first time: *Though now we must part, / I will be happy indeed / after this evening. / What might I have looked forward to / if we had not met today?*" H. McCullough, *Kokin Wakashū,* 95.

32. Rodd and Henkenius, *Kokinshū,* 330–331. See also H. McCullough, *Kokin Wakashū,* 214.

33. Takeoka, *Ise monogatari zen hyōshaku,* 767.

34. Quoted in Yura, *Ise monogatari kōsetsu,* 1:264.

35. Yura, *Ise monogatari kōsetsu,* 1:264.

36. Quoted in ibid., 1:267.

37. Vos, *A Study of the Ise-Monogatari,* 1:199.

38. H. McCullough, *Tales of Ise,* 96.

39. Ibid., 218, n. 1.

40. Quoted in Takeoka, *Ise monogatari zen hyōshaku,* 648. Marra perceptively notes that friendship links the presence of Aritsune in section 38 and section 82: "A believer in the value of true friendship (*dan* 38), Aritsune helps Prince Koretaka find a proper answer to a poem by Narihira during their visit to the prince's villa in Minase (*dan* 82)." Marra, *The Aesthetics of Discontent,* 49–50.

41. Quoted in Yura, *Ise monogatari kōsetsu,* 1:267.

42. Yura, *Ise monogatari kōsetsu,* 1:315.

43. Section 46 is missing from the Nurigome-bon, another influential version of the *Ise.* See Ichihara, *Ise monogatari nurigome-bon no kenkyū,* 6.

44. The only other use of the word *uruwashi* in the *Ise* is in episode 24, where it appears as a verb. A man urges his former wife to love her new husband as she had once loved him: *uruwashimi se yo* ("you should be affectionate [to him]") (Vos, *A Study of the Ise-Monogatari,* 1:191). The poem makes the woman realize how much she loved her former husband, and she dies searching for him. Takeoka describes the power of the word *uruwashi* this way: "We might say that the entire episode hinges on this wonderful word. The moment the woman heard it, she understood with her whole body, as if struck by a bolt of lightening, how deeply her husband had loved her to that day. It was natural that she should drop everything and go in pursuit of the man, who had wished her happiness in her new life and gone on his way alone" (*Ise monogatari zen hyōshaku,* 543).

45. Takeoka, *Ise monogatari zen hyōshaku,* 542.

46. The same rejection of the necessity of "seeing" for male friendships to survive is evident in the Chinese poetic tradition, where friendship between men is also idealized as being unaffected by long periods of absence. See ibid., 764.

47. Miner, Odagiri, and Morrell, *The Princeton Companion to Classical Japanese Literature,* 143.

48. M. Morris, "Waka and Form, Waka and History," 555.

49. In the general introduction to *A History of Japanese Literature,* Konishi stresses that the concept of implicitness should not be construed as a description of Japanese literature as irrational or nonintellectual. He further explains what he means by implicitness in a note (bracketed interpolations are the volume editor's): "It is difficult to explain my special usage [of naikōsei] adequately. The 'yin principle' is easy enough to turn to, but such are the manifold complexities stretching out

from the concepts of yin-yang thought that the exact meaning is hard to convey. The passive [shōkyoku—negativism or conservatism in the dictionary] may express some features of the idea, but I fear that many other features in my concept would thereby be lost. English 'implicitness' being fairly close to what I have in mind, I have ventured to use 'naikōsei' [usually defined by dictionaries as 'introversion,' etc.], although it is inadequate. I have had the suggestion (from Ulrich Mammitsch) of the German 'beredtes Schweigen' (meaningful or expressive silence)" (Konishi, *A History of Japanese Literature,* 1:16 n. 12).

50. Ibid., 2:359.

51. Vos, *A Study of the Ise-Monogatari,* 2:134–135.

52. Interestingly, Confucian-inspired avowals of devotion found in Chinese and Korean poetry from ministers intent on proving their loyalty to their emperor or king cast the gender binarism in opposite terms, with the lord occupying the masculine position and the minister the feminine.

53. Narihira was born in 825, his nephew Koretaka in 844, making Narihira almost twenty years the Prince's senior, but episode 82 constructs the symbolic seniority of the two in the opposite position.

54. Takeoka, *Ise monogatari zen hyōshaku,* 1216.

55. Ellipsis points are in the original.

56. Ellipsis points are in the original.

57. The movement toward intensification and deepening of friendship in the Aritsune and Koretaka episodes is almost diametrically opposed to the trajectory of erotic adventure in the tale, which finds the hero moving from one woman to another, as often as not rejected by them and ready to begin his amorous pursuits all over again elsewhere.

58. H. McCullough, *Tales of Ise,* 149.

59. Videen, *Tales of Heichū,* 30–31.

60. Ibid., 39.

61. Ibid.

62. Ibid., 50.

63. Ibid., 53.

64. Ibid.

65. Ibid., 59.

66. This episode of the *Heichū* appears also in a version of the *Yamato monogatari* called the Mikanagi-bon. Morimoto, *Heichū monogatari zenshaku,* 134.

67. Videen, *Tales of Heichū,* 63.

3. Poetic Sequences in the *Kagerō Diary*

1. See Mostow, "The Amorous Statesman and the Poetess."

2. Titles of poetic sequences are from Kawaguchi, *Kagerō nikki,* 134–136.

3. Sonja Arntzen describes the Machi Alley in a note as "a small street that ran

north and south between Muromachi Street and Nishi no Tōin Street." She adds, "Some commentators identify it as present day Shinmachi Street" [in Kyoto]. Arntzen, *The Kagerō Diary,* 68.

4. Kawaguchi, *Kagerō nikki,* 134 n. 3.

5. Seidensticker, *The Gossamer Years,* 173.

6. H. McCullough and W. McCullough, *A Tale of Flowering Fortunes,* 810 (quoted in Arntzen, *The Kagerō Diary,* 100).

7. Kawaguchi, *Kagerō nikki,* 134.

8. Arntzen, *The Kagerō Diary,* 100.

9. H. McCullough, *Classical Japanese Prose,* 127–128.

10. At other points in the text, the narrator defers to the Prince's status: "Noriakira had the aura of royal prestige about him, which can be felt in the respectful tone the author reserves for him in the diary. This was one of the high points in the author's married life, when she is able to participate in her husband's playful and courtly correspondence with royalty" (Arntzen, *The Kagerō Diary,* 100).

11. *Nikki* is usually translated as "diary" and is associated with autobiographical writing, but numerous scholars have noted that the *Kagerō* has many aspects of a poem-tale *(uta monogatari),* making it more a fictionalized memoir than a factual autobiography. See Arntzen, "Of Love and Bondage," 25–26.

12. Arntzen, *The Kagerō Diary,* 100.

13. Seidensticker, *The Gossamer Years,* 48. *The Gossamer Years,* Seidensticker's 1952 translation, was published in 1955 and revised in 1964. Page numbers are from the 1964 edition.

14. Ibid., 173 n. 61.

15. Ibid., n. 62.

16. H. McCullough, *Classical Japanese Prose,* 128–129.

17. Kawaguchi, *Kagerō nikki,* 135.

18. Ibid., 135 n. 21.

19. Kawaguchi interprets poem 2 as the narrator's reply to the Prince, not Kaneie's, on the basis of a multiple pun on *yo ni furu,* which has a range of meanings—"living," "growing old," "declining in the world," or "rain falling in the night." In the opening lines of the *Kagerō,* the author employs the phrase *yo ni furu* to suggest that she has lived a vain existence, and Kawaguchi sees these lines as possibly being echoed here. Kawaguchi, *Kagerō nikki,* 135.

20. Arntzen, *The Kagerō Diary,* 181.

21. Ibid., 104.

22. Seidensticker, *The Gossamer Years,* 49.

23. Arntzen, *The Kagerō Diary,* 105.

24. Kawaguchi, *Kagerō nikki,* 136 n. 4.

25. Seidensticker, *The Gossamer Years,* 48–49.

26. Ibid., 173 n. 64.

27. Arntzen, *The Kagerō Diary,* 103–105.

28. Ibid., 104.
29. Kawaguchi, *Kagerō nikki,* 136.
30. H. McCullough, *Classical Japanese Prose,* 129.
31. Arntzen, *The Kagerō Diary,* 104.
32. H. McCullough, *Classical Japanese Prose,* 130.
33. Arntzen, *The Kagerō Diary,* 106.
34. Seidensticker, *The Gossamer Years,* 49.
35. Ibid., 173.
36. Arntzen, *The Kagerō Diary,* 105–107.
37. Ibid., 106.
38. H. McCullough, *Classical Japanese Prose,* 130.
39. Seidensticker, *The Gossamer Years,* 49.
40. Kawaguchi, *Kagerō nikki,* 137.
41. H. McCullough, *Classical Japanese Prose,* 130.
42. Arntzen, *The Kagerō Diary,* 107.
43. Seidensticker, *The Gossamer Years,* 49.
44. Kawaguchi, *Kagerō nikki,* 137.
45. Arntzen, *The Kagerō Diary,* 107.
46. Kawaguchi, *Kagerō nikki,* 137 n. 22.
47. Arntzen, *The Kagerō Diary,* 107.
48. Seidensticker, *The Gossamer Years,* 50.
49. Arntzen, *The Kagerō Diary,* 107–111.
50. Ibid., 110. H. McCullough has the author sharing her carriage with the Prince's consort, which seems more plausible (*Classical Japanese Prose,* 131).
51. Ibid., 111.
52. Seidensticker, *The Gossamer Years,* 51.
53. Rodd and Henkenius, *Kokinshū,* 117.
54. Aki no no no kusa no tamoto ka hanasusuki ho ni idete maneku sode to miyuran. H. McCullough, *Kokin Wakashū,* 60–61.
55. Arntzen, *The Kagerō Diary,* 32–33.
56. Ibid., 15.
57. Arntzen contends that the author seems oblivious to the role Kaneie played in Takaakira's downfall: "Nowhere in her relation of the events concerning Takaakira's fall does she indicate even obliquely that she is aware her husband is one of the chief engineers of the conspiracy that brought Takaakira down" (*The Kagerō Diary,* 16).
58. Ibid., 148.
59. Ibid.
60. Ibid., 149.
61. Seidensticker, *The Gossamer Years,* 178 n. 139.
62. Arntzen, *The Kagerō Diary,* 151–153.
63. Kawaguchi, *Kagerō nikki,* 163 n. 16.
64. Ibid., n. 17.

4. *The Tale of Genji*

1. Field, *The Splendor of Longing,* 17.

2. Abe, *Kampon Genji monogatari,* 31.

3. Noted in reference to the secret of the Reizei Emperor's birth. Field, *The Splendor of Longing,* 42.

4. Ibid., 88.

5. Seidensticker, *The Tale of Genji,* 192.

6. Yamagishi, *Genji monogatari,* 2:49.

7. Ibid.

8. *Hakushi monjū,* 16:5, cited in Yamagishi, *Genji monogatari,* 2:447 n. 75.

9. Ibid., n. 79.

10. Tyler, *The Tale of Genji,* 251.

11. Ibid., n. 84.

12. Ibid., 251.

13. Ibid., n. 85.

14. Ibid., 252 n. 87.

15. Arthur Waley renders the poem this way: *The Tartar horse neighs into the northern wind; The bird of Yüeh nests on the southern bough* (Waley, *The Tale of Genji,* 293). Seidensticker's version: *The Tartar pony faces towards the north. The Annamese bird nests on the southern branch* (Seidensticker, *The Tale of Genji,* 245).

16. Yamagishi, *Genji monogatari,* 2:51.

17. Tyler, *The Tale of Genji,* 252.

18. Ibid.

19. Vos, *A Study of the Ise-Monogatari,* 239.

20. Ibid.

21. Studies of this problem include Abe, "*Genji monogatari* no shippitsu junjo"; Ishida, "Hahakigi no botō o megutte, aruiwa Hahakigi to Wakamurasaki"; Kadosaki, "*Genji monogatari* 'narabi no maki' no setsu no tenkai, *Kakaishō* igo no yokotate setsu hihan" and "*Genji monogatari* no narabi no maki ni tsuite." In English, see Gatten, "The Order of the Early Chapters in the *Genji Monogatari.*"

22. The structure of main chapters that are followed by chronologically contemporaneous but thematically autonomous chapters has historically been described by Genji scholars with the terms *hon no maki,* "main chapters," and *narabi no maki,* "lateral (or parallel) chapters." See Okada, *Figures of Resistance,* 342 n. 2; and Shirane, *The Bridge of Dreams,* 234 n. 13. The designation of main or lateral chapters illuminates an essential structural feature of the *Genji,* but it cannot be applied exactly to Abe's thematic formulation of a Kiritsubo narrative and a Broom Tree narrative in the first half of the tale.

23. Abe, *Genji monogatari kenkyū josetsu,* 939–1009.

24. Shirane, *The Bridge of Dreams,* 70–72.

25. Abe, *Kampon Genji monogatari,* 970.

26. Ibid., 32.

27. Ibid., 85.
28. Ibid.
29. Seidensticker, *The Tale of Genji*, 66.
30. Abe, *Kampon Genji monogatari*, 91.
31. Seidensticker, *The Tale of Genji*, 79.
32. Ibid., 82.
33. Abe, *Kampon Genji monogatari*, 107.
34. Seidensticker, *The Tale of Genji*, 73.
35. Abe, *Kampon Genji monogatari*, 95 n. 5.
36. Ibid., 91.
37. Seidensticker, *The Tale of Genji*, 70.
38. Abe, *Kampon Genji monogatari*, 150.
39. Ibid.
40. Seidensticker, *The Tale of Genji*, 117.
41. Ibid.
42. Ibid., 118.
43. Ibid.
44. Ibid.
45. Ibid., 120.
46. Ibid.
47. Ibid., 121.
48. Ibid.
49. Ibid., 123.
50. Ibid.
51. Ibid., 125.
52. Ibid., 127.
53. Ibid., 298.
54. Ibid.
55. Ibid., 301.
56. Ibid., 302.
57. Ibid.
58. Abe, *Kampon Genji monogatari*, 186.
59. Seidensticker, *The Tale of Genji*, 132.
60. Abe's argument is that "Momiji no Ga" (chap. 7) was written first as part of the primary Kiritsubo narrative, after which the author went back and wrote the "Broom Tree" (chap. 2) and other chapters comprising the secondary Broom Tree narrative.
61. Shirane, *The Bridge of Dreams*, 70.
62. Ibid., 71.
63. Field, *The Splendor of Longing*, 49.
64. Ibid.
65. Seidensticker, *The Tale of Genji*, 144.
66. Ibid., 145.

67. Ibid.
68. Ibid., 146.
69. Ibid.
70. Ibid.
71. Royall Tyler notes that "the image of waves breaking on a beach suggests erotic desire" and translates Genji's reaction to the poem as "She has no shame!" Tyler, *The Tale of Genji,* 149 n. 43.
72. Abe, *Kampon Genji monogatari,* 54.
73. Ibid., 55.
74. Seidensticker, *The Tale of Genji,* 42.
75. Margaret Childs argues that Utsusemi succeeded in resisting Genji in this scene. To my mind, later developments make it clear that such was not the case. For example, Genji always numbered her among his women and ultimately took responsibility for her later in life. See Childs, "The Value of Vulnerability."
76. Ibid., 45.
77. Abe, *Kampon Genji monogatari,* 60.
78. Ibid., 61.
79. Ibid.
80. Seidensticker, *The Tale of Genji,* 47.
81. Ibid., 48.
82. The dynamic of Genji and Tō no Chūjō's friendship here suggests that Abe Akio is correct in arguing that the Gen no Naishi episode in "Momiji no Ga" (chap. 7) was written first and inspired the Broom Tree narrative that precedes it in the present order of chapters.
83. Seidensticker, *The Tale of Genji,* 55.
84. Abe, *Kampon Genji monogatari,* 381.
85. Seidensticker, *The Tale of Genji,* 273.
86. Ibid., 343–344.
87. Ibid., 365.
88. Ibid., 367.
89. Ibid., 529.
90. Ibid., 388.

5. The Uji Chapters

1. Shirane, *The Bridge of Dreams,* 192.
2. Field, *The Splendor of Longing,* 224.
3. Field has a fine discussion of the ironies of the phrase in *The Splendor of Longing,* 224–225.
4. Seidensticker, *The Tale of Genji,* 781.
5. Abe, *Kampon Genji monogatari,* 1026–1027.
6. Waley, *The Tale of Genji,* 929 (my italics).
7. Seidensticker, *The Tale of Genji,* 782 (my italics).

8. Tyler, *The Tale of Genji,* 834 (my italics).

9. Abe, *Kampon Genji monogatari,* 1029.

10. Seidensticker, *The Tale of Genji,* 783.

11. Royall Tyler senses the oddity of this temporal leap and explains it this way in a note: "Not three twelve-month years but perhaps, in this way of counting, as little as eighteen months or so, starting in one year and ending in the second calendar year after it" (Tyler, *The Tale of Genji,* 835 n. 11). The explanation may shorten the time span, but it does not alter the significance of the gap in the action of the story.

12. Ibid., 840.

13. Ibid.

14. Seidensticker, *The Tale of Genji,* 790.

15. Tyler, *The Tale of Genji,* 841.

16. Ibid.

17. Abe, *Kampon Genji monogatari,* 1038.

18. Seidensticker, *The Tale of Genji,* 792.

19. Tyler, *The Tale of Genji,* 852.

20. Ibid.. 854.

21. Ibid.

22. Abe, *Kampon Genji monogatari,* 1054.

23. Seidensticker, *The Tale of Genji,* 808.

24. Abe, *Kampon Genji monogatari,* 1064.

25. Seidensticker, *The Tale of Genji,* 817.

26. Tyler, *The Tale of Genji,* 864.

27. Ibid., 871.

28. Seidensticker, *The Tale of Genji,* 739.

29. Ibid., 793.

30. Tyler, *The Tale of Genji,* 843.

31. Seidensticker, *The Tale of Genji,* 814.

32. Ibid., 816.

33. Ibid., 837.

34. Ibid., 838.

35. Field, *The Splendor of Longing,* 242–243.

36. Ibid., 255.

37. Ibid., 263.

38. Ibid., 262.

39. Ibid., 273.

40. Seidensticker, *The Tale of Genji,* 990.

41. Tyler, *The Tale of Genji,* 1014.

42. Ibid., 1021.

43. Ibid., 1023.

44. Ibid., 1043.

45. Ibid., 1057.

46. Ibid., 1059.

47. Field, *The Splendor of Longing,* 279.

48. Various theories assign identity to the Eighth Prince, the Suzaku Emperor, or other male figures in the tale.

49. Tyler, *The Tale of Genji,* 1097.

Afterword

1. Derrida, *Politics of Friendship,* 278–279.

2. *Nihon koten bungaku daijiten,* 4:15.

3. Kaneko Kinjirō, *Renga haikai shū,* 32:193–195. The poetic subject of the "Solo Sequence" alternates between male and female perspectives, but it is firmly male in the sub-sequence of verses 13–18. See Earl Miner's complete translation of Sōgi's "Solo Sequence" in *Japanese Linked Poetry,* 234–271.

4. For more on medieval and early modern *nanshoku,* see my introduction to *The Great Mirror of Male Love;* also Pflugfelder, *Cartographies of Desire;* and Leupp, *Male Colors.*

5. Konishi, *A History of Japanese Literature,* 2:99.

6. Miner, *Japanese Linked Poetry,* 21, 24, 32, 35–36.

7. *Nihon koten bungaku daijiten,* 1:161–162; also Vos, *A Study of the Ise-Monogatari,* 1:104–105.

8. Vos, *A Study of the Ise-Monogatari,* 1:149.

Works Cited

Abe Akio. *Genji monogatari kenkyū josetsu.* Tokyo: Tokyo Daigaku Shuppan Kai, 1959.

———. "*Genji monogatari* no shippitsu junjo." In *Kokugo to kokubungaku* (August–September 1939), reprinted in *Genji monogatari III,* Nihon bungaku kenkyū shiryō sōsho, 32–52. Tokyo: Yūseidō, 1971.

———. *Kampon Genji monogatari.* Tokyo Shōgakukan, 1992.

Arntzen, Sonja. "Of Love and Bondage in the *Kagerō Diary:* Michitsuna's Mother and Her Father." In *The Father-Daughter Plot: Japanese Literary Women and the Law of the Father,* edited by Rebecca L. Copeland and Esperanza Ramirez-Christensen, 25–48. Honolulu: University of Hawai'i Press, 2001.

———, trans. *The Kagerō Diary: A Woman's Autobiographical Text from Tenth-Century Japan.* Ann Arbor: Center for Japanese Studies, University of Michigan, 1997.

Bargen, Doris. *A Woman's Weapon: Spirit Possession in* The Tale of Genji. Honolulu: University of Hawai'i Press, 1998.

Borgen, Robert. *Sugawara no Michizane and the Early Heian Court.* Honolulu: University of Hawai'i Press, 1994.

Bowring, Richard. "The *Ise monogatari:* A Short Cultural History." *Harvard Journal of Asiatic Studies* 52.2 (1992).

Childs, Margaret. "The Value of Vulnerability: Sexual Coercion and the Nature of Love in Japanese Literature." *Journal of Asian Studies* 58 (1999).

Derrida, Jacques. *Politics of Friendship.* Translated by George Collins. New York: Verso, 1997.

Field, Norma. *The Splendor of Longing in* The Tale of Genji. Princeton, N.J.: Princeton University Press, 1987.

Gatten, Aileen. "The Order of the Early Chapters in the *Genji Monogatari.*" *Harvard Journal of Asiatic Studies* 41 (June 1981): 5–46.

Harich-Schneider, Eta. *Rōei: The Medieval Court Songs of Japan.* Tokyo: Sophia University Press, 1965.

Hirose Yuiji. "Irogonomi no kikōshi." In *Nihon bungaku no dansei zō,* edited by Nishijima Atsuya, 45–65. Tokyo: Sekai Shisōsha, 1994.

Ichihara Sunao. *Ise monogatari nurigome-bon no kenkyū.* Tokyo: Meiji Shoin, 1987.

Ishida Jōji. "Hahakigi no botō o megutte, aruiwa Hahakigi to Wakamurasaki." In *Genji monogatari Makura no sōshi kenkyū to shiryō,* edited by Murasaki Shikibu Kai, 46–52. Tokyo: Musashino Shoin, 1973.

Kadosaki Shin'ichi. "*Genji monogatari* 'narabi no maki' no setsu no tenkai, *Kakaishō* igo no yokotate setsu hihan." In *Tenri daigaku gakuhō* 51 (March 1965), reprinted in *Genji monogatari I* Nihon bungaku kenkyū shiryō sōsho, 177–193. Tokyo: Yūseidō, 1969.

———. "*Genji monogatari* no narabi no maki ni tsuite." In *Genji monogatari kōza,* vol. 2, edited by Yamagishi Tokuhei and Oka Kazuo, 168–197. Tokyo: Yūseidō, 1971–1972.

Kaneko Kinjirō et al., eds. *Renga haikai shū.* Nihon Koten Bungaku Zenshū, vol. 32. Tokyo: Shōgakukan, 1974.

Kaneko Motoomi and Emi Seifū, eds. *Wakan rōei shū shinshaku.* Tokyo: Meiji Shoin, 1942.

Katagiri Yōichi, ed. *Ise monogatari, Yamato monogatari.* Kanshō Nihon Koten Bungaku, vol. 5. Tokyo: Kadokawa, 1975.

Katagiri Yōichi et al., eds. *Taketori monogatari, Ise monogatari, Yamato monogatari, Heichū monogatari.* Nihon Koten Bungaku Zenshū, vol. 8. Tokyo: Shōgakukan, 1972.

Kawaguchi Hisao. "Kagerō nikki." In *Tosa nikki, Kagero nikki, Izumi Shikibu nikki, Sarashina nikki,* edited by Suzuki Tomotarō et al., 83–378. Nihon Koten Bungaku Taikei, vol. 20. Tokyo: Iwanami Shoten, 1965.

———, ed. *Wakan rōei shū.* Nihon Koten Bungaku Taikei, vol. 73. Tokyo: Iwanami, 1965.

Keene, Donald. *Seeds in the Heart.* New York: Henry Holt, 1993.

Kimbara Tadashi. *Heianchō kanshibun no kenkyū.* Fukuoka: Kyushu Daigaku, 1981.

Konishi Jin'ichi. *A History of Japanese Literature.* 5 vols. Princeton, N.J.: Princeton University Press, 1986.

LaMarre, Thomas. *Uncovering Heian Japan: An Archaeology of Sensation and Transcription.* Durham, N.C., and London: Duke University Press, 2000.

Leupp, Gary P. *Male Colors: The Construction of Homosexuality in Tokugawa Japan.* Los Angeles: University of California Press, 1995.

Mann, Susan. "The Male Bond in Chinese History and Culture." *American Historical Review* 105 (December 2000): 1600–1614.

———. "Women's History, Men's Studies: New Directions in Research on Gender in Late Imperial China." In *Gender and Medical History,* Papers from the Third International Conference on Sinology, History Section, 73–103. Taipei: Institute of Modern History, Academia Sinica, 2002.

Marra, Michele. *The Aesthetics of Discontent: Politics and Reclusion in Medieval Japanese Literature.* Honolulu: University of Hawai'i Press, 1991.

McCullough, Helen Craig, ed. *Classical Japanese Prose: An Anthology*. Stanford, Calif.: Stanford University Press, 1990.

———, trans. *Kokin Wakashū: The First Imperial Anthology of Japanese Poetry*. Stanford, Calif.: Stanford University Press, 1985.

———, trans. *Tales of Ise: Lyrical Episodes from Tenth-Century Japan*. Stanford, Calif.: Stanford University Press, 1968.

McCullough, Helen Craig, and William H. McCullough, trans. *A Tale of Flowering Fortunes: Annals of Japanese Aristocratic Life in the Heian Period*. 2 vols. Stanford, Calif.: Stanford University Press, 1980.

McCullough, William H. "Japanese Marriage Institutions in the Heian Period." *Harvard Journal of Asiatic Studies* 27 (1967): 103–167.

Miner, Earl. *Japanese Linked Poetry: An Account with Translations of Renga and Haikai Sequences*. Princeton, N.J.: Princeton University Press, 1979.

Miner, Earl, Hiroko Odagiri, and Robert E. Morrell, eds. *The Princeton Companion to Classical Japanese Literature*. Princeton, N.J.: Princeton University Press, 1985.

Miyake, Lynne K. "*The Tosa Diary:* In the Interstices of Gender and Criticism." In *The Woman's Hand: Gender and Theory in Japanese Women's Writing*, edited by Paul Gordon Schalow and Janet A. Walker, 41–73. Stanford, Calif.: Stanford University Press, 1996.

Morimoto Shigeru. *Heichū monogatari zenshaku*. Kyoto: Daigakudō Shoten, 1996.

Morris, Ivan. *The World of the Shining Prince: Court Life in Ancient Japan*. London: Peregrine, 1964. Reprint, 1986.

Morris, Mark. "Waka and Form, Waka and History." *Harvard Journal of Asiatic Studies* 46:2 (1986): 551–610.

Mostow, Joshua S. "The Amorous Statesman and the Poetess: The Politics of Autobiography and the *Kagerō Nikki*." *Japan Forum* 4.2 (October 1992): 305–315.

———. "Modern Constructions of *Tales of Ise:* Gender and Courtliness." In *Inventing the Classics: Modernity, National Identity, and Japanese Literature*, edited by Haruo Shirane and Tomi Suzuki, 96–119. Stanford, Calif.: Stanford University Press, 2000.

———. "Mother Tongue and Father Script: The Relationship of Sei Shōnagon and Murasaki Shikibu to Their Fathers and Chinese Letters." In *The Father-Daughter Plot: Japanese Literary Women and the Law of the Father*, edited by Rebecca L. Copeland and Esperanza Ramirez-Christensen, 115–142. Honolulu: University of Hawai'i Press, 2001.

Murase, Miyeko. *Bridge of Dreams: The Mary Griggs Burke Collection of Japanese Art*. New York: Metropolitan Museum of Art, 2000.

———. *The Tale of Genji: Legends and Paintings*. New York: George Braziller, 2001.

Nickerson, Peter. "The Meaning of Matrilocality: Kinship, Property, and Politics in the Mid-Heian Period." *Monumenta Nipponica* 48.4 (Winter 1993): 429–467.

Nihon koten bungaku daijiten. 6 vols. Tokyo: Iwanami, 1984.

Nishijima Atsuya. *Nihon bungaku no dansei zō*. Tokyo: Sekai Shisōsha, 1994.

Okada, H. Richard. *Figures of Resistance: Language, Poetry, and Narrating in the* Tale of Genji *and Other Mid-Heian Texts.* Durham, N.C.: Duke University Press, 1991.

Ōsone Shōsuke and Horiuchi Hideaki, eds. *Wakan rōei shū.* Shinchō Nihon Koten Shūsei, vol. 14. Tokyo: Shinchō, 1983.

Pflugfelder, Gregory. *Cartographies of Desire: Male-Male Sexuality in Japanese Discourse 1600–1950.* Berkeley and Los Angeles: University of California Press, 1999.

Rimer, J. Thomas, and Jonathan Chaves, eds. *Japanese and Chinese Poems to Sing: The Wakan rōei shū.* New York: Columbia University Press, 1997.

Rodd, Laurel Rasplica, and Mary Catherine Henkenius, trans. *Kokinshū: A Collection of Poems Ancient and Modern.* Princeton, N.J.: Princeton University Press, 1984.

Sarra, Edith. *Fictions of Femininity: Literary Inventions of Gender in Japanese Court Women's Memoirs.* Stanford, Calif.: Stanford University Press, 1999.

Schalow, Paul Gordon. "Five Portraits of Male Friendship in the *Ise monogatari.*" *Harvard Journal of Asiatic Studies* 60.2 (December 2000): 445–488.

———. Introduction to *The Great Mirror of Male Love,* by Ihara Saikaku, 1–46. Stanford, Calif.: Stanford University Press, 1990.

———. "The Invention of a Literary Tradition of Male Love: Kitamura Kigin's *Iwatsutsuji.*" *Monumenta Nipponica* 48.1 (1993): 1–31.

Schalow, Paul Gordon, and Janet A. Walker, eds. *The Woman's Hand: Gender and Theory in Japanese Women's Writing.* Stanford, Calif.: Stanford University Press, 1996.

Seidensticker, Edward, trans. *The Gossamer Years.* Revised ed. Rutland, Vt.: Tuttle, 1964.

———, trans. *The Tale of Genji.* New York: Knopf, 1976.

Shirane, Haruo. *The Bridge of Dreams: A Poetics of* The Tale of Genji. Stanford, Calif.: Stanford University Press, 1987.

Takahashi Tōru. *Irogonomi no bungaku to ōken: Genji monogatari no sekai e.* Tokyo: Shintensha, 1990.

Takeoka Masao. *Ise monogatari zen hyōshaku: Kochūshaku jūisshū shūsei.* Tokyo: Yūbun Shoin, 1987.

Tsukahara Tetsuo. *Ise monogatari no shōdan kōsei.* Tokyo: Shintensha, 1988.

Tyler, Royall, trans. *The Tale of Genji.* New York: Viking, 2001.

Ury, Marian. "Chinese Learning and Intellectual Life." In *The Cambridge History of Japan,* vol. 2, edited by Donald H. Shively and William H. McCullough, 341–389. Cambridge: Cambridge University Press, 1999.

Videen, Susan Downing, trans. *Tales of Heichū.* Cambridge, Mass: Council on East Asian Studies, Harvard University Press, 1989.

Vos, Frits. *A Study of the Ise-Monogatari: With the Text According to the Den-Teika-Hippon and an Annotated Translation.* Vols. 1 and 2. The Hague: Mouton, 1957.

Waley, Arthur, trans. *The Tale of Genji.* New York: Modern Library, 1993.

Watson, Burton, trans. *The Complete Works of Chuang Tzu.* New York: Columbia University Press, 1968.

Yamagishi Tokuhei, ed. *Genji monogatari,* vol. 2. Nihon Koten Bungaku Taikei, vol. 15. Tokyo: Iwanami Shoten, 1959.

Yokota-Murakami, Takayuki. *Don Juan East/West: On the Problematics of Comparative Literature.* Albany: State University of New York Press, 1998.

Yura Takuo. *Ise monogatari kōsetsu.* Tokyo: Meiji Shoin, 1985.

Index

About the Author

Paul Gordon Schalow teaches Japanese literature in the Department of Asian Languages and Cultures at Rutgers University. He earned his Ph.D. in Japanese literature with a specialization in Edo period fiction from Harvard University. His previous publications include a translation of Ihara Saikaku's *The Great Mirror of Male Love* (1990) and an edited volume (with Janet A. Walker) entitled *The Woman's Hand: Gender and Theory in Japanese Women's Writing* (1996).

Production Notes for *Schalow / A Poetics of Courtly Male Friendship in Heian Japan*

Cover and interior designed by the University of Hawai'i Press production staff with text and display in Palatino

Composition by Josie Herr

Printing and binding by The Maple-Vail Book Manufacturing Group

Printed on 60# Text White Opaque, 426 ppi